SALE OF GOODS:

READING AND APPLYING THE CODE
Second Edition

By

Carol L. Chomsky
Professor of Law
University of Minnesota Law School

and

Christina L. Kunz
Professor of Law
William Mitchell College of Law

AMERICAN CASEBOOK SERIES®

Mat #40176714

American Casebook Series and West Group are trademarks registered in the U.S. Patent and Trademark Office.

COPYRIGHT © 2002 By WEST GROUP

© 2004 West, a Thomson business
      610 Opperman Drive
      P.O. Box 64526
      St. Paul, MN 55164–0526
      1–800–328–9352

ISBN 0–314–14975–9

TEXT IS PRINTED ON 10% POST CONSUMER RECYCLED PAPER

To Steve, Aaron, and Emma

CLC

To Alex and Charlotte

CLK

Preface to Students

The Uniform Commercial Code (UCC) is one of the classic codes in American law. This book's primary subject is Article 2 of the UCC, a pivotal portion of the Code that provides many of the rules of law governing sales of goods. You will be introduced, as well, to other portions of the UCC that interact with Article 2 and to several significant commercial law statutes that provide additional context for problem-solving related to sales of goods.

As appropriate for teaching a body of law governed by statute, the book focuses your attention on close textual analysis of Article 2. Cases—the mainstay of most law school texts—are included only when necessary to introduce governing rules of law not derivable from the statute itself. Thus, you will find fewer cases included here than in traditional law school texts. You will learn how the Code works by parsing the statutory language and exploring its interpretation in response to "reading" problems designed to guide your analysis. In the process, you will learn how to approach and master any statute. After helping you make sense of the statutory words, the book presents a series of application problems, ranging from simple to complex, that will help you assess your understanding of the statute. As its title makes explicit, the book thus focuses on two essential skills for any statutory analysis: reading statutory text critically and determining how to apply it to facts. Although you already may have had some experience reading and applying statutes, this book will help you strengthen and extend those skills and knit them together into a comprehesive ability to use code-based rules to solve complex problems.

This book appears at a critical juncture in the history of Article 2, and your study of the statute will be affected by that fact. Article 2 was written in the 1940s by Karl Llewellyn, an important figure in American jurisprudence (and quite a character in his own right). In 1952, Article 2 was approved by the National Conference of Commissioners on Uniform State Laws (NCCUSL) and the American Law Institute (ALI), which, during the next two decades, promoted and achieved its enactment by the legislatures of 49 states and the District of Columbia, creating a truly uniform law for sales of goods across the country. Although Article 2 worked fairly well for its first half-century, some practitioners and commentators urged revisions in order to better facilitate sales of goods in a changed business and technological world. A drafting committee of NCCUSL (to which Professor Kunz was an official observer) undertook such a revision, and the resulting set of amendments was adopted by both NCCUSL and the ALI in 2003.

This book is focused primarily on unamended Article 2, because that is the version in effect in every jurisdiction as of this writing. However, the amendments may well be enacted in several states in the upcoming year and in more states in years to come, so a lawyer-to-be needs to know both the amended and unamended versions. This book therefore has a secondary focus on amended Article 2. The text and problems involving amended Article 2 are marked with a "2003" box in the margin.

UCC Article 1, which provides definitions of terms and other foundational provisions for the entire Code, was revised in August 2001, and the 2001 version has been enacted in several states, with more likely to follow in the upcoming years. The new version of Article 1 is a "revision" because it involved considerable rewriting and renumbering of sections, while the new version of Article 2 involves only amendments to Article 2, considerably less rewriting, and no renumbering of sections. We have thus referred throughout the text to "revised" or "unrevised" Article 1 but to "amended" or "unamended" Article 2.

We have written the text with the unrevised version of Article 1 (2000) as the primary focus and the revised version of Article 1 (2001) as the secondary focus. A concordance of Article 1 sections appears on page xxix, listing the equivalent sections of the 2000 and 2001 versions. We have also provided parallel citations to the unrevised and revised versions the first time we introduce a section of Article 1.

We hope you enjoy this hands-on approach to learning the Code, developed based on our insights from years of teaching. We have worked hard to craft a book that enables you to master this subject and its skills, so that you truly can "own the Code."

Carol L. Chomsky
Christina L. Kunz
May 2004

Acknowledgments

This book grew out of our experiences teaching a remarkable set of unpublished teaching materials written by a colleague, Professor Daniel S. Kleinberger. His grasp of the potential of a problem- and statute-based teaching approach inspired both of us to begin to write some of our own problems and eventually our own assignments. In our conversations, we still refer back to Dan's fact situations and questions, as well as his chosen cases. Thank you, Dan.

We also appreciate the assistance that our respective law schools have given this project, scheduling our courses and exams in a coordinated fashion, freeing up our summers, providing word processing and messenger services, and photocopying course materials as we wrote them. Special thanks to Deans Harry J. Haynsworth, E. Thomas Sullivan, and Alex Johnson. Most of all, we would like to thank Cal Bonde, our wizard word processor, who helped us to create the format of the book; established and maintained a document management system for our various edited versions, semester by semester; typed some of our handwritten edits; formatted every assignment; and was part of our e-mail round-robin between the two schools. She has survived two editions of the book, with unflagging grace and good humor.

We acknowledge the late Robert Hudec, professor from the University of Minnesota Law School, whose insightful student handout on the parol evidence rule was the source on which Problem 12-12 was based.

For the second edition, we relied on the excellent research assistance of Justin Kaufman, Matthew Krohn, Kirstin Kanski, Jacob Sellers, C. Blair Buccicone, Jennifer Callahan, and Christianne Riopel in tracking down lines of cases and checking the finer points of sales law. The index and tables were carefully generated by Christina Kilby and Rian Radtke.

This book represents a truly collaborative effort, as we wrote, discussed, edited, taught, and rewrote the materials. We early adopted the practice of meeting weekly to review whatever we had taught that week as well as new edits to chapters of the manuscript. We owe many thanks to Sebastian Joe's Original Ice Cream Cafe (on Franklin Avenue) and Coffee News (on Grand Avenue), our usual coffee haunts, for tolerating our long and animated conversations as we debated interpretations and explored our vision of the Code and how to teach it effectively. We thank our families and friends, who suffered through our mutual obsession with Article 2. And finally we thank our students, who confirmed the value of our approach by enthusiastically embracing the materials and by learning the Code well enough to challenge our own understandings.

West Group has enabled us to publish the book in the format we wanted, giving us free rein to develop these newly conceived and carefully formatted teaching materials. Our thanks to Douglas Powell, Pamela Siege, Louis Higgins, and Staci Herr. In addition, the following material appears by permission of West Group:

> *Bartus v. Riccardi*, 284 N.Y.S.2d 222 (City Ct. 1967)
> *City of Wood River v. Geer-Melkus Construction Co.*, 444 N.W.2d 305 (Neb. 1989).
> *Daitom, Inc. v. Pennwalt Corp.*, 741 F.2d 1569 (10th Cir. 1984).
> *East River Steamship Corp. v. Transamerica Delaval, Inc.*, 106 S. Ct 2295 (1986).
> *Evans Industries, Inc., v. International Business Machines Co.*, No. Civ.A. 01-0051, 2004 WL 241701 (E.D. La. Feb. 6, 2004)
> *Nanakuli Paving and Rock Company v. Shell Oil Company, Inc.*, 664 F.2d 772 (9th Cir. 1981)
> *Pass v. Shelby Aviation, Inc.*, 2000 WL 388775 (Tenn. Ct. App.).
> *Patterson v. Her Majesty Industries, Inc.*, 450 F. Supp. 425 (E.D. Pa. 1978).
> *Wilson v. Scampoli*, 228 A.2d 848 (D.C. Ct. App. 1967).

Summary of Contents

Table of Contents

Table of Statutes and Regulations

Table of Cases

Table of Secondary Authorities

Concordance of Article 1 Sections[1]

2000 version	2001 version
1-101	1-101(a)
1-102(1)	1-103(a)
1-102(2)	1-103(a)(1)-(3)
1-102(3)	1-302(a), (b) (1st and 2nd sentences)
1-102(4)	1-302(c)
1-102(5)	1-106
1-103	1-103(b)
1-104	1-104
1-105	1-301 (with significant changes)
1-106	1-305
1-107	1-306
1-108	1-105
1-109	1-107
1-201(1)-(20), (22)-(24), (28-40), (42)-(43), (45-(46)	1-201(1)-(20), (22)-(24), (28)-(40), (42)-(43), (45)-(46)
1-201(25)	1-202(a)-(c)
1-201(26)	1-202(d), (e)
1-201(27)	1-202(f)
1-201(37) (all but 1st paragraph)	1-203
1-201(44)	1-204
1-202	1-307
1-203	1-304
1-204(1)	1-302(b) 3rd sentence
1-205	1-303(b)-(e), (g)
1-206	deleted
1-207	1-308
1-208	1-309
1-209	1-310
2-208	1-303(a), (e), (f)
new	1-101(b)
new	1-102
new	1-108
new	1-201(b)(10a), (30a), (33a), (39a)

---

[1] For current status of adoption by the states, see www.nccusl.org/nccusl/default.asp.

Assignment 1: Scope of Article 2 ("Sale" of "Goods")

§§ 2-102; 2-103(1)(a), (d); 2-105(1), (2); 2-106(1); 2-107(1), (2); 2-304; 2-501(1)

An Overview of Article 2

This course focuses on Article 2 of the Uniform Commercial Code (UCC). We begin with an overview of the organization of Article 2. Knowing its structure will help you when you have to recall or go in search of a particular section and will provide a context for your study of each section.

Article 2 is divided into seven "Parts," each dealing with a different aspect of the law relating to sales of goods. The title of each Part is a general guide to the contents; your understanding of the title of each Part will increase as you learn the sections within each Part. Here is a brief description of the Parts:

PART 1:   SHORT TITLE, GENERAL CONSTRUCTION AND SUBJECT MATTER
Laying the foundation: scope of Article 2, definitions

PART 2:   FORM, FORMATION AND READJUSTMENT OF CONTRACT
Creating an enforceable obligation: formation and modification of contracts, statute of frauds, parol evidence, assignment and delegation

PART 3:   GENERAL OBLIGATION AND CONSTRUCTION OF CONTRACT
Determining the parties' obligations: warranty obligations, meaning of delivery terms, default terms, unconscionability limitation

PART 4:   TITLE, CREDITORS AND GOOD FAITH PURCHASERS
Passing title to the goods: when title passes, what kind of title passes, rights of third-party purchasers

PART 5:   PERFORMANCE
Fulfilling delivery and payment obligations: seller's tender, buyer's payment, buyer's inspection, liability for damage to goods before and during performance

PART 6:   BREACH, REPUDIATION AND EXCUSE
Dealing with the goods and contract during performance: buyer's acceptance, rejection, or revocation of acceptance of goods; anticipatory repudiation; right to adequate assurance of performance; impossibility and impracticability

PART 7:   REMEDIES
Remedies for failure of performance: claiming or reclaiming goods, liability for damages, specific performance, statute of limitations

2003   PART 8:   TRANSITION PROVISIONS
Applicability of pre- and post-amendment provisions

Progressing from Part 1 through Part 7 roughly approximates the chronological analysis of a problem involving a possible contract for sale of goods. For example, if presented with such a problem, you are likely to ask the following series of questions:

- Is this a transaction within the scope of Article 2? (Part 1)
- Was an enforceable contract created? (Part 2)
- What are the rights and obligations created by the contract? (Parts 3 and 4)
- Did the parties perform their obligations? (Part 5)
- What are the parties' rights and responsibilities in the absence of full performance? (Parts 6 and 7)

The divisions described here are not precise; that is, cross-references, definitions, and interlocking provisions will keep you flipping back and forth among the Parts. Nevertheless, the rough organization outlined here should be a helpful guide for situating your study of the individual statutory provisions.

When you look at the table of contents for the Uniform Commercial Code, you can see that Articles 2 through 9 focus on specific types of commercial transactions—sales and leases of goods, commercial paper, electronic funds transfers, letters of credit, secured transactions, and so on. Articles 1, 10, and 11 are general-purpose articles that govern any transaction that is within the scope of any other article in the Code. They contain definitions, effective dates, repeals of inconsistent legislation, and other provisions applicable to all articles. In this textbook, you will be introduced to the parts of Article 1 that are particularly relevant to Article 2 concerns.

Learning the UCC

In this assignment, you will be introduced to two critical concepts used in defining the scope of Article 2: "sale" and "goods." This assignment does much more than teach you how the Code defines and uses those terms, however. It guides you through a method for learning statutory law, a method you can use throughout this course and every other time you are called upon to analyze and apply a statute or other code language, such as regulations and court rules.

Learning to read and understand a statute, particularly a code with interwoven provisions, is both a skill and an art, and it is different in many ways from reading and understanding cases. Case holdings can be articulated in narrow or broad terms, and can be tied more or less closely to the facts of the case. Even a court's statement of the legal rule it is following may legitimately be re-articulated and reinterpreted by a creative legal analyst. Statutes, on the other hand, are written as general rules, and the rules change only if the legislature amends them. The precise language in the statute is decisive. Though paraphrasing and re-articulating a statutory rule may sometimes assist your analysis and explanation, you must return to the precise words of the statute in order to find your authority. Every word in a statute is operative and therefore meaningful; there are no *dicta*.

This does not mean that statutes are somehow clear on their face and require no interpretation. Because they are drafted as general rules, even well drafted statutory provisions require analysis and interpretation in order to determine how to apply them to real circumstances. Perhaps because a statute represents an effort to establish broad but precise rules, statutory language is also often more difficult, more convoluted, or more awkward than ordinary writing. Ambiguities, vagueness, internal contradiction—any or all of these may complicate your task. You may need to draw on your understanding of the purpose of the statute, on legislative history, and on public policy to help understand the words. Moreover, statutory meanings sometimes change over time, based on judicial interpretation, though all such interpretations must still be tied to the text itself.

The starting place for understanding a statute is always the statutory text. Even the simplest statutory section requires close reading and attention to detail. More complicated sections require, in addition, that you determine how multiple clauses and subsections relate to one another and, perhaps, to other statutory sections. Learning how a statute works by reading it—not by being told by someone else how it works—is a skill you may not have mastered yet. You will become more adept at statutory reading and analysis only with practice, so your work with Article 2 will lead you not only to an understanding of that portion of the Uniform Commercial Code, but also to a better facility in working with all statutes.

Because each person has different preferred learning styles—visual, auditory, experiential, abstract—each of you must learn for yourself how you can best approach and learn the statute. Start with the suggestions outlined here and experiment for yourself as you progress through the material.

Foundational Principles for Article 2
and a Seven-Step Method For Learning a Statute

The seven steps listed below, explained in detail in the pages that follow, will provide you with a cohesive and comprehensive method for learning to read, learn, and use statutory language:

STEP 1. *Make a "jot" list of the general subject matter of the statutory provisions.*

STEP 2. *Read the statutory provisions closely, identify defined words, and annotate the statute.*

STEP 3. *Rewrite the statutory rules.*

STEP 4. *Read and annotate the Official Comments and supplement your annotations of the statute.*

> **STEP 5.** *Check cross-references.*
> **STEP 6.** *Diagram at the macro level.*
> **STEP 7.** *Create a diagram of the "Really Big Picture."*

We begin our consideration of Article 2 by showing you how to use these seven steps to explore the section that defines the scope of Article 2 (2-102) and six sections that provide critical definitions and terms necessary to understand that scope (2-103, 2-105, 2-106, 2-107, 2-304, 2-501).

STEP 1. *Make a "jot" list of the general subject matter of the statutory provisions.*

If you are working with multiple sections (as you often will be), you should make a brief list of all the sections and their general subject matters to give you an easy way to begin connecting the sections. For example, **your first task in Assignment 1 is to scan the assigned statutory sections, listed below, and complete the list of their topics.** Beware of simply using the caption for the section if it seems incomplete or perhaps a bit inaccurate.

Section #	Topic
2-102	scope of Article 2 (transactions in goods)
2-103(1)(a), (d)	definitions of buyer, seller[1]
2-105(1), (2)	
2-106(1)	

2003 [1] UCC Article 2 was amended in 2003 by its drafting organization, the National Conference of Commissioners on Uniform State Laws (NCCUSL), and its co-sponsor, the American Law Institute (ALI). (See Preface to this textbook for more information.) The 2003 amended version adds other definitions in 2-103, which will be introduced later, and moves the definition of "seller" to 2-103(1)(o).

Section #	Topic
2-107(1), (2)	
2-304	
2-501(1)	

Sometimes you can create this "jot list" at the beginning of an assignment; sometimes you will find it easier to do after you have looked closely at each section independently.

STEP 2. *Read the statutory provisions closely, identify defined words, and annotate the statute.*

ALL learning about a statute must start with reading the statutory section(s) closely and probably rereading at least once. It may be helpful at this stage (especially if a section contains long or convoluted sentences with multiple phrases and qualifiers) to identify the grammatical structure of each sentence: Where is the subject? the verb? Where do qualifying clauses begin and end? What words do they qualify?

You will probably want to annotate the Code sections, underlining and writing marginal notes to highlight critical concepts and terms. At this early stage, be sure to identify words that are or may be defined elsewhere or for which you need further explanation. At the end of the Official Comments for each section is a listing of "Definitional Cross References." Be sure to note those cross references, but be aware that some defined words may not appear in this list. **Look now at 2-103(2) and (3), which contain indices of important definitions for Article 2. Also look at 1-201, which contains more than forty definitions applicable throughout the Code unless they are supplanted by particular provisions in other parts of the Code or "the context otherwise requires."** You will be expected to use 2-103 and 1-201 regularly to locate defined words used elsewhere in the Code. Consider flagging them in your Code volume for easy reference.

Annotating the Code will help you to learn the content of the statute in greater depth and also will make the statute more approachable and memorable when you return to it later (perhaps in an exam or in law practice). You should continue to add explanations and cross-references as your understanding of a section expands and you identify connections with other portions of the Code and the accompanying comments.

STEP 3. *Rewrite the statutory rules.*

This is the most critical step in learning a statute. Rewriting will require time, effort, and creativity to complete, especially if a section is particularly confusing or cumbersome. The text of any statutory section states one or more rules of law. Trying to explain those rules by simply repeating the language of the section involves no analysis of the section and will not further your real understanding of what the statutory language means. To ensure that you truly understand the rules stated in the section and to help you identify the way the rules operate and detect ambiguities and confusions, you should rewrite the rules in your own language in a form that reflects the structure of the rule.

Even a paraphrase of what each segment or phrase means can be useful and will help you avoid errors arising from incomplete understanding of the language, but most rewrites go further. On the next several pages, you will find illustrations of various methods of rewriting, applied first to a simple section containing the definition of a "sale" (2-106(1)) and then to a much more complex provision detailing the events necessary for "identification" to occur (2-501(1)). You should try different methods of rewriting each rule or rules as you study them. Some methods will work better for you than others; some methods will work better for some sections than for others. If you work through statutory provisions in the manner suggested, they will be *yours*—you will know them in a very different way than if you simply read them without pulling them apart and putting them back together.

a.   **Closely read 2-106, which contains the definition of "sale." Write the definition here:**

Now consider the following ways to restate that definition:

You might create a **bullet list** of the elements of the rule established in the section, and, where applicable, the consequences of satisfying the standard. Note the inclusion of definitional cross-references, which may be critical to understanding the meaning of and connections among sections:

> *A transaction is a sale (2-106) if there is*
> - *Passing of title*
> - *From "seller" to "buyer" (2-103)*
> - *For a "price" (2-304)*

Alternatively, you might create an **"if/then" paraphrase** to list the elements and the legal consequence of satisfying those elements:

> *IF there is*
> - *(1) passing of title*
> - *(2) from seller to buyer (2-103)*
> - *(3) for a price (2-304)*
> *THEN there is a "sale"*

If you are graphically inclined, you might draw a **flow chart or diagram**:

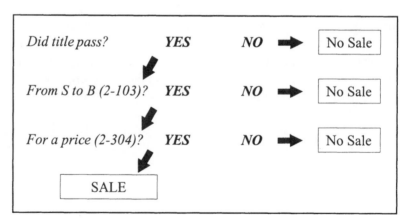

b.   Identification is the process of designating which particular items are the goods being sold—not just 500 loaves of bread but *those* 500 loaves. Section 2-501(1) governs how and when "identification" of goods occurs. Studying 2-501(1) is an instructive exercise because the seemingly straightforward language of the section hides subtle complexities that can be seen only when you attempt a structured rewrite of the text. The discussion of 2-501(1) below is quite complex, and understanding it will require substantial effort. If you perform the reading tasks requested and follow the analysis closely, you will both learn the rules regarding identification of goods (important later in the book) and appreciate the value of the various rewrite methods illustrated. In answering the questions below, be sure you can specify the statutory language that supports your answer. We suggest that you note the statutory rules revealed in your answers so you can better see how to organize them effectively into a meaningful rewrite.

Begin by reading the first sentence of 2-501(1) and then answer the following questions:

1.   What are the consequences when goods are identified?

2.   Do goods have to exist to be identified?

3.   Do goods have to conform to the contract requirements in order to be identified?

Now read the second sentence of 2-501(1). How and when does identification occur under this provision?

Now read the third sentence of 2-501(1), which contains subparts 2-501(1)(a), (b), and (c). Then answer the following questions:

1.   When do none of these subsections apply?

2.   Under what circumstances does 2-501(1)(a) apply? If it does apply, when are the goods identified?

3.   Under what circumstances does 2-501(1)(c) apply? If it does apply, when are the goods identified?

4.   Does 2-501(1)(c) specify the time of identification of the goods in a contract for sale of crops if the crops are already growing at the time the contract is entered?

5.   Under what circumstances does 2-501(1)(b) apply? To answer, you must also read 2-105(2), which contains an important definition. If 2-501(1)(b) does apply, when and how are the goods identified?

With these details in mind, review the following rewrites, and consider which one(s) explicate 2-501 better. Also think about which one(s) suit your learning style best. Remember that you usually will use only one of these rewrite methods for each section you study.

Bullet list:

- *Goods can be identified only after they exist.*
- *Parties may agree explicitly how and when goods will be identified (as long as identification occurs only after the goods exist).*
- *If parties make no explicit agreement about identification, then,*
  - *for **goods that exist and are designated at the time of contracting**, identification occurs when contract is made.*
  - *for **crops that are not yet growing at time of contracting but are nonetheless designated at that time**, identification occurs when crops are planted OR otherwise become growing crops if*
    - *crops are to be harvested within 12 months after contracting OR*
    - *crops are to be harvested next normal harvest after contracting*
  - *for **young that are not yet conceived at time of contract but are nonetheless designated at that time**, identification occurs when young are conceived if*
    - *it's a sale of unborn young to be born within 12 months after contracting*
  - *for **other "future goods"** (that is, goods didn't exist or weren't designated at time of contract), identification occurs when goods are shipped, marked, or otherwise designated by seller as goods to which the contract refers*

CONSEQUENCES OF IDENTIFICATION OF EXISTING GOODS:

Buyer obtains "special property" AND insurable interest
EVEN THOUGH
- *Goods are nonconforming AND*
- *Buyer has option to return or reject the goods*

If/then paraphrase:

a. What happens upon identification?

IF goods are
    (a) existing AND
    (b) identified to contract
EVEN THOUGH
    (c) goods are nonconforming AND
    (d) buyer has option to return or reject
THEN
    Buyer obtains "special property" and insurable interest

b. How and when does identification occur?

    i.   *IF **parties agree explicitly** upon timing or manner of identification of existing goods,*
        THEN that identification prevails over default provisions (ii through v)

    ii.   *IF contract is for sale of **goods already existing and designated at time of contracting***
        THEN identification occurs when contract is made

    iii.   *IF contract is for sale of **unborn young not conceived at time of contracting but to be born within 12 months after contracting and designated before conception as subject matter of the contract***
        THEN identification occurs when young are conceived

    iv.   *IF contract is for sale of **crops not yet growing at time of contracting but designated as the subject matter of the contract and to be harvested within 12 months after contracting OR to be harvested at next normal harvest season after contracting***

> *THEN identification occurs when crops are planted or otherwise become growing*
>
> v.   *IF contract is for sale of **future goods** not listed in iii or iv above*
> *THEN identification occurs when goods are shipped, marked or otherwise designated by the seller as goods to which the contract refers*

Flowchart or diagram:

Time Of Identification (If
Parties Do Not Agree Explicitly)

Kind of Goods	*When identification occurs*
Goods existing and designated at time of contracting	*When contract made*
Unborn young designated but not conceived at time of contracting, will be born within 1 year after contracting	*When young conceived*
Crops designated but not yet growing at time of contracting, to be harvested within 1 year after contracting or next normal harvest	*When crops planted or otherwise become growing*
Future goods not described above	*When goods shipped, marked, or otherwise designated by S as goods for the contract*

Paraphrase:

Concepts and rules about identification:

- *The goods must exist at the time of identification.*

- *Parties may by explicit agreement decide when and how identification is to occur (as long as goods exist at time of identification).*

- *If the parties don't specify the time for identification, the Code offers default rules:*

  - *If at the time the contract is created the goods exist and are designated as being the goods associated with the contract, then that is the time when identification occurs.*

  - *If the contract is for unborn livestock or growing crops, there are special provisions about when identification occurs (see 2-501(1)(c)).*

  - *If the contract is for other kinds of future goods (which don't exist or were not designated at the time the contract is made), then identification occurs when the seller ships the goods, marks them, or otherwise designates that these goods are the ones associated with the contract.*

STEP 4.   ***Read and annotate the Official Comments and supplement your annotations of the statute.***

The Official Comments were written by the drafters of the UCC to explain the provision and were available to the enacting legislatures. They thus form a part of the legislative history for the Code. The comments are not enacted language in most states, but they can help you to understand the purpose intended by the drafters and may give you examples of applications. For example, comment 5 to 2-501 tells you that identification may occur when a seller identifies a fungible bulk as the source of goods being sold.

Skim the comments for each section, to ascertain the topic(s) and subsection(s) covered in each comment. Highlight or annotate the comments, noting the connections to code subsections, to help you remember and return to the appropriate comments when you need them later. You might place comment numbers next to the portions of the Code section discussed in those comments. Read the comments as you need them to understand the finer analytical points of particular subsections. Add those points to your rewrite or your annotation of the section.

STEP 5. *Check cross-references.*

The Code contains many cross-references to other Code sections:

- Some sections refer to other sections, sometimes by section number and sometimes merely by topic.
- Some comments refer to other sections, again, sometimes by section number and sometimes merely by topic.
- Following the comments is a list of "Cross References." For reasons we never have figured out, this list uses "Point" to refer to "Comment," so Point 1 lists the cross-reference sections from Comment 1, even if Comment 1 didn't explicitly give the section numbers.
- Following the Cross References list is a list of "Definitional Cross References." This list is often incomplete, but it does provide one means of finding definitions. See Step 2 *above* for the other means of finding definitions.

You should always check the Definitional Cross References and read the definitions of words you have not previously encountered that appear in the sections or subsections you are exploring. (At first, this will be a chore, but you will need to look up fewer and fewer definitions as you become familiar with the frequently used defined terms.)

Other cross-references require finer judgment calls. If a statutory provision is "subject to" or "except as provided in" another section, you will want to at least check the topic of or even skim that section. Cross-references in comments need not be checked unless the comment has left you wanting further clarification. Other cross-references may or may not need to be checked, depending on the nature of the issue you're exploring. During this course, you will develop judgment about which cross-references to check or to fully read, and which ones you may safely skip or defer reading.

STEP 6.   *Diagram at the macro level.*

For each related group of sections (within one or more assignments), draw a flowchart or diagram illustrating how those sections relate to one another. Include section numbers and topics but refrain from including the details of the statute so that you can concentrate on the big picture in this step. Do not be dismayed to find that you need to revise the flowchart after you have worked through the problems. Consider using a pencil or erasable pen for this step.

On the next page is an example of a macro-level flowchart of the scope of Article 2, starting with 2-102 ("[T]his Article applies to transactions in goods . . ."). The flowchart then moves to 2-105 for the definition of "goods," which in turn leads to 2-107, dealing with goods to be severed from realty. The 2-105 definition of "goods" uses the defined terms "identification" and "contract for sale," so the flowchart refers to the sections that define *those* terms. The definition of "sale" in turn uses the defined terms "seller" and "buyer" and also requires an understanding of the meaning of "price."

After reviewing this sample flowchart, you may wish to create your own macro-level flowchart of these sections delineating the scope of Article 2. It is the act of seeing and noting the interconnections that will ensure that you understand and will remember them.

Diagram: Scope of Article 2

STEP 7. *Create a diagram of the "Really Big Picture."*

At the end of each subject unit, you should try to integrate all of that unit's material together in a "master" flowchart or timeline diagram. Your goal at this stage is to show the interrelationships among the clusters of sections included

---

[2] In the 2003 amended version, the definition of "goods" appears in 2-103(1)(k) and the references to future goods appear in 2-105(1).

in each separate assignment. Those interrelationships might be cross-references among sections or chronological steps in a larger analysis. Ultimately, you should be able to pull together all the units into a chart or diagram that shows the progression of analysis for a sale-of-goods transaction, with cross-references to the sections that govern particular aspects of the analysis. You are likely to exclude from your master diagram much of the detail regarding each step of the analysis in order to see the "big picture." Your master diagram can (and should) refer to more detailed rewrites of those sections.

Using Cases

It is important to learn how a statute works by reading and analyzing the statutory provisions themselves, as outlined in Steps 1 through 7 above, because the statute itself, not a court's interpretation of the statute, is always the primary authority for problem-solving and litigation in cases arising under the Code. However, judicial interpretations and applications of a statute may add to your primary understanding of the statute by clarifying an uncertain point, by denoting which of several possible interpretations of a provision some or most courts have chosen, or by illustrating the ways a court may apply a provision to facts. This textbook includes cases *only* for the purpose of showing how the cases supplement the rules in the Code, *not* for showing what the Code says.

When you read any cases included in this book—after first reading and analyzing the relevant statutory provisions yourself—you should determine what the case adds to your understanding of the relevant Code section. Then integrate those additional points into your section rewrite, your jot list, and/or your flowchart or diagram, as appropriate. Do not dwell on the procedural posture or facts of the case very much, except as they are helpful to give you a context for understanding how the statute is applied. Be sure, however, to question the court's analysis. As always, the statute is the primary authority, and courts sometimes make mistakes in their rulings. Indeed, as you become proficient in reading and understanding the Code, you may find an uncomfortably large number of cases in which courts have misconstrued the Code. You should learn to trust your own analysis so you can question case precedent when appropriate and lead the next court to a more accurate outcome.

Reading and Applying the Code

In most of the assignments that follow, you will find two sets of problems. The initial set—called "Reading the Code"—is designed to help you understand the rules you can derive directly from the Code sections and Official Comments, as illustrated above in your responses to the questions about 2-501. The concluding problems—"Applying the Code"—give you the opportunity to apply your understanding to fact situations. "Reading the Code" problems are not a substitute for engaging in the seven-step method described above. Rather, answering the reading questions posed in the assignment will help you fine-tune your rewriting of the rules and help you determine if your rewrite is complete and accurate.

Once you have familiarized yourself with the statutory sections in an assignment—through creating jot lists, reading, annotating, and rewriting the Code, and answering the reading questions—you are ready to tackle the application problems. You will find that your understanding of the abstract rules in the Code gains considerable depth by applying the rules to realistic fact situations. You will need to identify which statutory sections apply to a particular set of facts, determine which language in the sections controls, and articulate the analysis that determines the answer (or the likely or arguable answer) to the question asked.

That last step—articulating the analysis—is especially important. It is not enough to know the right answer. You must be able to explain why you're right—whether to a judge or to a client or to the teacher and your classmates. Although your audience in class is familiar with the same basic material from which you draw your analysis, you should not assume that your listeners have all understood the material in the same way that you have or that they have reached the same answer by the same path. When you share your analysis of a problem, therefore, you should be prepared to explain the following:

1.   A brief statement of the problem (the facts): We've all read the problem, but we read a lot of problems, and we need to be reminded which one this is, without restating the whole thing.

2.   A brief statement of the main issues: This helps to focus your analysis and your audience. "The question is whether the actions of the buyer constituted acceptance of the goods" goes beyond the facts and begins

the analysis. This step is particularly important in complex problems where the issue or issues will not be obvious.

3.   Your step-by-step analysis: Your analysis should clearly and methodically take your audience from problem to solution. If the problem is complex, a road map of the sub-issues you intend to address will make your oral analysis easier to follow. Be sure that your analysis includes answers to these questions:

- Which statutory sections did you use to respond to the issue(s) raised? Which precise language in those sections controlled or guided the outcome? If it's not obvious (i.e., it wasn't simply listed in the assignment), how did you find the relevant section?

- What statutory ambiguities made solving the problem more difficult? How did you resolve those ambiguities?

- Which facts were most salient in your application? Why?

Your classmates also will be depending upon you to be clear and thorough enough for them to check their own responses. Remember that your classroom presentation of a problem's solution is a rehearsal for a common event in law practice: explaining your analysis to a judge or to another attorney or even to a client (though perhaps in the latter case you wouldn't refer to the statutory sections in the same way).

Reading the Code

Problem 1-1. The Scope Provision. Recalling the diagram on page 17 and the title of this book, you may wonder why 2-102 defines the scope of Article 2 as "transactions in goods," rather than just "sales of goods."

(A)   Read the first sentence of 2-106(1). How does this section narrow the scope of application of Article 2? What is the effect of the "unless" clause?

(B)   Read the rest of 2-106(1). Draw a diagram or picture of the scope of Article 2 that demonstrates the relationships among "present sale," "contract to sell," "contract for sale," and "transaction in goods." Where would a lease of goods fit into your diagram? What about a gift of goods? A sale of services or real estate?

(C)   Based on your answers to (A) and (B), which of the following statements best articulates the scope of Article 2?

      (1)   Unless the context otherwise requires, this Article applies to transactions in goods.
      (2)   Unless the context otherwise requires, this Article applies to sales of goods.
      (3)   Unless the context otherwise requires, this Article applies to contracts for sale of goods.

Problem 1-2. "Goods."

(A)   Read 2-107(1) and (2) and comments 1 and 2. What does each subsection require for a contract to be a contract for sale of goods?

(B)   Read 2-105(1) and (2) and comments 1 and 5, and recall 2-107(1) and (2). Draw a diagram representing the meaning of "goods." (Hint: Use a pencil or erasable pen.) Your diagram should show the placement of and relationships among the following:

(A)   things movable at the time of identification to the contract for sale

(B)   specially manufactured goods

(C)   money in which the price of the goods is paid

(D)   investment securities

(E)   things in action

(F)   unborn young of animals

(G)   growing crops

(H)   minerals, oil and gas or the like, or a structure or its materials, to be removed from realty by the seller

(I)   minerals, oil and gas or the like, or a structure or its materials, to be removed from realty by the buyer

(J)   minerals, oil and gas or the like being sold with the realty

(K)   timber to be cut and sold separately from the realty

(L)   things attached to realty (but not minerals, oil, gas, or the like; or timber; or a structure or its materials), being sold apart from the realty, and capable of being severed without material harm to the realty

(M)   things attached to realty (but not minerals, oil, gas, or the like; or timber; or a structure or its materials) being sold with the realty

(C)   If the subject of a contract for sale is a shed to be removed from the real estate by the buyer, is it a sale of goods under Article 2? Is the answer governed by 2-107(1)? by 2-107(2)?

Applying the Code

Problem 1-3. Do each of the following contracts involve "goods," as that term is used in 2-105 and 2-107?[3]

(A)   Brenda engages a brick mason to tuckpoint the bricks on one side of her house. Tuckpointing is the process of grinding or drilling or chiseling out the old crumbly mortar and replacing it with fresh mortar.

(B)   Bonita owns a thousand acres of land and sells half of her acreage to her neighbor.

(C)   Stacy owns a business. Some of her customers do not pay on time. She transfers the debts that are more than 90 days overdue to a collection agency, which pays her 50 cents on the dollar.

---

[3] If a contract involves non-goods as well as goods, the contract is not necessarily within the scope of UCC Article 2. Assignment 2 discusses when Article 2 applies to these "mixed" transactions.

(D)   Yang takes over someone else's business by "buying" the name of the business and the business goodwill. No inventory or equipment changes hands.

(E)   Hal arranges with a tailor to have a custom-fitted suit sewn for him.

(F)   Consider a homeowner who contracts to sell her house to Buyer #1. The purchase agreement says the sale includes the curtain rods, lighting fixtures, gas stove, built-in dishwasher, and refrigerator, but it expressly excludes the antique chandeliers in the foyer and dining room. The homeowner sells the chandeliers to Buyer #2, a shop that sells antique lamps; an employee of the shop comes out to remove the chandeliers, leaving a few neatly capped wires hanging out of an electrical junction box where each chandelier hung. Are the items sold to Buyer #1 with the house within the scope of 2-107(1), 2-107(2), or neither? Are the chandeliers within the scope of 2-107(1), 2-107(2), or neither?

Problem 1-4. Do each of the following transactions involve a "contract for sale" per the Article 2 definition? If so, is it a present sale or a contract to sell? If the transaction involves something other than or in addition to a contract for sale, what would you call that part of the transaction?

(A)   Gary rents furniture for his new apartment, paying a monthly fee to the rental agency. At the end of two years, he can opt to rent for another two years, in which case the agency will deliver new furniture to him.

(B)   A friend gives his lifetime collection of baseball cards to Rob. Rob takes his friend out to dinner to thank him.

(C)   Jane clips a newspaper coupon good for a free pack of computer paper when presented at a local computer and office product store. One week later, she visits the store, picks up a pack of paper, and presents both the coupon and the paper to the cashier.

(D)   A grain dealer and a farmer agree that the dealer will deliver seed to the farmer and will buy the resulting wheat crop from the farmer at a specified price per bushel.

2003

Note on the Amended Definition of "Goods"

The 2003 amended version of Article 2 includes a revised definition of "goods," which appears in 2-103(1)(k). The new definition explicitly includes "future goods" and excludes "information" and "the subject matter of foreign exchange transactions" but is otherwise identical to the current version. The most significant change is the exclusion of "information" from the definition of "goods." As reflected in Official Comment 7 to the 2003 amended version, the drafters intend the revised "goods" definition to exclude (from Article 2) those transactions that involve "information not associated with goods" but to include many transactions involving so-called "smart goods"—goods with information attached or integrated. As in other "mixed transactions" (e.g., goods *and* services, goods *and* realty), the courts will decide whether Article 2 applies to sales of various kinds of smart goods (goods *and* information). Assignment 2 addresses the standard used in making such determinations, and how it might apply to transactions involving both goods and information. As the comment further notes, Article 2 may apply to a transaction including information, but "nothing in this Article alters, creates, or diminishes intellectual property rights."

Assignment 2: Scope and Mixed Transactions

§§ 1-103, 2-102

     Assignment 1 examined 2-102 and the related cluster of sections that specify which transactions are expressly and clearly within the scope of Article 2. However, section 2-102 does not settle the more difficult issue of how Article 2 applies to transactions that involve both a sale of goods and some other type of transaction. As you saw in Assignment 1, goods are not the only subject of contracting; the contract could focus on services, realty, intellectual property, or other intangible rights. Nor is a sale the only kind of transfer of interest; a transaction could involve a lease, a bailment, a gift, an assignment, or other transfer. (Contracts involving a lease of goods are covered by Article 2A.[1]) Contracts that do not involve a sale or lease of goods are governed by the common law and other statutes besides Article 2 or 2A of the Uniform Commercial Code.

     Article 2 does not specify how it applies to mixed transactions, so 1-103 directs you to the law outside of the UCC for an answer. Section 1-103[2] allows the "principles of law and equity" to supplement the UCC to the extent that the UCC does not displace other law (usually the common law) on a particular issue.[3] If a contract involves a sale of goods *and* some other non-sale-of-goods aspect, the courts can choose to (1) divide the contract into separate parts, with each part governed by the relevant body of law, or (2) treat the whole contract as falling entirely within the scope of one body of law or the other.

     Even if a mixed transaction is considered to fall within the scope of Article 2, it still may be necessary to look outside of Article 2 for rules of law

---

[1] Article 2A was added in 1987 to reflect the growth of the leasing industry. It was drafted to match the language, organization, and policies of Article 2 (and to some extent Article 9) as much as possible, so your knowledge of Article 2 will enable you to understand much of Article 2A even though this textbook does not cover Article 2A directly.

[2] Subsection 1-103(b) in revised Article 1.

2003   [3] In addition, the 2003 amended version includes a new section, 2-108, which explicitly lists some of the statutes and rules that prevail over Article 2 in the event of a conflict. *See also* the Note on Certificate-of-Title Acts in Assignment 15.

applicable to the non-sale-of-goods component of the contract.   For example, in a mixed goods-and-services contract, the parts of Article 2 dealing with formation and enforceability (e.g., the Statute of Frauds and the parol evidence rule) apply equally well to services and goods, but other portions of Article 2 (e.g., provisions on delivery, tender, and warranty) don't apply well or at all to questions related to services. In the absence of applicable Article 2 provisions, one may have to look elsewhere (to general principles of contract law) to determine legal consequences.

Even when a statute does not apply directly, courts can choose to apply a statute by analogy to a situation outside the express scope of the statute. Thus, courts have the discretion to apply portions of Article 2 to non-sale-of-goods transactions when the transaction is analogous to a sale of goods or when the underlying policies of that portion of Article 2 are consistent with the policies that the court wishes to apply to the transaction. See 1-102 comment 1.[4]

Parties are concerned about (and litigate over) which body of law governs their transactions because some rules of law governing goods and non-goods transactions differ dramatically, even though many provisions (much of contract formation, for instance) are largely the same. For instance, here are five major differences between the bodies of law governing goods and services (somewhat simplified, to show the big picture):

Issue	Law governing contracts for services	Law governing contracts for sales of goods
Differing offer and acceptance	mirror-image rule	battle of forms (2-207)
Irrevocable offer	option contract, Restatement (2d) §§ 45 (offer for unilateral contract), 87 (bid relied upon)	same, plus firm offer (2-205)

---

[4] In revised Article 1, this comment appears in 1-103 comment 1.

Issue	Law governing contracts for services	Law governing contracts for sales of goods
Implied warranty of performance quality	services will be performed in a reasonable and workerlike fashion	goods will be fit for their ordinary purpose and of fair average quality; pass without objection in the trade; run of even kind and quality; be adequately packaged, contained, and labeled; and conform to promises and affirmations on label or container (2-314)
Standard for performance	performance may be rejected only if material breach	goods may be rejected if not conforming in all respects (with some exceptions) (2-601)
Statute of limitations	varies from state to state, and depending on cause of action (2 to 10 years, generally)	breach suit must be brought within 4 years of when cause of action accrues (2-725)[5]

Note that questions about body of law are not resolved by contract clauses in which the parties agree on "choice of law" (which state's or country's law governs the contract),[6] "choice of forum" (which court will decide disputes about the contract), or a means of alternative (non-judicial) dispute resolution (ADR) to resolve the parties' contractual disputes.

---

[5] Considerably changed in the 2003 amended version. *See* Assignment 23.

[6] Choice of law clauses are governed by 1-105 (1-301 in revised Article 1).

Reading the Code (and its Case Law)

Problem 2-1. Three Approaches to Mixed Transactions. Sometimes a mixed transaction can be viewed as consisting of two or more separate contracts. Whether a contract is "divisible" in this fashion is a question of law, and depends on whether the parties intended such a separation of the contract's parts. Typically courts consider whether the parties gave a single assent to the whole transaction or instead assented separately to several things, and whether a unified price was paid for the whole transaction or instead separate consideration was given for different performances. If dividing the transaction into its separate parts results in a sale-of-goods part and a non-sale-of-goods part, the court then applies the proper body of law to each part of the contract. Read *Pass v. Shelby Aviation, Inc.*, at page 35, which shows one court's solution to the issue of mixed transactions for nondivisible contracts.

(A)   Identify and describe the two alternative approaches that the *Pass* court discussed to determine whether Article 2 governs a nondivisible mixed-transaction agreement.

(B)   Which approach did the court adopt, and what was the result of applying that approach?

(C)   List the factors that the *Pass* court used in applying its approach.[7]

---

[7] Some courts applying the predominant purpose approach have not used factors, but instead have adopted a more holistic approach, looking at the overall thrust or purpose of the contract, as well as the "reasonable totality of the circumstances," *DeFilippo v. Ford Motor Co.*, 516 F.2d 1313 (3d Cir. 1975). *See also Bonebrake v. Cox*, 499 F.2d 951 (8th Cir. 1974). The factors articulated in *Pass* are helpful references even if a court adopts the holistic approach.

(D)   How would the rejected approach have resolved the issue of which body of law applied to the agreement in *Pass*?

Applying the Code (and its Case Law)

Problem 2-2. For each of the following fact situations, determine whether the contract is divisible and apply the predominant purpose factors used in *Pass* to determine whether Article 2 governs the transaction.

(A)   Briana engages a brick mason to come to her house and tuckpoint the bricks on one side of her house. Tuckpointing is the process of grinding or drilling or chiseling out the old crumbly mortar and replacing it with fresh mortar. The mason's bid, which Briana accepts, states the following: "Tuckpoint brick on south side with mortar to match color and style of rest of house; protect garden below; clean-up." The mason spends 14 hours removing the old mortar and 8 hours adding the new mortar. She bills Briana at the rate of $55 per hour, plus $185 for the mortar and other supplies.

(B)   Charles arranges to buy a van from a dealer that specializes in customizing new vans. On the purchase agreement for the vehicle, Charles specifies his choice of the design of the hand-painted exterior and interior trim, the hand-painted design on the exterior wheel cover on the back of the van, the CD/DVD system and screens to be installed in the van, and the custom sunroof to be added. These items add 12% additional cost to the van. Charles stops by the dealer twice to check over the work being done on the van.

(C)   Pieter enters into an agreement to have a swimming pool contractor build a swimming pool in his back yard. The pool that the contractor installs is made of prefabricated fiberglass sections and a vinyl liner, assembled and sealed together on site. The agreement includes specifications for 47 items, including excavation, steel reinforcement ribs, the plaster finish, pump and filtration system, poolside tile and concrete, and the contractor's responsibility for obtaining construction permits. The cost of the pool as a whole is $7,980. The bill does not itemize any of the costs. In addition, the contractor offers to sell Pieter, and Pieter decides to buy, $1,200 in pool equipment, including a detachable diving board, two removable pool ladders, and a "skimmer" (an aquatic robot that continuously vacuums the water surface for debris).

Software, "Smart Goods," and Article 2

During the past two decades, courts have split on whether the licensing or assignment of software is a sale of goods, or whether the embedded intellectual property and its licensing prevents that result. Some courts have ruled that software transactions (especially those involving off-the-shelf software sold on the mass market) are governed by Article 2, and most of those courts have applied Article 2 directly, rather than by analogy. Certainly a disc containing software is goods, because it is "a thing movable at the time of identification," and that piece of goods is being transferred by sale, in the sense that the buyer is gaining title to the disc in return for the price. However, that analysis ignores the intellectual property aspect of the transaction, as well as its licensing or assignment provisions. Other courts have instead ignored the goods aspect of software purchases or ruled that the non-sale-of-goods aspects were the predominant purpose of the transaction so Article 2 did not apply to the transaction.

Scope questions are complicated further for transactions that involve "smart goods"—the fast-expanding category of goods with embedded software or other information. Examples include cars, video games, hand-held computer games, sophisticated watches, microwave ovens, DVD players, and televisions. In a jurisdiction in which software alone would not be within Article 2, sale of the goods with embedded software (smart goods) would be a mixed transaction, to be judged under the predominant purpose test.

2003   Perhaps the most contentious issue in the drafting of the 2003 amended version of Article 2 was whether smart goods should be within the scope of Article 2, by way of the definition of "goods."[8] Consumer groups and industry interests (manufacturers of software, computers, and smart goods) were keenly interested in the drafting outcome on this issue and advocated strongly divergent positions. Ultimately, the only solution that could garner sufficient support for NCCUSL and ALI approval was to exclude "information" from the definition of "goods" and otherwise to leave the issue to the courts. "Information" is not defined. The comment to amended 2-103(1)(k) (the definition of "goods") emphasizes that mixed transactions in goods and information are sometimes in and sometimes out of the scope of Article 2, but nothing in Article 2 alters, creates, or diminishes intellectual property rights (which are governed by federal and other state laws). The comment states that the purchase of an automobile is a transaction in goods and is governed by Article 2, even though it contains computer programs. It also states that Article 2 does not apply to an online

---

2003   [8] In the 2003 amended version, "goods" is defined in 2-103(1)(k).

download of software or "an architect's provision of architectural plans on a computer disc."[9]

2003   **Problem 2-3.** Determine which of the following smart goods are within Article 2. Use the "goods" definition in the 2003 amended version (2-103(1)(k)), the accompanying comment, and the predominant purpose test. If you cannot reach a definite result, articulate the arguments for each possible result.

(A)   Bryce buys a microwave oven at a large retail store that sells appliances and other electronics. He receives a receipt that lists the model, manufacturer, and price of the microwave oven. The box containing the microwave lists the features of the oven, including a probe that can be inserted into meat so that the microwave can adjust the cooking time and intensity according to the internal temperature of the meat. This feature is powered by software inside the oven. So is the defrosting feature, which determines the defrosting time and intensity based on the user's keypad input of the weight of the frozen meat. Other portions of the microwave oven are electronic and mechanical working parts.

(B)   Kaely buys a GameGirl hand-held computer game which allows her to play electronic versions of games such as Boggle, Scrabble, chess, and Monopoly by pressing buttons on the keyboard on the control module. To play each game, she inserts a card containing the game into the control module. She can buy additional games as they are issued by the manufacturer of the control module. She buys the control module and cards for four games at a shopping

---

[9] The Uniform Computer Information Transactions Act (UCITA) takes a different approach by applying the gravamen test to mixed transactions of information and goods. UCITA § 103(b)(1). However, UCITA was adopted in only two states (Maryland and Virginia), did not gain endorsement by the ALI or the ABA, and was removed from NCCUSL's legislative agenda in August 2003, so its influence on this issue is mainly as a commentary source, rather than as a binding statute.

mall store that sells computer games. The receipt merely lists the five items by brand names and prices.

(C)   Molly buys the latest hardback volume of the Harry Potter series at midnight of the first day on which the book is available. She buys the book at a nearby bookstore, which is hosting a Harry Potter party, complete with costumes and games.

Pass v. Shelby Aviation, Inc.

2000 WL 388775
(Tenn. Ct. App. Apr. 13, 2000)

Judge LILLARD delivered the opinion of the court, in which Judge HIGHERS and Judge FARMER joined.

This is an interlocutory appeal in a breach of warranty case. The plaintiffs' decedents were killed in an airplane crash. The estates sued the aviation company that performed the annual inspection on the airplane, on a theory of breach of warranty. The trial court denied the defendant's motion to dismiss, holding that the transaction was subject to the warranty provisions of Article 2 of the Uniform Commercial Code. Permission for interlocutory appeal was granted on this issue. We reverse, utilizing the predominant purpose test to determine if a mixed transaction of goods and services is subject to the Uniform Commercial Code, and holding that the transaction in this case was predominantly the provision of a service, not subject to the warranty provisions of the UCC.

This breach of warranty case arises out of the crash of a single engine Piper airplane owned and piloted by Max E. Pass, Jr. ("Mr. Pass"). On April 15, 1994, Mr. Pass and his wife, Martha N. Pass ("Mrs. Pass"), departed in the aircraft from Plant City, Florida, bound for Clarksville, Tennessee. Somewhere over Alabama the couple flew into turbulence. Mr. Pass lost control of the aircraft, and the plane crashed to the ground outside of Opelika, Alabama. Neither Mr. nor Mrs. Pass survived the crash.

The Defendant/Appellant in this case, Shelby Aviation, Inc. ("Shelby Aviation"), is a fixed base operator that services aircraft at Charles Baker Airport in Millington, Tennessee. On December 29, 1993, approximately four and a half months prior to the flight in which he was killed, Mr. Pass took his airplane to Shelby Aviation for inspection and service. In servicing the aircraft, Shelby Aviation replaced both rear wing attach point brackets (also called "attach point fittings") on the plane.

Three and one half years after the crash, Max E. Pass, Sr., father of Max Pass, Jr. and administrator of his estate, and Shirley Williams, mother of Martha N. Pass and administratrix of her estate, filed suit against Shelby Aviation. The lawsuit alleged that the rear wing attach point brackets sold and installed by Shelby Aviation were defective because they lacked the bolts necessary to secure them to the airplane. The Plaintiffs asserted claims against the Defendant for breach of common law warranty, and for breach of express and implied warranties under Article 2 of the Uniform Commercial Code ("UCC"), which

governs the sale of goods.[1] The Plaintiffs' complaint alleged that the Defendant's employees "failed to provide and install the bolts necessary to secure the rear wing attach point brackets to the fuselage of the aircraft," that the missing bolts "resulted in a failure of both wings to withstand the torque routinely applied to an aircraft during turbulence," and that as consequence the right wing separated from the aircraft in flight, causing Mr. Pass to lose control and the airplane to crash.

On January 28, 1998, Shelby Aviation filed a motion to dismiss, under Tennessee Rule of Civil Procedure 12.06, asserting that the Plaintiffs failed to state a claim upon which relief can be granted. Shelby Aviation contended that the transaction with Max Pass, Jr. had been primarily for the sale of services, rather than of goods, and that consequently the transaction was not covered by Article 2 of the Uniform Commercial Code. Shelby Aviation further contended that all common law warranties had been subsumed into the UCC upon its adoption in Tennessee.

After the Plaintiffs filed their response to its motion to dismiss, Shelby Aviation filed a reply to the Plaintiffs' response, which included the affidavit of Shelby Aviation president, Joe

---

[1] The statute of limitations for bringing an action for breach of a contract for sale under Article 2 of the UCC is four years from the date the cause of action accrues. Tenn.Code Ann. § 47-2-725(1). A cause of action accrues when the breach occurs, and a breach of warranty occurs when tender of delivery is made. Tenn.Code Ann. § 47-2-725(2).

McElmurray ("McElmurray"). In this affidavit, McElmurray stated that Mr. Pass had brought his plane to Shelby Aviation for an annual inspection, which was required by regulations of the Federal Aviation Administration; that all parts replaced on the plane were installed pursuant to the requirements of the annual inspection; and that the parts sold had not come from stock maintained by Shelby Aviation but instead had been ordered specifically for Mr. Pass' airplane.

On September 28, 1998, the trial court denied Shelby Aviation's motion to dismiss. On October 21, 1998, Shelby Aviation filed a motion for permission to file an interlocutory appeal of the trial court's denial of its motion to dismiss. On January 28, 1999, the trial court issued an order granting Shelby Aviation's motion for permission to file an interlocutory appeal. The trial court's order states, in relevant part:

> The transaction between Mr. Pass and Shelby Aviation involved both the rendering of services and the sale of goods. Plaintiffs' Complaint was filed December 12, 1997, alleging breach of Article 2 warranties. In response, Defendant filed a Motion to Dismiss under Tenn.R.Civ.P. 12.02(6). Defendant contends that the transaction at issue is not covered by Article 2. This Court denied Defendant's Motion to Dismiss. The determinative issue and the issue to be appealed is whether the transaction between Mr. Pass and Shelby Aviation is governed by Article 2.

On March 9, 1999 this Court granted Defendant's application for interlocutory appeal.

On appeal, Shelby Aviation raises three issues: 1) whether the trial court erred in denying Shelby Aviation's motion to dismiss the Plaintiffs' claims for breach of express and implied warranties under the UCC on the basis that the mixed transaction between it and Max Pass, Jr. was not governed by the UCC under the predominant factor test; 2) whether the trial court erred in denying Shelby Aviation's motion to dismiss the Plaintiffs' claim for breach of common law warranty on the basis that such warranty was subsumed into Article 2 of the Uniform Commercial Code upon Tennessee's adoption of the UCC; and 3) whether the trial court erred in denying Shelby Aviation's motion to dismiss the Plaintiffs' claims for breach of implied and express warranties under Article 2 of the UCC on the basis that such warranties were effectively disclaimed by Shelby Aviation.

Since the trial court's decision to deny Shelby Aviation's motion to dismiss was predicated on not just on the pleadings, but the "entire record in the cause," we treat the trial court's denial of Shelby Aviation's motion as the denial of a motion for summary judgment. Tenn.R.Civ.P. 12.02 . . . . [O]ur review of the trial court's denial of Shelby Aviation's motion for summary judgment is *de novo* on the record before this Court. *Warren v. Estate of Kirk,* 954 S.W.2d 722, 723 (Tenn.1997).

Shelby Aviation first argues that it is entitled to judgment as a matter of law on the Plaintiffs' claims for breach of the express and implied warranties of Article 2 of the UCC because the transaction between it and Max Pass, Jr. was not subject to Article 2. Shelby Aviation contends that the contract between it and Max Pass was one predominantly for service, rather than the sale of goods, and as such, falls outside of the UCC. The Plaintiffs assert that the contract was predominantly for the sale of goods, and therefore subject to the express and implied warranties on the sale of goods provided by Article 2 of the UCC.

Article 2 of the Uniform Commercial Code, adopted by Tennessee, governs the sale of goods. Many contracts, however, like the one at bar, involve a mixture of both goods and services. The problem in such "mixed" transactions is to determine whether Article 2 governs the contract. Most jurisdictions follow one of two different approaches to address the problem. *Neibarger v. Universal Cooperatives, Inc.,* 486 N.W.2d 612, 622 (Mich.1992). The first approach, sometimes called the "gravamen test," looks to that portion of the transaction upon which the complaint is based, to determine if it involved goods or services. *In re Trailer and Plumbing Supplies,* 578 A.2d 343, 345 (N.H.1990); *Anthony Pools v. Sheehan,* 455 A.2d 434, 441 (Md.1983). The other approach, known as the "predominant factor" or "predominant purpose test," looks at the transaction as a whole to determine whether its predominant purpose was the sale of goods or the provision of a service. *Insul-Mark Midwest, Inc. v. Modern Materials, Inc.,* 612 N.E.2d 550, 554 (Ind.1993). In *Hudson v. Town and Country True Value Hardware,* 666 S.W.2d 51 (Tenn.Ct.App.1984), a mixed transaction involving a contract for the sale of both goods and real estate, Tennessee elected to follow the predominant factor approach, finding it "preferable to adopt a test that views the transaction as a whole." *Id.* at 54.

The predominant factor test, as applied to a mixed transaction of goods and services, was described by the Eighth Circuit Court of Appeals in *Bonebrake v. Cox,* 499 F.2d 951 (8th Cir.1974):

> The test for inclusion or exclusion [in the U.C.C.] is not whether they [contracts] are mixed, but granting that they are mixed, whether their predominant factor, their thrust, their purpose, reasonably stated, is the rendition of services with goods incidentally involved (e.g. contract with artist for painting) or is a transaction of sale, with labor incidentally involved (e.g., installation of a water heater in a bathroom).

Id. at 960.

Under the predominant factor test, the transaction between Shelby Aviation and Mr. Pass is examined to determine whether its predominant purpose was the sale of goods or the sale of services. If it was predominantly a contract for the sale of goods, it falls under the UCC, and the warranty provisions of Article 2 apply. If it was predominantly a contract for service, it falls outside the UCC, and the warranty provisions of Article 2 are inapplicable.

In order to determine whether the predominant purpose of a mixed transaction is the sale of goods or the provision of a service, we examine the language of the parties' contract, the nature of the business of the supplier of the goods and services, the reason the parties entered into the contract (i.e. what each bargained to receive), and the respective amounts charged under the contract for goods and for services. *Ogden Martin Sys. of Indianapolis, Inc. v. Whiting Corp.*, 179 F.3d 523, 530-31 (7th Cir.1999) (citing *Insul-Mark Midwest, Inc. v. Modern Materials, Inc.*, 612 N.E.2d 550, 555 (Ind.1993)); *Coakley & Williams, Inc. v. Shatterproof Glass Corp.*, 706 F.2d 456, 460 (4th Cir.1983). None of these factors alone is dispositive. *BMC Industries, Inc. v. Barth Industries, Inc.*, 160 F.3d 1322, 1330 (11th Cir.1998). The party seeking application of the UCC bears the burden of proof to show that the predominant purpose of the contract was the sale of goods. *Insul-Mark*, 612 N.E.2d at 555; *Northwestern Equipment, Inc. v. Cudmore*, 312 N.W.2d 347, 351 (N.D.1981). The Indiana Supreme Court describes the analysis:

> To determine whether the predominant thrust of a mixed contract is to provide services or goods, one looks first to the language of the contract, in light of the situation of the parties and the surrounding circumstances. Specifically one looks to the terms describing the performance of the parties, and the words used to describe the relationship between the parties.

Beyond the contractual terms themselves, one looks to the circumstances of the parties, and the primary reason they entered into the contract. One also considers the final product the purchaser bargained to receive, and whether it may be described as a good or a service.

Finally, one examines the costs involved for the goods and services, and whether the purchaser was charged only for a good, or a price based on both goods and services. If the cost of the goods is but a small portion of the overall contract price, such fact would increase the likelihood that the services portion predominates.

Insul-Mark, 612 N.E.2d at 555 (citations omitted).

In this case, Shelby Aviation argues that the predominant factor, thrust and purpose of its transaction with Mr. Pass was the sale of services, with the sale of goods incidentally involved. Shelby Aviation notes the language in the invoice, which refers to the plane being brought in for "repair" and "100 hour inspection." Shelby Aviation also observes that the nature of its business is primarily service. The Plaintiffs argue that the predominant factor was the sale of goods. In analyzing the costs of the goods and services, the Plaintiffs argue that the cost to install the parts should be included within the cost of the parts. If it is, the Plaintiffs assert that 75% of the total amount charged by Shelby Aviation was for the sale of goods.

The written document evidencing the transaction is the invoice prepared by

Shelby Aviation. The invoice is preprinted with a handwritten description of repairs performed and parts used. In the top left hand corner, blocked off from the rest of the writing, is a preprinted paragraph that states that the owner is authorizing "the following repair work to be done along with the necessary material." On the top right hand side, under a heading entitled "Description," the box stating "annual 100 hour periodic inspection" is checked. On the left side of the invoice, beneath the authorization for repair, is a section entitled "Part number and description" with a handwritten list of the parts used and the amount charged for each. The right hand lower side of the page, under the heading "Service Description" lists the service performed and the amount charged. Finally, the bottom left corner of the page contains a block for "owner's signature" acknowledging "acceptance of repaired plane." As a whole, the invoice clearly emphasizes the repair and inspection aspect of the transaction, indicating that the predominant purpose was the sale of service, with the sale of goods incidental to that service.

We must also consider the nature of Shelby Aviation's business. The Plaintiffs' complaint asserts that Shelby Aviation is "in the business of maintenance, service, storage, and upkeep of aircraft." Shelby Aviation's president stated in his affidavit that the parts sold to Mr. Pass in conjunction with the service performed on his airplane were ordered specifically for his airplane. In addition, the invoice indicates that one part installed by the defendant, the right engine mag, was supplied by Mr. Pass.

Shelby Aviation argues that if it were primarily in the business of selling parts, rather than service, it would not have permitted a customer to supply his own part to be installed. Overall, the nature of Shelby Aviation's business appears to be service rather than the sale of parts.

It is also clear that Mr. Pass took the plane to Shelby Aviation primarily to have a service performed, i.e., the annual inspection. What the purchaser sought to procure when he entered into the contract is a strong indication of the predominant purpose of the contract. *See Stafford v. Int'l Harvester Co.,* 668 F.2d 142, 147 (2nd Cir.1981) ("underlying nature of a hybrid transaction is determined by reference to the purpose with which the customer contracted with the defendant"); *Northwestern Equipment Inc. v. Cudmore,* 312 N.W.2d 347, 349 (N. D.1981) ("Bonebrake test looks to the predominant purpose or thrust of the contract as it would exist in the minds of reasonable parties"). In *Neibarger v. Universal Cooperatives, Inc.,* 486 N.W.2d 612, 622 (Mich.1992), the Michigan Supreme Court described its analysis of the purpose of the parties' dealings:

> If the purchaser's ultimate goal is to acquire a product, the contract should be considered a transaction in goods, even though service is incidentally required. Conversely, if the purchaser's ultimate goal is to procure a service, the contract is not governed by the UCC, even though goods are incidentally required in the provision of this service.

Id. Thus, the "final product" Mr. Pass "bargained to receive" appears to be the annual inspection of his airplane. *Insul-Mark,* 612 N.E.2d at 555.

The last factor to be considered is the respective amounts charged under the contract for goods and services. By adding the labor charge to install the parts sold to the cost of the parts themselves, the Plaintiffs calculate that 75% of the amount Shelby Aviation charged is attributable to the sale of goods rather than service. The Plaintiffs cite no case law in support of this method of calculation. Indeed, at least one case appears to indicate that the cost of labor for installing parts would *not* be included in the cost of the goods for purpose of ascertaining the predominant purpose of the contract. *See Ogden Martin Systems of Indianapolis, Inc. v. Whiting Corp.,* 179 F.3d 523, 531 (7th Cir.1999). If the cost of labor is not considered part of the cost of goods, the percentage of the invoice attributable to goods is 37%.[2]

Regardless of how the percentage of the cost of goods is calculated, viewing the transaction as a whole, we must conclude that the predominant purpose of the transaction was the provision of a service rather than the sale of goods. The language of the invoice, the nature of the defendant's business, and the purpose for which Max Pass took his airplane to Shelby Aviation all indicate that service was the predominant factor in the transaction. Even where the cost of goods exceed the cost of the services, the predominant purpose of the contract may still be deemed the provision of service where the other factors support such a finding. *See Northwestern Equipment, Inc. v. Cudmore,* 312 N.W.2d 347, 351 (N.D.1981). Therefore, we hold that the transaction between Shelby Aviation and Max Pass, Jr. was predominantly a contract for service, with the sale of goods incidentally involved. As such, it is not subject to the warranty provisions of Article 2 of the UCC. Shelby Aviation is entitled to judgment as a matter of law on the Plaintiffs' UCC breach of warranty claims.

. . . .

The decision of the trial court denying Shelby Aviation's motion for summary judgment on the UCC breach of warranty claims is reversed, and the case is remanded to the trial court for further proceedings consistent with this Opinion.

. . . .

---

[2] A tally of the separate charges on the invoice Shelby Aviation prepared for Max Pass, Jr. reveals that Mr. Pass was charged $654.37 for parts, and $1,132.50 for services. Plaintiffs point out that this does not add up to the total amount of the invoice, and that Shelby Aviation apparently overcharged Max Pass by $375 by adding the inspection charge twice when it tallied the total bill.

Assignment 3: Interpretive Guidelines for Construing the Code

§§ 1-102; 1-103; 1-109; 1-201(3), (11), (42); 1-203; 1-205; 2-208; 2-209(1), (4); 2-302; 2-305; 2-306; 2-307; 2-308; 2-309; 2-725(1)

This assignment introduces the goals of the Uniform Commercial Code, as articulated in the statute, and other interpretive devices used to discern the Code's meaning. The foundational concepts in this assignment reappear in many other assignments, because they determine the content of the contract and delineate the boundaries of the parties' freedom of contract.

Reading the Code

Problem 3-1. Purposes and Construction of the UCC.

(A)   Read 1-102(1) and (2).[1] Do the articulated purposes of the UCC increase or decrease the weight that one jurisdiction should give to other jurisdictions' rulings that interpret and apply UCC provisions?

(B)   Read 1-102(3), (4), and comments 2 and 3.[2] Does the UCC encourage or discourage freedom of contract? What are the limits on parties' freedom of contract?

(C)   Read 1-102(5)[3] and 1-109[4] for your own information. These are fairly standard rules for reading statutes, at least those that have not yet been corrected for gender neutrality.

---

[1] Section 1-103(a) in revised Article 1.

[2] Section 1-302 and comments 1 and 2, with some changes, in revised Article 1.

[3] Section 1-106 in revised Article 1.

[4] Section 1-107 in revised Article 1.

Problem 3-2. Mandatory versus Default Provisions. A crucial skill in reading the UCC is to be able to determine whether

- a particular provision is **mandatory** and therefore cannot be abrogated by the parties' agreement or
- the provision is a **default** provision (also known as a gap-filler), which becomes part of the contract if the parties do not expressly or impliedly agree upon their own term on that topic.

As 1-102(4)[5] notes, not all default provisions are marked with the words "unless otherwise agreed," so you sometimes will have to determine whether a particular Code provision is a mandatory or a default provision based on the guidance in 1-102 as well as your sense of which kinds of provisions must be binding on all parties, regardless of their wish to avoid a particular rule.

Read the provisions in the following list and then divide them between mandatory and default provisions, in the chart on the next page. We have filled in several examples to get you started.

     1-203[6]
     2-302
     2-307
     2-308
     2-309[7]
     2-725(1)[8]

---

[5] Section 1-302(c) in revised Article 1.

[6] Section 1-304 in revised Article 1.

2003 [7] Subsection (3) is slightly changed, though not in substance, in the 2003 amended version.

2003 [8] Section 2-725 is changed in major respects in the 2003 amended version (see Assignment 23), but the status of the section as a mandatory or default rule remains the same.

Mandatory provisions	Default provisions
• Purposes of UCC, construction rules, variation by agreement (1-102) • Principles of law and equity supplement Code unless displaced by particular UCC provisions (1-103)[9] • Output and requirements terms (2-306(1))	• Best efforts required in exclusive dealings agreement (2-306(2))

Problem 3-3.   Agreement, Contract, Course of Dealing, Course of Performance, and Usage of Trade. Read 1-201(3), (11), (42);[10] 1-205 (and comments 1, 2, 4, 5, and 7); and 2-208 (and comment 3).[11]

---

[9] Section 1-103(b) in revised Article 1.

[10] Subsections 1-201(b)(3), (12), and (40) in revised Article 1.

[11] Section 2-208, which contains the definition of course of performance, has become difficult to find in some statutory supplements. In the 2001 revision of Article 1, the definition of course of performance appears in 1-303, along with the provisions on course of dealing and usage of trade. The Article 1 revision necessitated a conforming amendment to Article 2 that deleted 2-208. Post-2001 versions of Article 2 thus may not contain 2-208. You should be able to find 2-208 (which is still in effect in all the jurisdictions that have not adopted revised Article 1) either in an appendix to revised Article 1 (containing the conforming amendments to the revision) or in strikeout font in the section of the supplement containing the 2003 amendments to Article 2. If you find 2-208, flag the page so you can find it easily again. If you can't find it in your supplement, use the course-of-performance provision in 1-303, which makes only small changes in the wording of the definition in order to make it parallel

(A)   How are course of performance and course of dealing different? How are they similar?

(B)   Can a usage of trade apply to a consumer (a person who buys for personal, family, or household use)?

(C)   Construct an equation (or two or three) that represents the relationships among the following items:

Agreement	Contract	Course of dealing
Course of performance	Parties' language	Usage of trade
Rules imposed by law		

For example: $A + B + C = D$; $D + E + F = X$

Note that "+" doesn't mean "and" in the sense that all of the items must be present; some items can be a null or empty set.

(D)   To which part of which equation does the defined word "term" apply?

---

the definitions of course of performance and usage of trade.

Problem 3-4. Hierarchy of Terms and Provisions.

(A)   List the following items in hierarchical order, indicating which item prevails over which other item(s) in the event of a conflict. Explain why the order makes sense:

Course of dealing	Course of performance	Parties' language
Usage of trade	Default provisions	Mandatory provisions

(B)   Read the following note on "Overlaps" and explain how it changes your answer to (A).

Overlaps among Course of Performance, Modification, and Waiver

Commentators and courts have concluded that course of performance, modification, and waiver have inevitable areas of overlap, even though they each have non-overlapping areas as well. Read 2-208(3)[12] and comment 3, and 2-209(1), (4) and comment 4.

By definition, a course of performance can help explain an express term of the contract. (2-208(1)).[13] If the requirements of 2-208 are satisfied, repeated occasions for performance, knowledge of the performance by the other party, and an opportunity for that party to object a court of performance may also create a modification of the contract under 2-209. However, a course of performance does not always effect a modification, because the express terms or mandatory provisions may "trump" the course of performance.

A course of performance may also establish a waiver by demonstrating an intentional relinquishment of a known right or privilege. However, a course

---

[12] 1-303(f) in revised Article 1. See note 11 for instructions on how to find 2-208 in the statutory supplement.

[13] 1-303(d) in revised Article 1.

of performance does not always constitute a waiver, because many courses of performance do not involve giving up a benefit.

It's easier to distinguish between a waiver and a modification. A modification of a contract must be mutually agreed to and cannot be retracted, although the parties subsequently may agree to rescind or modify the modification. A waiver of a term is effected by the party to whose benefit the term runs, and that party can subsequently retract the waiver if the requirements of 2-209(5) are satisfied. A course of performance in a particular transaction thus may establish a waiver or a modification, but not likely both and perhaps not either.

Problem 3-5. Open Price Terms.

(A)   Read 2-305. Subsection (1) says that a contract for sale may be formed even though a price is not fixed. Subsection (4) says that if no price is fixed, there is no contract. Explain how these subsections can be reconciled.

(B)   Under what two sets of circumstances may a single party to a contract set the sales price?

(C)   Under what three sets of circumstances may a court choose a "reasonable price" to establish the price of goods in a sales contract?

Applying the Code

Problem 3-6. Read 2-306 and comments 2, 3, and 5. Label each of the following as usage of trade, course of dealing, course of performance, output term, requirements term, or exclusive dealing term. If you cannot decide between two answers, consider the contractual purpose of the clause.

(A)   A coal distributor agrees to furnish an electrical power utility all of the coal that the utility will need for the upcoming winter heating season.

(B)   The current contract and three previous contracts between a battery manufacturer and an automobile assembly plant call for weekly deliveries of automobile batteries. Although the written agreements were silent on time and exact place of delivery, the manufacturer delivered the batteries to Dock #15 between 8 and 10 a.m. each Monday morning under the previous agreements.

(C)   In the steel industry, the cost of freight is always calculated from Pittsburgh, no matter where it is being shipped from (or so we've heard).

(D)   A department store chain obtains the right to be the only retailer selling a particular line of clothing, in return for the chain's promise to feature the clothing prominently in its paper and online advertising.

(E)   A florist is under a year-long contract to deliver a fresh bouquet to the front desk of a nearby company each week. By the end of the first month, the florist has delivered each of the four bouquets in a plastic vase.

(F)   Not Just for Pigs, Inc. is a small company that hand-makes chocolate truffles that are in great demand regionally. It makes an arrangement with a grocery store chain to furnish half of the truffles it produces during the upcoming calendar year to the grocery store chain.

Problem 3-7. Bario Todd is a respected artist whose medium is raku pottery (raku is a pottery firing process that uses reduction rather than oxidation to produce iridescent and black finishes). Todd is contemplating selling his pots at a local gallery. The gallery has proposed an arrangement under which Todd would furnish enough raku pots so that the gallery would always have at least five pots on hand for sale.

(A)   What does Article 2 call this kind of arrangement? (Choose among the items listed in the introduction to Problem 3-6.)

(B)   As his attorney, what cautions would you raise about this arrangement? What drafting alternative(s) would you propose to alleviate your concerns?

Assignment 4: Contract Formation by Offer and Acceptance or by Conduct

§§ 1-204, 2-204, 2-205, 2-206, 2-207(1), first sentence of 2-207(3)

The Article 2 rules on contract formation appear in 2-204 through 2-207,[1] but much of sale-of-goods contract formation remains governed by the common law, as allowed by 1-103.[2] If your memory of the basic rules of contract formation is rusty, locate those rules in a treatise or other study aid and refer to them while completing this assignment.

Section 2-207 actually covers two issues: whether a contract is formed, and, if so, what its terms are. Subsection (1) and the first sentence of (3) deal with contract formation and will be covered in this assignment. Subsection (2) and the remainder of (3) determine the terms of the contract; they will be covered in Assignment 5.

Reading the Code

Problem 4-1. Firm Offers. Recall that, under the common law, an offer may generally be withdrawn before acceptance but is irrevocable when consideration has been paid to keep it open, thereby creating an option contract. In addition, Restatement (Second) §§ 45 and 87(2) also make offers irrevocable in some situations (see page 26). Section 2-205 provides an additional means by which an offer may be made irrevocable. Read 2-205 and comments 3 and 4. Also note the definitional cross-references. For the time being, assume that a merchant is any person who is in business; Assignment 7 will cover the definition of merchants under 2-104.

(A)   Section 2-205 establishes that an offer will be irrevocable under what specific circumstances?

2003 [1] Sections 2-204 through 2-206 in the 2003 amended version.

[2] Section 1-103(b) in revised Article 1.

(B)   For how long is the offer irrevocable?

(C)   Read comment 4. What does the final "but" clause mean? Why is it needed?

(D)   Read comment 3. If an offer otherwise meeting 2-205 is expressly irrevocable for more than three months, is 2-205 inapplicable? If not, what result? Does your answer change if the offeree gave consideration to keep the offer open?

(E)   What is the difference between a signed written offer from a merchant saying, "This offer lapses after May 31" and an offer that says, "This offer is irrevocable through May 31"? Which one might be governed by 2-205? What is the meaning of "This offer is good until June 1"?

Problem 4-2. Formation in General. Read 2-204 as well as the accompanying comment. Subsection (1) identifies circumstances that result in creation of a contract, and subsections (2) and (3) identify circumstances that will not prevent a finding that a contract was made. This section was written to make uniform the rules governing contract formation for sales of goods, even though the common law of some states was to the contrary of one or more subsections. Subsection (3) has been widely applied by analogy to non-sale-of-goods circumstances.

(A)   Under 2-204(1), what must be established to prove contract formation?

(B)   Under 2-204(2) and (3), what circumstances are specifically identified as not preventing contract formation?

Problem 4-3. Acceptance by Promise or Conduct. Read 2-206.

(A)   Select the statement that best describes the relationship between 2-206(1)(a) and (1)(b) (up to the comma):

1.   They cover the same factual circumstances.
2.   They cover entirely different factual circumstances.
3.   Their coverage overlaps partially but not completely.
4.   Subsection (a) is a subset of (b).
5.   Subsection (b) is a subset of (a).

(B)   To prevent a would-be accommodation shipment from being an acceptance, how would a seller indicate to the buyer that a shipment is offered only as an accommodation?   What are the meanings of "seasonable" and "notify"?

(C)   In the last clause of 2-206(1)(b) (after the comma), what does "such a shipment of nonconforming goods" constitute, if it is not an acceptance?

(D)   If "such a shipment of nonconforming goods" is an acceptance, what else is it? See comment 4.

Problem 4-4. Battle of Forms, Round 1. Read 2-207(1), the first sentence of 2-207(3), and comments 1 and 7.

(A)   Based on comment 1, what two fact situations does 2-207(1) cover? For the remainder of this Problem, ignore the first fact situation about confirmations, which will be covered in Problem 4-5.

(B)   Reorder the clauses of 2-207(1) into if/then/regardless-of/unless form. (As instructed in (A), omit the portions of 2-207(1) that pertain to confirmations.)

(C)   Recall that non-sale-of-goods contracts are governed by the mirror image rule, under which the acceptance must match the offer. Does 2-207(1) displace the common law mirror image rule? See comments 1 and 2. Does Article 2 seek to increase or decrease the number of contracts formed?

(D)   Restate the first sentence of subsection 2-207(3) as an if/then paraphrase.

(E)   Must the rules in 2-207(1) and the first sentence in (3) be applied in a certain sequence, or can counsel choose whichever rule is favorable?

Problem 4-5. Battle of Forms, Round 2. Subsection 2-207(1) applies not only to "definite and seasonable expressions of acceptance," but also to written confirmations. Comment 1 indicates that a confirmation is a document sent "where an agreement has been reached either orally or by informal correspondence between the parties and is followed by one or both of the parties sending formal memoranda embodying the terms so far as agreed upon and adding terms not discussed." Does a confirmation create a contract? If not, what purpose does a confirmation serve?

In view of your answer, you should be able to see that 2-207(1) creates a legal fiction with respect to a confirmation by saying that a confirmation *"operates* as an acceptance." It does this in order to apply 2-207(2) (covered in Assignment 5) to confirmations, in order to resolve whether the additional or different terms in the confirmation become part of the contract.

Applying the Code

Problem 4-6. Definite and Seasonable Expression of Acceptance. Read the following text very carefully, and make sure that you can articulate the main points and answer the questions at the end.

The application of 2-207(1) often depends upon determining what constitutes "a definite and seasonable expression of acceptance." As comment 2 indicates, "a proposed deal which in commercial understanding has in fact been closed is recognized as a contract" even though the acceptance contains additional or different terms. According to one commentator:

> [T]he response of the offeree operates as an acceptance if a reasonable [person] in the position of the offeror would assume that an agreement had been made despite differences in the exchanged forms. In this connection, reasonable belief that the contract has been made must take into account the words that were used by the offeree, where they appeared in his form, whether they were printed, typed, or handwritten, along with the total commercial setting of the transaction, including course of dealing and usage of trade. In case of doubt, the court ought to decide in favor of the existence of a contract, because the chances are good that both parties intended to create one when they exchanged their forms, and moreover, the ambiguities of the offeree's purported acceptance ought to be resolved against him in close cases . . . .

William D. Hawkland, *Uniform Commercial Code Series* § 2-207:2, at 2-271 to -272 (2001).

Some courts interpreting 2-207(1) have paraphrased "definite . . . expression of acceptance" as meaning that the document responding to the offer manifests an acceptance and does not "diverge[] significantly as to a dickered term." *U.S. Industries, Inc. v. Semco Manufacturing, Inc.*, 562 F.2d 1061, 1067 (8th Cir. 1977).

- A "dickered term" (or some courts use the phrase "dickered-for term") is a term that the parties have negotiated and agreed upon, or a term specified by a party in non-form language. Examples commonly include the type of goods, their price, quantity, and delivery date. *General Electric Co. v. G. Siempelkamp GmbH & Co.*, 29 F.3d 1095, 1098 (6th Cir. 1994); *Gardner Zemke Co. v. Dunham Bush, Inc.*, 850 P.2d 319, 323 (N.M. 1993).
- A divergence was found to be "significant" when an offer listed the price as $1.55 per ton and the responsive document listed the price as $1.85 per ton. *Howard Construction Co. v. Jeff-Cole Quarries, Inc.*, 669 S.W.2d 221, 229 (Mo. Ct. App. 1983) (mentioning an example from White & Summers' treatise: an offer for 200,000 pounds of lard at 10¢ per pound and an acknowledgment at 15¢ per pound).
- A would-be acceptance was found to diverge significantly as to the dickered terms where the offer (a subcontractor's bid to a general contractor) gave an 8% payment discount if contractor paid in full within ten days of invoice, while the response gave an 8% discount but required contractor to pay only 90% of the cost of materials furnished within the preceding month, and allowed contractor to retain 10% of the price until completion of the project. *Herm Hughes & Sons, Inc. v. Quintek*, 834 P.2d 582, 585 (Utah Ct. App. 1992).

Consider the following facts. Are any contracts created? If so, by which actions?

(A)   After negotiations, Buyer orders 1,000 units of goods at $50 per unit in a purchase order that also contains a set of standard terms. Seller sends Buyer an acknowledgment promising to send 900 units, on a form that contains standard terms that differ from the Buyer's. After Buyer receives the acknowledgment but has done nothing else, Seller denies that a contract exists.

(B)   After negotiations, Buyer orders 450 "red" seat cushions at $50 per unit in a purchase order that also contains a set of standard terms. Seller sends Buyer an acknowledgment promising to send 450 "scarlet" seat cushions on a form that contains standard terms that differ from the Buyer's. After Buyer receives the acknowledgment, Seller denies that a contract exists.

(C)   Offeror sends purchase order. Offeree responds with a pre-printed "Order Verification" postcard that says, "Your order has been received and is being processed."

Problem 4-7. Expressly Conditional "Acceptance." Read the following text very carefully, and make sure that you can articulate the main points and answer the questions at the end.

A contract does not result under 2-207(1) if the "acceptance is expressly made conditional on assent to the additional or different terms." The courts are unanimous that, to have this result, the condition must be express (not implied), using language such as "provided that," "subject to," "but only if," or other language that makes it clear that the would-be acceptance is effective only if the additional or different terms are included in the agreement. In this sense, 2-207(1) is consistent with the policy and effect of 2-206(1), which indicates that an offeror can specify how the offer is to be accepted but must do so unambiguously. Similarly, the offeree can specify whether the response is or is not intended to be an acceptance, but must do so expressly and unambiguously.

However, the courts are split regarding whether a would-be acceptance is "expressly conditional" if it says that acceptance is conditional on the offeree's additional or different terms or only if it makes acceptance conditional on the offeror's *assent* to the offeree's additional or different terms.

• The former rule was applied in *Construction Aggregates Corp. v. Hewitt-Robins, Inc.*, 404 F.2d 505, 508 (7th Cir. 1968), in which seller responded to buyer's order with a letter stating that seller's acceptance was predicated on certain modifications, including a substitute warranty clause. Buyer made no written objection to the terms in seller's letter but requested only a change in the payment terms, which seller granted. The court ruled that seller's letter was a counter-offer, rather than an acceptance, because it was expressly conditional on the stated modifications.

• On the other hand, the latter rule was applied in *Dorton v. Collins & Aikman Corp.*, 453 F.2d 1161, 1168 (6th Cir. 1972), in which the court held that a response to an offer is expressly conditional and therefore not an acceptance only if it "clearly reveals that the offeree is unwilling to proceed with the transaction unless he is assured of the offeror's assent to the additional or different terms therein." "Expressly" means "directly and distinctly stated or expressed rather than implied or left to inference." *Id.* The court would have found the acceptance to have been expressly conditional if the seller had insisted on the buyer signing and delivering it back to the seller. Instead, the seller's acceptance said the seller would consider the buyer's failure to object to seller's additional terms within ten days to indicate acquiescence to those additional terms. Because usually assent cannot be shown by silence, the court ruled that the seller's acceptance was *not* expressly conditional on the buyer's assent to the additional terms. This more stringent approach, requiring that the acceptance expressly demand affirmative approval of the additional or different terms, seems to be the majority approach.

Consider the following facts. Does a contract exist? If so, by which actions?

(A) Offeror sends purchase order. Offeree responds with a pre-printed "Order Verification" that says, "We will ship your order in 4-6 business days. Please note that all sales are made subject to terms noted below." The Order Verification contains form language with several terms additional to and different from those contained on the original purchase order.

(B)   Offeror sends purchase order. Offeree responds with a "Purchase Acknowledgment" saying "We accept your order, but only if you agree to the terms in our standard contract, listed on the back of this confirmation." The pre-printed terms on the back of the Purchase Acknowledgment list several terms additional to and different from those contained on the original purchase order.

(C)   Same facts as (B) above. There is no further communication between the parties. Offeree later ships the ordered goods. Offeror receives and keeps the goods without objection.

Problem 4-8. Scope of 2-207(1). Subsection 2-207(1) specifies that it applies to confirmations only if they are written, but it doesn't limit its application to acceptances that are written. Which portions of 2-207 and its comments furnish arguments for or against applying 2-207(1) to oral acceptances? The answer to this question determines the scope of application of the rules in both 2-207(1) and (2).

Problem 4-9. Contract Formation in an Electronic Setting. Students of commercial law need to be conversant with the electronic commerce statutes that interact with the UCC and enable contracts to be formed in electronic media. This Problem acquaints you with the basic vocabulary, rules, and statutes governing electronic contract formation. A problem in Assignment 6 focuses on the enforceability of electronic contracts under the statute of frauds.

Read the following text very carefully, and make sure that you can articulate the main points and answer the questions at the end.

The rise of electronic commerce has posed special issues of contract formation, many of which have been addressed by a trio of statutes:[3]

- Uniform Electronic Transactions Act (UETA), completed in 1999 and enacted in 42 states and the District of Columbia as of March 2004;[4]
- Electronic Signatures in Global and National Commerce Act (E-Sign), enacted at the federal level in 2000; and
- revisions of the UCC, including the 2003 amendments to UCC Article 2.

These statutes differ somewhat in scope of application:

- UETA: electronic records and electronic signatures relating to a transaction, if both parties to the transaction have "agreed"[5] to conduct the transaction by electronic means;
- E-Sign: any transaction in or affecting interstate or foreign commerce;
- Art. 2: contract for sale of goods

Because each subsequent act borrowed from previous act(s), the three acts overlap quite a bit. E-Sign's definitions and rules are already the law in every jurisdiction (remember that E-Sign is a federal statute), and very similar provisions appear in UETA.[6] Thus, even if a state has not yet enacted the 2003

---

[3] A fourth statute, the Uniform Computer Information Transactions Act (UCITA), was enacted in only Maryland and Virginia and has since been withdrawn from legislative enactment efforts by NCCUSL.

[4] For a current list of states enacting UETA, see www.nccusl.org.

[5] UETA borrows the UCC's meaning of "agreed," so a person might "agree" to do business electronically expressly or implicitly (by conduct, course of performance, course of dealing, or usage of trade). Comment 4 to UETA § 5 notes that a person presenting a business card with an e-mail address might be "agreeing" to do business electronically.

[6] Although the supremacy clause of the United States Constitution would allow E-Sign to pre-empt UETA, E-Sign explicitly allows states to enact laws that modify, limit, or supersede part of E-Sign (the part relevant to our Article 2 topics) if the state law is
  • an enactment of UETA or
  • an alternative set of procedures or requirements for use or acceptance of electronic records and signatures, so long as they are consistent with E-Sign and do not favor one technology over another (and if enacted after E-Sign, include a specific reference to E-Sign; the 2003 amendments to Article 2 contain such a reference in § 2-108(4)).
State enactments of UETA (and state statutes complying with the second bullet point) therefore take precedence over E-Sign, to the extent the two statutes are inconsistent. The

amendments to Article 2 related to electronic commerce, many of the same rules are already in effect, because of E-Sign and UETA.

Consider the following facts and answer the questions posed, as you read the pertinent portions of the acts (some of which have been paraphrased for ease of understanding).

A bookseller sets up a web site on which customers can order used books. The web site's terms of use say that all orders are "subject to availability," and that statement appears at the top of the ordering screen. Each customer can fill an electronic "shopping cart" with items from the web site's electronic catalog and then must furnish a credit card number and agree to pay the requisite amount by clicking a clearly labeled "I Agree" button. The web site's software then checks the bookseller's automated inventory report to make sure that the ordered books are in stock and issues an automated e-mail to the customer stating when the ordered items will be shipped. The buyer gets the e-mail. The bookseller ships the ordered books to the customer, who receives them and finds them to be acceptable.

(A)   Have any electronic records been used between the parties? If so, identify them. Use the definitions below:

Definition	Authority
"Record" means information that is inscribed on a tangible medium or that is stored in an electronic or other medium and is retrievable in perceivable form.	E-Sign § 106(9); UETA § 2(13); UCC 2-103(1)(m) (2003)
"Electronic record" means a record created, generated, sent, communicated, received, or stored by electronic means.	E-Sign § 106(4); UETA § 2(7); UCC 2-103(1)(h) (2003)
"Electronic" means relating to technology having electrical, digital, magnetic, wireless, optical, electromagnetic, or similar capabilities.	E-Sign § 106(2); UETA § 2(5); UCC 2-103(1)(f) (2003)

---

more non-uniform the UETA enactment, the more likely it is that the enactment must instead meet the requirements in the second bullet above, in order not to be pre-empted (in whole or in part) by E-Sign.

(B)   Have any of the electronic records you noted in (A) been "sent" or "received"? If so, identify when. Note any additional facts you need to know. Use the rules below:

Rule	Authority

(a) unless otherwise agreed, an electronic record is sent when it
    (1) is addressed properly or otherwise directed properly to an information processing system that the recipient has designated or uses for the purpose of receiving electronic records and from which the recipient is able to retrieve the electronic record,
    (2) is in a form capable of being processed by that system, and
    (3) enters an information processing system outside the control of the sender.
	UETA § 15(a)

(b) Unless otherwise agreed between a sender and the recipient, an electronic record is received when it
    (1) enters an information processing system that the recipient has designated or uses for the purpose of receiving electronic records and from which the recipient is able to retrieve the electronic record and
    (2) is in a form capable of being processed by that system.
	UETA § 15(b)

(C)   Did the electronic records contain any electronic signatures? Use the definitions below:

Definition	Authority
"Electronic signature" means an electronic sound, symbol, or process attached to or logically associated with a record and executed or adopted by the person with the intent to sign the record.	E-Sign § 106(5); UETA § 2(8);
"Sign" means, with present intent to authenticate or adopt a record: (i) to execute or adopt a tangible symbol; or (ii) to attach to or logically associate with the record an electronic sound, symbol, or process.	UCC 2-103(p) (2003)

(D)   Are any electronic agents involved in the contract formation process? Use the definition below.

Definition	Authority
"Electronic agent" means a computer program or an electronic or other automated means used independently to initiate an action or respond to electronic records or performances in whole or in part, without review or action by an individual.[7]	E-Sign § 106(3); UETA § 2(6); UCC 2-103(g) (2003)

---

[7] Note that an "electronic agent" is not really an "agent," because agency law requires an agent to be a person. Computer software running on a computer is a machine programmed by a person and set in motion by a person, but it is not an agent.

(E)   Which actions, if any, form a contract between the bookseller and the customer? Use the rules below, as well as common law rules.

Rule	Authority
Record, signature, or contract can't be denied legal effect or enforceability solely because it's in electronic form.	E-Sign § 101(a); UETA § 7(a),(b); UCC 211(1), (2) (2003)
A contract can be formed between an electronic agent and an individual or between two electronic agents.[8]	E-Sign § 101(h); UETA § 14(1); UCC 2-204(1), (4) (2003)
A contract is formed between an electronic agent and an individual if the individual takes actions it is free to refuse to take or makes a statement, and the individual has reason to know the actions or statement will (i) cause the electronic agent to complete the transaction or performance; or (ii) indicate acceptance of an offer, regardless of other expressions or actions by the individual to which the electronic agent cannot react.[9]	UCC 2-204(4)(b) (no E-Sign provision) (UETA § 14(2) contains a similar rule that doesn't go as far)
Such a contract doesn't include terms provided by an individual if the individual had reason to know that the agent couldn't react to the terms as provided.[10]	UCC 2-211(4) (2003) (no UETA or E–Sign provisions)
Receipt of an electronic communication can have a legal effect, even if no individual is aware of the receipt.	UETA § 15(e); UCC 2-213(1) (2003)

---

[8] Such as when software programmed as a shopping "bot" buys from an automated web site.

[9] Identical to UCITA § 206(b).

[10] Similar to UCITA § 206(c).

(F)   Would your answer to (E) differ in a jurisdiction not enacting UETA or the 2003 amendments to Article 2? Could the same result be reached under common law?

2003   Problem 4-10. Battle of Forms, Round 3.

Read 2-206(3) and comments 2 and 3 in the 2003 amended version.

(A)   In what respects does 2-206(3) differ from unamended 2-207(1)?

(B)   Which, if any, of these differences affect the outcome of an offer-acceptance dispute? Do amended 2-206(3) and its comments settle the *Construction Aggregates-Dorton* split (see page 57)?

Assignment 5: Determining the Content When Offer and Acceptance Differ: Battle of Forms

§ 2-207(2), (3)

You have already seen in Assignment 4 that, under Article 2, a contract may be formed even though the acceptance contains additional or different terms from the offer (2-207(1)). And if the writings do *not* show agreement sufficient to satisfy 2-207(1), a contract may still be formed by conduct (2-207(3)). Saying that a contract has been formed leaves an important question unanswered, however: What are the terms of that contract? Section 2-207 attempts to answer that question, but it contains ambiguities and contradictions, and it leaves some critical questions unanswered. The materials in this assignment are designed to help you understand the remainder of 2-207 as it is currently applied and to recognize the interpretational problems. The assignment will also introduce you to the substantial changes to 2-207 made in the 2003 amendments.

Reading the Code

Problem 5-1. Terms in Contracts Created by Conduct. To make sense of this complicated section, you should consider separately each of several paths through the provision. First, look at 2-207(3) and Comment 7. The second sentence of 2-207(3) states a rule for determining contract terms. The first sentence tells you when that rule applies. Rewrite and paraphrase the subsection as an if/then statement:

IF these facts are established:

THEN this is the rule for determining the contract terms:

Problem 5-2. Additional Terms in Contracts Created by Offer and Acceptance. As we saw in Assignment 4, section 2-207(1) tells us that under certain conditions a response to an offer can operate as an acceptance even though the purported acceptance *adds new terms* or *contains different terms* than the offer. We will first consider what happens when the purported acceptance *adds new terms*.

(A)   Read 2-207(2). If the parties are *not* both merchants, what happens to additional terms in the acceptance? Under what circumstances will such terms become part of the contract?

(B)   If the parties *are* both merchants, what happens to additional terms in the acceptance? Under what circumstances will such terms become part of the contract?

(C)   Read the first sentence of 2-207 comment 6. Why is this statement incorrect if read literally?

Problem 5-3. Material Alteration. Under 2-207(2)(b), to determine if an additional term will become part of the contract, you may have to determine whether the new term would "materially alter" the contract.

(A)   What do comments 4 and 5 suggest as a general standard for determining whether an additional term would "materially alter" the contract?

(B)　　　Comment 4 gives the following examples of clauses that *would* materially alter a contract:

- negating implied warranties that would normally attach to a sale;
- demanding near perfect compliance with quantity terms where usage of trade allows greater leeway;
- reserving to seller the power to cancel the entire contract if buyer doesn't pay a single invoice when due;
- requiring that complaints be made much sooner than usual or reasonable.

Comment 5 gives the following examples of clauses that *would not* materially alter a contract:

- giving seller the same or a slightly greater exemption from performance than already granted by Article 2 under circumstances of impracticability;
- requiring that complaints be made within a time limit that is customary and reasonable;
- if the goods are being sold for immediate resale, providing for inspection by the ultimate purchaser;
- providing credit terms or interest within the range of trade practice, and not interfering with credit bargained for;
- limiting remedies in a reasonable manner in accordance with the relevant Article 2 provisions.

From reviewing these examples, what questions might you ask a client to help you determine whether an additional term would be considered a material or nonmaterial alteration?

Problem 5-4. Different Terms in Contracts Created by Offer and Acceptance. Now that you have seen the operation of 2-207 on *additional* terms, we must consider what effect the section has on *different* terms:

(A)   What makes a term "different" rather than "additional" for the purposes of 2-207(1)?

(B)   What—if anything—does the text of 2-207(2) explicitly tell us about what happens to *different terms* that are contained in the acceptance?

(C)   Read comment 3 to 2-207, the caption for 2-207, and 1-109. Based on these sources, what more can you say about how to treat *different* terms appearing in an acceptance?

(D)   Your answers to (B) and (C) should convince you that 2-207(2) fails to give clear guidance regarding how to treat different terms. One possibility might be to apply 2-207(2) to different as well as to additional terms. What would be the result of doing so? Would the different terms always, never, or sometimes become part of the contract?

(E)   Applying 2-207(2) is not the only option for handling different terms. Read *Daitom, Inc. v. Pennwalt Corp.*, at page 85. What three alternatives does *Daitom* give for handling different terms? Be sure that for each alternative you can explain how that alternative can be supported by reference to the code, comments, and policy underlying the code. Do you agree with *Daitom*'s description of how 2-207(2) would work if applied to different terms?

Problem 5-5. Additional and Different Terms in Acceptances.

(A)　　Consider the following chart, which displays four possibilities of agreement and disagreement between offer and acceptance as to a particular term. "Version A" represents one substantive choice of term, e.g., "1% monthly interest on unpaid balances." "Version B" represents a different substantive choice *on the same subject matter*, e.g., "No interest on unpaid balances." Fill in the final column, indicating which version of the term, if any, will be in the contract, or what rule will be used to select the term.

Term in the offer	Term in the acceptance	Term in the contract
Version A	Version A	
Version A	(Silent)	
(Silent)	Version A	
Version A	Version B	

(B)　　Under the common law, if an offer and acceptance did not match, the "acceptance" would be considered a counteroffer. If the parties nonetheless began performance, the counteroffer would often be considered the articulation of contract terms that had been accepted by performance, thereby giving preference to the "last form" exchanged between the parties. Under similar circumstances, does 2-207 give a preference to the first form, the last form, or neither, in determining which terms are part of the contract?

Problem 5-6. Additional and Different Terms in Confirmations.

(A)   Recall the way in which 2-207 treats additional terms in an acceptance. Under 2-207, what happens to additional terms in a confirmation sent by one of the parties to the transaction?

(B)   Read comment 6 to 2-207 (except for the first sentence) and recall the meaning of "confirmation" as used in 2-207(1). What happens if both parties send confirmations that contain additional terms that conflict with each other? What happens if one or both parties send a confirmation that contains terms that conflict with the agreement reached before the confirmation was sent?

(C)   Consider the following chart, which displays the range of scenarios that may occur regarding agreement, disagreement, and silence when one or both parties send confirmations after they agree to a contract. As in Problem 5-5, "Version A" represents a term on a particular subject matter (e.g., "Complaints as to delivered goods must be made within 60 days"), while "Version B" and "Version C" represent different terms *on the same subject matter* (e.g., "All complaints of defect to be made within 90 days" and "Seller must be notified of any defects within 120 days"). Fill in the final column, indicating what the term in the contract will be or what rule will be used to select the term.

Term agreed to before confirm-ation(s) sent	Term in confirmation from first party	Term in confirmation from second party	Term in final contract
(Silent)	Version A	(Silent)	
(Silent)	Version A	Version B	
Version A	(Silent)	(Silent)	
Version A	Version B	(Silent)	
Version A	Version B	Version B	
Version A	Version B	Version C	

Problem 5-7. Overview of 2-207. Before proceeding to the application problems below, you should construct a flowchart or other rewrite of 2-207 based on the analysis reflected in your answers to Problems 5-1 to 5-6. This exercise will help you pull together the parts of 2-207 and will serve as a foundation for applying the section. (You may wish to do your flowchart on a separate sheet of paper.)

Applying the Code

Problem 5-8. Consider the following short scenarios, designed to ensure that you can navigate your way through the multiple paths in 2-207. For each one, determine (1) what subsection of 2-207 (if any) determines which terms are in the contract, and (2) whether the offeror's or offeree's terms control or what standard you would use to answer that question. Assume all parties are merchants. In answering these questions, you will find it helpful to consider first whether the contract is formed by offer and varying acceptance, by prior agreement followed by one or more confirmations, or by conduct.

(A)   Offeror sends a purchase order saying, "This offer may be accepted only on the terms specified herein." Offeree responds with a document saying "Your order is accepted" but the document adds a new term on a minor subject not covered in the original purchase order. Would your answer be different if the purchase order instead said, "This offer expressly conditioned on your acceptance of these terms"?

(B)   Offeror sends purchase order with a set of standard terms and a cover letter specifying that seller must agree to all of buyer's terms. Offeree responds with a "Confirmation" containing standard terms, some of which differ from those in the offer and specifying that "Acceptance is subject to agreement to all terms contained herein." There is no further written communication. Offeree ships the ordered goods within the time specified in the order. Offeror receives and keeps the goods.

(C)   Offeror sends purchase order with no mention of a delivery date. Offeree responds with a preprinted "Order Verification" saying, "Your order is accepted. Shipment will be made in three business days."

(D)   Same as (C), but the "Order Verification" also contains on the reverse side a pre-printed term specifying, "Goods sold without warranty."

(E)   Offeror sends an offer to sell a specified quantity of goods to buyer at a specified price. On the back is a pre-printed set of terms, including one that specifies, "Seller warrants against defects for six months" and another that provides for arbitration of disputes. Offeree responds with a "Purchase Order" repeating the quantity and price from the seller's form. On the reverse side is a pre-printed term specifying "One Year Warranty Against Defects."

(F)   Ritz Department Store sends a purchase order for perfume gift sets on Friday, December 3, specifying delivery of goods by December 14. Offeree responds on December 8 with a "Sales Verification" repeating the quantity and price from the purchase order and stating, "Shipment will arrive within ten business days."

(G)   Buyer and Seller agree by phone on sale of goods to Buyer at a specified price. Buyer and Seller each send confirming documents repeating the agreed-upon terms on quantity and price. On the back of Buyer's form is a pre-printed provision specifying that Seller will pay any attorney fees that Buyer incurs if enforcement of the contract in court is necessary and identifying the law of Texas (where the Buyer is located) as the law to be applied to any such dispute. On the back of Seller's form is a preprinted provision specifying that the law of New York (where Seller is located) will apply to any dispute.

Problem 5-9.   Apple Aircraft Rentals ("Apple"), sends the following communication to Primara Aircraft on June 1:

> We are ordering from you ten (10) Primara Cloudgrazer aircraft at the price stated in your price quotation, subject to our standard terms and conditions (attached).

The standard terms include this one:

> Vendor agrees to reimburse Apple for any amounts owed by Apple to third parties because of defects in vendor's product.

The next day, Primara sends the following response:

> We accept. Please note that the sale includes the terms contained on the back of this acceptance form.

The back of the form contains the following terms:

     (i)   Any claims of defect in equipment must be submitted in writing within 60 days of detection;

     (ii)   Primara will not pay any consequential damages to Buyer for any liability of Buyer to third parties arising from use of Primara's aircraft;

     (iii)   Any dispute between us is to be governed by binding arbitration.

There is no further correspondence between the two companies relating to terms. Three weeks later Primara seeks to deliver the aircraft to Apple. Apple refuses to accept the planes, claiming there was no contract. Primara claims breach of contract and seeks to enforce the binding arbitration provision that it asserts is part of the contract.

(A)   Do these communications create a contract? If so, which of the terms specified by Apple or Primara are part of the contract, and why? In formulating your answer, consider the following information about arbitration procedure, drawn from an American Arbitration Association publication:[1]

- "Under the standard AAA [American Arbitration Association] rules, the procedure is relatively simple: legal rules of evidence are not applicable; there is no motion practice or court conference; there is no requirement for transcripts of the proceedings or for written opinions of the arbitrators. Although there is no formal discovery process, the AAA's rules allow the arbitrator to require production of relevant documents, the deposition of factual witnesses, and an exchange of reports of expert witnesses."
- "The arbitrator shall be the judge of the relevance, materiality, credibility and weight of the evidence offered, and conformity to legal rules of evidence shall not be necessary."
- "The arbitrator may grant any remedy or relief that the arbitrator deems just and equitable and within the scope of the agreement of the parties."
- The parties may provide by agreement that the arbitrators give effect to substantive rules of law, but in the absence of such an agreement, the arbitrator is not bound to do so.
- Judicial review of arbitration awards is limited, and awards generally may not be challenged on the grounds that they do not follow substantive or procedural rules of law.

---

[1] American Arbitration Association, *Resolving Commercial Financial Disputes—A Practical Guide*, available at www.adr.org.

(B)   Would your answer to (A) be different if the communications concerned a single Primara Cloudgrazer aircraft being purchased by a flying enthusiast for use in pleasure excursions?

(C)   Would your answer to (A) be different if a previous dispute between Primara and Apple had been handled by arbitration?

(D)   Would your answer to (A) be different if the order by Apple was the fifth such order from Primara and after each order Primara sent the same response, including the three terms on the back of the acceptance form?

"Terms in the Box"

What happens when a buyer receives goods along with documents that purport to contain terms of the contract? Are the documents to be considered acceptances or confirmations so that the effect of their contents is governed by 2-207(2)? Does 2-206(1) furnish any guidance about which terms become part of a contract formed by shipment of the goods? Does it matter if the seller's documents say the goods should be returned if the additional terms are not satisfactory? If the parties agreed to price, quantity, and other particulars before shipment, is the contract already formed so that the documents are an offer to modify under 2-209?

Recent cases involving computer hardware and software have generated two interesting lines of reasoning about whether such "terms in the box" become part of the contract. Because many sellers and buyers are affected by these kinds of "terms in a box," it is important to be familiar with the competing cases and rationales, as well as to determine if there is controlling authority on this point in the particular jurisdiction involved in a dispute. This remains a highly contested issue related to sales of goods.

In one line of cases, the terms delivered in the box were found to be part of the contract:

*   In *ProCD v. Zeidenberg,* a software vendor placed a notice of enclosed terms on the outside of the boxes, the shrinkwrap license terms were inside the boxes, and those terms gave buyers a right to return the software for a refund if the terms were unacceptable. Consumer buyer bought a package of vendor's software from a retail store, used the software rather than returning it, and disregarded the enclosed license terms restricting buyer's dissemination of the software on the Web. The vendor sought an injunction based on the terms of the shrinkwrap license. The court held that the vendor, as master of the offer, had specified which acts would constitute acceptance of the offer, and the

buyer had accepted the license terms in the way specified by the vendor, per UCC 2-204. Section 2-207 was held to be irrelevant because there was only one form.[2] *ProCD v. Zeidenberg*, 86 F.3d 1447 (7th Cir. 1996) (J. Easterbrook) (citing *Carnival Cruise Lines*[3]).

- In *Hill v. Gateway 2000, Inc.,* buyer ordered a computer by telephone from the manufacturer, who shipped the computer in a box containing additional terms and a statement that those terms became part of the contract unless the buyer returned the computer within thirty days. Buyer did not return the computer, and the manufacturer sought to enforce the additional terms. The court held that the terms (including the contested arbitration clause) were an offer from the manufacturer, which offer the buyer accepted by not returning the computer. *Hill v. Gateway 2000, Inc.*, 105 F.3d 1147 (7th Cir. 1997) (J. Easterbrook) (citing *ProCD* and *Carnival Cruise Lines*).

The courts in *ProCD* and *Hill* reasoned that the contract was formed only after the buyer received all terms from the seller, so those terms were accepted when the buyer tore open the shrinkwrap or kept the goods, even though the buyer may not have actually seen the terms.

In another line of cases, the courts used 2-204, 2-207, and 2-209 to reach the opposite result—that the "terms in the box" did not become part of the contract:

- In *Step-Saver Data Systems, Inc. v. Wyse Technology*, buyer, a value-added retailer, ordered multiple copies of software by phone, and seller, the software manufacturer, promised to ship. Buyer then sent a purchase order detailing the terms, and seller responded with shipment and an invoice with nearly identical terms (price, quantity, shipping, payment). On each software package was printed a "box-top license," which specified that buyer had a non-transferable license, disclaimed all

---

[2] A later court declined to follow this reasoning because 2-207(1) and (2) can indeed apply to a single-form transaction (*see Klocek* on page 80).

[3] In *Carnival Cruise Lines, Inc. v. Shute*, 499 U.S. 585 (1991), buyers purchased passage on a cruise ship through a travel agent, and the cruise line later sent them tickets with a Florida forum selection clause. The Court upheld the unnegotiated clause in the form contract because the buyers received notice of the forum clause before the cruise and because the clause was enforceable under previous precedents on enforceable forum-selection clauses.

warranties except a single express warranty, limited buyer's remedies to return and replacement, excluded all damages, provided that the box-top license was the final and complete agreement of the parties, specified that buyer's opening of the box was acceptance of the box-top terms, and instructed buyer to return the box unopened within fifteen days for a refund if buyer did not accept the terms. The parties repeated this sequence over perhaps six to eight shipments for a total of 142 software copies. The court held that (1) the parties' performance (seller's shipment and buyer's acceptance of the goods and payment) had formed a contract, (2) the contract was sufficiently definite under 2-204(3) without the box-top terms, (3) buyer never agreed to the box-top license as a final expression or modification of the parties' agreement so the integration clause was not binding, (4) the box-top license was similar to a written confirmation under 2-207(1) rather than a conditional acceptance,[4] (5) the warranty disclaimer and the remedy limitation in the box-top agreement would materially alter the parties' agreement under 2-207(2) and so did not become part of the agreement,[5] and (6) the repeated use of the box-top license did not create a course of dealing between the parties. *Step-Saver Data Systems, Inc. v. Wyse Technology*, 939 F.2d 91 (3d Cir. 1991).

•   In *Arizona Retail Systems, Inc. v. Software Link, Inc.,* buyer, a value-added retailer, ordered either an evaluative copy or a live copy of software from the manufacturer (who was one of the defendants in *Step-Saver*). The manufacturer sent both an evaluative copy and a live copy, which were wrapped together in shrink-wrap plastic with an attached license agreement that claimed to be triggered upon buyer opening the plastic; accompanying materials stated that buyer could return the

---

[4] The court did not satisfactorily explain why it needed to analyze the issue of conditional acceptance under 2-207(1) when the parties had already formed a contract by that point. A subsequent court noted that the *Step-Saver* court's approach was erroneous in this respect and refused to follow that part of the *Step-Saver* reasoning (*see Arizona Retail Systems* above).

[5] The *Step-Saver* court seemed to use 2-207(3) for its analysis of the parties' contract formation by performance, then shifted to 2-207(1) to analyze seller's conditional acceptance arguments, and finally used 2-207(2)(b) to determine whether the disclaimer and remedy limitation were added to the agreement. The court never explained why it did not instead apply the remainder of 2-207(3) (the knock-out rule) to determine the terms of the agreement.

materials if not satisfied. Buyer tested the evaluation disk, read the license agreement, and decided to keep the software. The court held that buyer accepted the license terms to that particular software shipment by not returning the software or by tearing open the shrinkwrap plastic. Subsequently, buyer made numerous purchases of the same software by phone with manufacturer, who promised to ship promptly and did not mention the license agreement. Manufacturer then shipped the software with a shrinkwrap license agreement attached to the packaging. The court held that the license agreement was either (1) an additional set of terms that were material alterations under 2-207(2)(b) and therefore were not part of the contract or (2) a proposal to modify under 2-209 to which buyer did not expresssly assent (borrowing the *Step-Saver* analysis). *Arizona Retail Systems, Inc. v. Software Link, Inc.*, 831 F. Supp. 759 (D. Ariz. 1993).

• In *Klocek v. Gateway, Inc.,* the record was "woefully unclear" as to how and where a contract was formed so the court considered multiple contract formation scenarios. The buyer purchased a computer from the manufacturer, who shipped the goods or gave the goods to the buyer in person, with Standard Terms and Conditions enclosed in the box. The terms included an arbitration clause and also stated that buyer would be deemed to have accepted those terms by not returning the goods within five days. For purposes of ruling on a motion to dismiss, the court assumed that the buyer made an offer in person or by catalog order, which offer the seller accepted by completing the sales transaction in person or agreeing to ship the catalog order or shipping the computer to buyer, per 2-206. The court then reasoned that the terms enclosed with the shipment were not conditional and so not a counteroffer, but instead were either an expression of acceptance or a written confirmation under 2-207(1). Because buyer was not a merchant, those enclosed terms did not become additional terms to the contract under 2-207(2) unless buyer agreed to them. Buyer's lack of consent caused the same result under 2-209. Buyer never assented to the five-day return term and so could not be said to assent to the enclosed terms by keeping the goods for more than five days, nor did buyer assent to the enclosed terms in any other way. "Express assent cannot be presumed by silence or mere failure to object." The court denied the manufacturer's motion to dismiss. *Klocek v. Gateway, Inc.*, 104 F. Supp. 2d 1332 (D. Kan. 2000) (expressly rejecting *ProCD* and *Hill*).

In this *Step-Saver* line of cases, the courts held that the contracts were created *before* the additional terms were received by the buyer or that the additional terms were included in the seller's acceptance. The courts then used 2-207 or 2-209 to determine whether those additional terms became part of the contract.

Problem 5-10. The *ProCD/Hill* and *Step-Saver* lines of cases reach different outcomes because they reach different conclusions regarding when and how the sales contracts were formed. To help clarify those analyses, consider the following transaction: A consumer buyer places an order for goods on the seller's web site, providing a credit card for payment. Seller ships the goods and includes in the shipment a "Confirmation of Order" that contains additional terms and instructs the buyer to return the goods if the terms are not acceptable. Answer the questions below, which ask you to enumerate the ways in which the contract might be considered formed and the implications of each formation method for determining the content of the contract. Place your answers in the chart that follows part (C). In formulating your answer, you may draw upon the case descriptions above, but the questions ask you to make your own independent analysis of how the statute operates, not to discuss and apply the cases themselves.

(A)   At what points in the described transaction might a court find a sales contract was created? You should be able to identify at least 3 or 4 different moments that might signal contract formation and to suggest why each one should (or should not) be considered to have created the contract. Place your answers in column 1 of the chart below.

(B)   For each moment you identified in (A), what section of Article 2 would you point to as establishing or governing that contract formation? Place your answers in column 2 of the chart below.

(C)   For each theory of contract formation noted in your answers to (A) and (B), do the seller's terms in the box become part of the contract? What statutory provisions support your result? Place your answers in column 3 of the chart below.

(A) Moment of contract formation	(B) UCC section governing contract formation	(C) Do terms in the box become part of the contract? Under what UCC section?

(D)   Given the variations reflected above, as the lawyer for a manufacturer who sells products directly to consumers, both merchants and non-merchants, through catalog and web purchases as well as in its own retail locations, what advice would you give to help your client maximize the chances that its terms will be binding on buyers?

2003 **Problem 5-11. "Battle of Forms" Under the 2003 Amendments.** Read the 2003 amended version of 2-207 and its comments. Note that comment 5 states that the 2003 amendments do not address the conflict between the *ProCD/Hill* and *Step Saver* lines of cases, the drafters preferring to take no position on the issue. As you have seen, *ProCD/Hill* and *Step-Saver* differ on whether 2-207 applies to "terms in a box," so changing the content of 2-207 does not affect that debate.

(A)   Rewrite the amended version of 2-207 using a bullet list, if-then paraphrase, flowchart, or diagram.

(B)   Make a list of the significant differences between the amended and unamended versions of 2-207. (*Tip:* This question asks you to compare the pre- and post-amendment versions of 2-207 and identify the changes based only on reading the two sets of rules. Questions (C) and (E) ask you to compare the two versions by considering how they would apply in particular fact situations. If you prefer to learn by looking at the "forest" before identifying individual "trees," you may wish to answer this question before completing the charts in (C) and (E) below. If, instead, you prefer to learn by studying the "trees" in order to figure out what the "forest" looks like, you may wish to complete the charts first, then answer this question.)

(C)   The chart below reproduces the scenarios presented in Problem 5-5, dealing with additional and different terms in an acceptance. Transcribe your answers from Problem 5-5 into the third column, then complete the final column by indicating which term will be included in the final contractual agreement under the 2003 amended version of 2-207.

Term in the offer	Term in the acceptance	Term in the contract (pre-amendment)	Term in the contract under 2003 amendments
Version A	Version A		
Version A	(Silent)		
(Silent)	Version A		
Version A	Version B		

(D)   Consider again the fact scenario presented in Problem 5-10. Under the 2003 amended version of 2-207, do the seller's terms in the box become part of the contract?

(E)   The chart below reproduces the scenarios presented in Problem 5-6, dealing with "different" terms in confirmations. Transcribe your answers in Problem 5-6 into the fourth column, then complete the final column by indicating which term will be included in the final contractual agreement under the 2003 amended version of 2-207.

Term agreed to before confirmation(s) sent	Term in confirmation from first party	Term in confirmation from second party	Term in final contract (pre-amendment)	Term under 2003 amendments
(Silent)	Version A	(Silent)		
(Silent)	Version A	Version B		
Version A	(Silent)	(Silent)		
Version A	Version B	(Silent)		
Version A	Version B	Version B		
Version A	Version B	Version C		

**Daitom, Inc.,
Plaintiff-Appellant,
v.
Pennwalt Corp.,
Defendant-Appellee**

741 F.2d 1569 (10th Cir. 1984)

Before BARRETT, DOYLE and LOGAN, Circuit Judges.

WILLIAM E. DOYLE, Circuit Judge.

I. STATEMENT OF THE CASE

This is an appeal from the grant of summary judgment against Daitom, Inc.

(Daitom), the plaintiff below. The result was dismissal by the United States District Court for the District of Kansas of all three counts of Daitom's complaint.

Daitom had brought this diversity action in federal court on March 7, 1980 against Pennwalt Corporation and its Stokes Vacuum Equipment Division (Pennwalt). Counts I and II of Daitom's complaint alleged breach of various express and implied warranties and Count III alleged negligent design and manufacture by Pennwalt of certain rotary vacuum drying machines sold to and used commercially by Daitom in the production of a vitamin known properly as dextro calcium pantothenate and commonly as Vitamin B-5.

Daitom is a Delaware chartered corporation having its principal place of business in Kansas. It was formed to implement a joint venture between Thompson-Hayward Chemical Company, Inc. of Kansas City, Kansas and Daiichi-Seiyakii Co., Ltd., of Tokyo, Japan. Pennwalt is a Pennsylvania chartered corporation with its principal place of business in Pennsylvania.

Daitom requests a reversal of the district court's grant of summary judgment against Daitom on all counts of its complaint and seeks a remand for a trial on the merits.

We have concluded that there should be a reversal with respect to Counts I and II, together with a remand to the district court for a trial on the merits of those claims. On the other hand, we have concluded that there should be an affirmance of the summary judgment against Daitom on Count III of its complaint.

II. FACTS

The essential facts so far as they pertain to the issues presented in this appeal are as follows.

For the purpose of implementing its joint venture, Daitom planned to construct and operate a manufacturing plant to commercially produce dextro calcium pantothenate. The design of the plant was undertaken and handled on behalf of Daitom by Kintech Services, Inc. (which company will be referred to as Kintech), an engineering design firm located in Cincinnati, Ohio. Kintech had the responsibility not only for designing

the plant; it also was responsible for investigating various means of drying the product during the production process, and for negotiating the purchase of certain equipment to be used in the plant. Included in the equipment was automated drying equipment to be used in removing methonol and water from the processed vitamin as part of the purification process.

There were numerous tests made and conducted at Kintech's request by equipment manufacturers. Kintech formulated specifications for the automated drying equipment. (This is referred to as Kintech Specification 342, Record, Volume I, at 59-65). On behalf of Daitom, Kintech invited various vendors to bid on the needed equipment.

Pennwalt, on September 7, 1976, submitted a proposal for the sale of two rotary vacuum dryers with dust filters and heating systems to dry dextro calcium pantothenate. The typewritten proposal specified the equipment to be sold, the f.o.b. price, and delivery and payment terms. A pre-printed conditions of sale form was also attached to the proposal and explicitly made an integral part of the proposal by the typewritten sheet.

Kintech recommended to Daitom that Pennwalt's proposal be accepted and on October 5, 1976, well within the thirty-day acceptance period specified in the proposal, Daitom issued a purchase order for the Pennwalt equipment. The purchase order consisted of a pre-printed form with the identification of the specific equipment and associated prices typewritten in the appropriate blank spaces on the front together with seventeen lengthy "boilerplate" or "standard" terms and conditions of sale on the back. In addition, on the front of the purchase order in the column marked for a description of the items purchased, Daitom typed the following:

> Rotary vacuum dryers in accordance with Kintech Services, Inc. specification 342 dated August 20, 1976, and in accordance with Stokes proposal dated September 7, 1976.

The two rotary vacuum dryers and the equipment that went along with them were manufactured by Pennwalt and delivered to Daitom's plant in early May 1977. For the reason that there had been no construction of Daitom's plant, the crated equipment was not immediately installed. Instead, it was stored outside in crates. On June 15, 1978, the dryers were finally installed and first operated by Daitom. Daitom notified Pennwalt of serious problems with the operation of the dryers on June 17, 1978.

Daitom's contention was that the dryers suffered from two severe defects: 1) they were delivered with misaligned agitator blades causing a scraping and damaging of the dryer interiors and an uneven distribution of the products being dried; and 2) they were undersized necessitating an overloading of the dryers and a "lumping up" of the product rendering it unsuitable for further use. Pennwalt's repair personnel visited the Daitom plant to investigate the alleged operating difficulties, but Daitom contends the dryers were not repaired and have never performed as required under the specifications and as represented by Pennwalt. This was the basis for the lawsuit.

This suit was brought in federal court on March 7, 1980, after Pennwalt's alleged failure to correct the difficulties with the dryers. On Pennwalt's motion, the district court granted summary judgment against Daitom on all three counts of its complaint. The court dismissed Counts I and II after applying section 2-207 of the Uniform Commercial Code (U.C.C.) and finding that Daitom's breach of warranties claims were barred by the one-year period of limitations specified in Pennwalt's proposal. The court further concluded that alleged damages in Count III for the negligent design and manufacture of the dryers were not available in tort; the sole remedy being in an action for breach of warranties which here was barred by period of limitations. Consequently, summary judgment was granted against Daitom. Daitom's subsequent motion for reconsideration was denied by the district court on June 3, 1982, and following that, this appeal took place.

III. DISCUSSION

A. The Issues

It is to be noted that the district court granted summary judgment against Daitom on Counts I and II of the complaint, finding the breach of warranties claim barred by the one-year period of limitations which was set forth in Pennwalt's proposal. In ruling against Daitom the court followed a three step analysis. First, it concluded that pursuant to U.C.C. § 2-207(1), a written contract for the sale of the rotary dryers was formed by Pennwalt's September 7, 1976 proposal and Daitom's October 5, 1976 purchase order accepting that proposal. Second, the court found that the one year period of limitations specified in Pennwalt's proposal and shortening the typical four-year period of limitations available under the U.C.C. became part of the contract of sale and governed the claims for breach of warranties. Thus, the court accepted the proposal that was contained in the documents that had been submitted by the defendant-appellee. . . .

Daitom has challenged the district court's findings as to the terms which became a part of the contract. Daitom argues that its October 5, 1976 purchase order did not constitute an acceptance of Pennwalt's September 7, 1976 proposal. Instead, Daitom claims that its purchase order explicitly made acceptance conditional on Pennwalt's assent to the additional or different terms in the purchase order. As a consequence, Daitom argues, pursuant to U.C.C. § 2-207(1),[1] the exchanged writings of the parties did not form a contract, because Pennwalt failed to assent to the additional or different terms in the purchase order. The most relevant additional or different terms Daitom alleges were in its purchase order were the terms reserving all warranties and remedies available in law, despite Pennwalt's limitation of warranties and remedies in its proposal. In a sense Pennwalt argues it enjoyed an exclusive right to set the conditions.

---

[1] The parties, throughout this litigation and through their briefs, agree that the law of Pennsylvania governs their warranty claims. The parties further agree that Pennsylvania has adopted the provisions of the Uniform Commercial Code and that for the purpose of this action the Pennsylvania statute does not modify the U.C.C. provisions. See 13 Pa.C.S.A. § 2207 (Purdon's 1984). Therefore, throughout this memorandum the relevant code sections will be referred to only by the U.C.C. numeral designation.

Daitom argues that on their face the writings failed to create a contract, and, instead, that a contract was to be formed by the conduct of both parties, pursuant to § 2-207(3), and the resulting contract consisted of the terms on which the writings agreed, together with "any supplementary terms incorporated under any other provision of [the UCC]." Therefore, Daitom concludes, the resulting contract governing the sale of the rotary dryers incorporated the U.C.C. provisions for express warranties (§ 2-313), implied warranties (§§ 2- 314, 2-315), and a four year period of limitations.

As an alternative argument, Daitom contends that even if its October 5, 1976 purchase order did constitute an acceptance of Pennwalt's September 7, 1976 proposal and did form a contract, all conflicting terms between the two writings were "knocked out" and did not become part of the resulting contract, because of their being at odds one with the other. Therefore, Daitom concludes once again that the resulting contract consisted of only those terms in which the writings agreed and any supplementary or "gap-filler" terms incorporated under the provisions of the U.C.C.; specifically §§ 2-313, 2- 314, 2-315, 2-725.

. . . .

After considering the record in the instant case, it is apparent that the substantive law was not correctly applied and that summary judgment against Daitom on Counts I and II was improper. The fundamental feature with respect to this is this court's determination of whether any terms in the parties' writings conflicted and, if so, which terms became part of the resultant contract.

B. The Applicable Law

The district court found the dispute between Daitom and Pennwalt involved a "transaction in goods," between persons who are "merchants" and, therefore, was governed by Article 2 of the U.C.C. U.C.C. §§ 2-102, 2-104. The district court also stated that the dispute is a classic example of the "battle of the forms."

As previously noted, there has been agreement that the law of Pennsylvania governs these claims for breach of warranty and Pennsylvania has adopted the provisions of the U.C.C. Section 2-207 of the U.C.C. was specifically drafted to deal with the battle of the forms and related problems. U.C.C. § 2-207, Comment 1.

Section 2-207 has been commented on in one case as a "murky bit of prose," (Southwest Engineering Co., Inc. v. Martin Tractor Co., Inc., 205 Kan. 684, 473 P.2d 18, 25 (1970)), and as "one of the most important, subtle, and difficult in the entire code, and well it may be said that the product as it finally reads is not altogether satisfactory." (Duesenberg & King, 3 Sales and Bulk Transfer Under the Uniform Commercial Code, § 3.03 at 3-12 (1984)). The Pennsylvania Supreme Court has not addressed the issues presented by this case. In the absence, therefore, of an authoritative pronouncement from the state's highest court, our task is to regard ourselves as sitting in diversity and predicting how the state's highest court would rule. Pennsylvania Glass Sand Corporation v. Caterpillar Tractor Company, 652 F.2d 1165, 1167 (3rd Cir.1981). This court must also follow any intermediate state court decision unless other authority convinces us that the state supreme court would decide otherwise. Delano v. Kitch, 663 F.2d 990, 996 (10th Cir.1981), cert. denied, 456 U.S. 946, 102 S.Ct. 2012, 72 L.Ed.2d 468 (1982). Also, the policies underlying the applicable legal doctrines, the doctrinal trends indicated by these policies, and the decisions of other courts may also inform this court's analysis. Pennsylvania Glass Sand, supra, at 1167 (3rd Cir.1981). With these standards in mind, we proceed to consider and analyze the case.

C. The writings and the contract.

[The court concludes that Daitom's purchase order was an acceptance of Pennwalt's proposal, despite its inclusion of terms additional to and different from those in the offer. The court rejected Daitom's claim that certain provisions made the acceptance expressly conditional on assent to the additional or different terms, applying the standard articulated in *Dorton v. Collins & Aikman Corp.,* 453 F.2d 1161 (6th Cir. 1972).]

Having found an offer and an acceptance which was not made expressly conditional on assent to additional or different terms, we must now decide the effect of those additional or different terms on the resulting contract and what terms became part of it. The district court simply resolved this dispute by focusing solely on the period of limitations specified in Pennwalt's offer of September 7, 1976. Thus, the court held that while the offer explicitly specified a one-year period of limitations in accordance with § 2-725(1) allowing such a reduction, Daitom's acceptance of October 5, 1976 was silent as to the limitations period. Consequently, the court held that § 2-207(2) was inapplicable and the one-year limitations period controlled, effectively barring Daitom's action for breach of warranties.

While the district court's analysis undertook to resolve the issue without considering the question of the application of § 2-207(2) to additional or different terms, we cannot accept its approach or its conclusion. We are unable to ignore the plain implication of Daitom's reservation in its boilerplate warranties provision of all its rights and remedies available at law. Such an explicit reservation impliedly reserves the statutory period of limitations; without such a reservation, all other reservations of actions and remedies are without effect.

The statutory period of limitations under the U.C.C. is four years after the cause of action has accrued. U.C.C. § 2-725(1). Were we to determine that this four-year period became a part of the contract rather than the shorter one-year period, Daitom's actions on breach of warranties were timely brought and summary judgment against Daitom was error.[2]

We realize that our conclusion requires an inference to be drawn from a construction of Daitom's terms; however, such an inference and construction are consistent with the judicial reluctance to grant summary judgment where there is some reasonable doubt over the existence of a genuine material fact. See Williams v. Borden, Inc., 637 F.2d 731, 738 (10th Cir.1980). When taking into account the circumstances surrounding the application of the one-year limitations period, we have little hesitation in adopting the U.C.C.'s four-year limitations reservation, the application of which permits a trial on the merits. Thus, this court must recognize that certain terms in Daitom's acceptance differed from terms in Pennwalt's offer and decide which become part of the contract. The district court certainly erred in refusing to recognize such a conflict.[3]

The difficulty in determining the effect of different terms in the acceptance is the imprecision of drafting evident in § 2-207. The language of the provision is silent on how different terms in the acceptance are to be treated once a contract is formed pursuant to § 2-207(1). That section provides that a contract may be formed by exchanged writings despite

---

[2] Daitom filed its complaint on March 7, 1980. While the parties dispute when the cause of action accrued and the period of limitations began to run, resolution of the dispute is unnecessary if this court concludes the four-year limitations period controls. Even if it is found the action accrued in May 1977 on delivery of the dryers to Daitom's plant, the four-year period of limitations had not expired on March 7, 1980 when the complaint was filed.

[3] There is some indication in its memorandum and order that had the district court considered the effect of the conflicting terms, it would have applied § 2-207(2)(b) and concluded that the terms in Pennwalt's offer controlled because Daitom's conflicting terms would have materially altered the content. Memorandum and Order at 11. Because we hold, infra, that conflicting terms should not be analyzed pursuant to § 2-207(2), this conclusion of the district court is also in error.

the existence of additional or different terms in the acceptance. Therefore, an offeree's response is treated as an acceptance while it may differ substantially from the offer. This section of the provision, then, reformed the mirror-image rule; that common law legal formality that prohibited the formation of a contract if the exchanged writings of offer and acceptance differed in any term.

Once a contract is recognized pursuant to § 2-207(1), 2-207(2) provides the standard for determining if the additional terms stated in the acceptance become a part of the contract. Between merchants, such additional terms become part of the resulting contract unless 1) the offer expressly limited acceptance to its terms, 2) the additional terms materially alter the contract obligations, or 3) the offeror gives notice of his or her objection to the additional terms within a reasonable time. Should any one of these three possibilities occur, the additional terms are treated merely as proposals for incorporation in the contract and absent assent by the offeror the terms of the offer control. In any event, the existence of the additional terms does not prevent a contract from being formed.

Section 2-207(2) is silent on the treatment of terms stated in the acceptance that are different, rather than merely additional, from those stated in the offer. It is unclear whether "different" terms in the acceptance are intended to be included under the aegis of "additional" terms in § 2-207(2) and, therefore, fail to become part of the agreement if they materially alter the contract. Comment 3 suggests just such

an inclusion.[4] However, Comment 6 suggests that different terms in exchanged writings must be assumed to constitute mutual objections by each party to the other's conflicting terms and result in a mutual "knockout" of both parties' conflicting terms; the missing terms to be supplied by the U.C.C.'s "gap-filler" provisions.[5] At least one commentator, in support of this view, has suggested that the drafting history of the provision indicates that the word "different" was intentionally deleted from the final draft of § 2-207(2) to preclude its treatment under that subsection.[6] The plain

---

[4] Comment 3 states (emphasis added):

Whether or not *additional or different* terms will become part of the agreement depends upon the provision of subsection (2).

It must be remembered that even official comments to enacted statutory text do not have the force of law and are only guidance in the interpretation of that text. In re Bristol Associates, Inc., 505 F.2d 1056 (3rd Cir.1974) (while the comments to the Pennsylvania U.C.C. are not binding, the Pennsylvania Supreme Court gives substantial weight to the comments as evidencing application of the Code).

[5] Comment 6 states, in part:
Where clauses on confirming forms sent by both parties conflict each party must be assumed to object to a clause of the other conflicting with one on the confirmation sent by himself.... The contract then consists of the terms expressly agreed to, terms on which the confirmations agree, and terms supplied by the Act, including subsection (2).

[6] See D.G. Baird & R. Weisberg, Rules, Standards, and the Battle of the Forms: A Reassessment of § 2-207, 68 Va.L.R. 1217, 1240, n. 61.

language, comments, and drafting history of the provision, therefore, provide little helpful guidance in resolving the disagreement over the treatment of different terms pursuant to § 2-207.

Despite all this, the cases and commentators have suggested three possible approaches. The first of these is to treat "different" terms as included under the aegis of "additional" terms in § 2-207(2). Consequently, different terms in the acceptance would never become part of the contract, because, by definition, they would materially alter the contract (i.e., the offeror's terms). Several courts have adopted this approach. E.g., Mead Corporation v. McNally-Pittsburg Manufacturing Corporation, 654 F.2d 1197 (6th Cir.1981) (applying Ohio law); Steiner v. Mobil Oil Corporation, 20 Cal.3d 90, 141 Cal.Rptr. 157, 569 P.2d 751 (1977); Lockheed Electronics Company, Inc. v. Keronix, Inc., 114 Cal.App.3d 304, 170 Cal.Rptr. 591 (1981).

The second approach, which leads to the same result as the first, is that the offeror's terms control because the offeree's different terms merely fall out; § 2-207(2) cannot rescue the different terms since that subsection applies only to additional terms. Under this approach, Comment 6 (apparently supporting a mutual rather than a single term knockout) is not applicable because it refers only to conflicting terms in confirmation forms following oral agreement, not conflicting terms in the writings that form the agreement. This approach is supported by Professor Summers. J.J. White & R.S. Summers, Uniform Commercial Code, § 1-2, at 29 (2d ed. 1980).

The third, and preferable approach, which is commonly called the "knock-out" rule, is that the conflicting terms cancel one another. Under this view the offeree's form is treated only as an acceptance of the terms in the offeror's form which did not conflict. The ultimate contract, then, includes those non-conflicting terms and any other terms supplied by the U.C.C., including terms incorporated by course of performance (§ 2-208), course of dealing (§ 1-205), usage of trade (§ 1-205), and other "gap fillers" or "off-the-rack" terms (e.g., implied warranty of fitness for particular purpose, § 2-315). As stated previously, this approach finds some support in Comment 6. Professor White supports this approach as the most fair and consistent with the purposes of § 2-207. White & Summers, supra, at 29. Further, several courts have adopted or recognized the approach.   E.g., Idaho Power Company v. Westinghouse Electric Corporation, 596 F.2d 924 (9th Cir.1979) (applying Idaho law, although incorrectly, applying § 2-207(3) after finding a contract under § 2-207(1)); Owens-Corning Fiberglass Corporation v. Sonic Development Corporation, 546 F.Supp. 533 (D.Kan.1982) (Judge Saffels applying Kansas law); Lea Tai Textile Co., Ltd. v. Manning Fabrics, Inc., 411 F.Supp. 1404 (S.D.N.Y.1975); Hartwig Farms, Inc. v. Pacific Gamble Robinson Company, 28 Wash.App. 539, 625 P.2d 171 (1981); S.C. Gray, Inc. v. Ford Motor Company, 92 Mich.App. 789, 286 N.W.2d 34 (1979).

We are of the opinion that this is the more reasonable approach, particularly when dealing with a case such as this where from the beginning the offeror's specified period of limitations would expire before the equipment was even installed. The approaches other than the "knock-out" approach would be inequitable and unjust because they invited the very kind of treatment which the defendant attempted to provide.

Thus, we are of the conclusion that if faced with this issue the Pennsylvania Supreme Court would adopt the "knock-out" rule and hold here that the conflicting terms in Pennwalt's offer and Daitom's acceptance regarding the period of limitations and applicable warranties cancel one another out. Consequently, the other provisions of the U.C.C. must be used to provide the missing terms.

This particular approach and result are supported persuasively by the underlying rationale and purpose behind the adoption of § 2-207. As stated previously, that provision was drafted to reform the infamous common law mirror-image rule and associated last-shot doctrine that enshrined the fortuitous positions of senders of forms and accorded undue advantages based on such fortuitous positions. White & Summers, supra at 25. To refuse to adopt the "knock-out" rule and instead adopt one of the remaining two approaches would serve to re-enshrine the undue advantages derived solely from the fortuitous positions of when a party sent a form. Cf., 3 Duesenberg & King at 93 (1983 Supp.). This is because either approach other than the knock-out rule for different terms results in the offeror and his or her terms always prevailing solely because he or she sent the first form. Professor Summers argues that this advantage is not wholly unearned, because the offeree has an opportunity to review the offer, identify the conflicting terms and make his or her acceptance

conditional. But this joinder misses the fundamental purpose of the U.C.C. in general and § 2-207 in particular, which is to preserve a contract and fill in any gaps if the parties intended to make a contract and there is a reasonable basis for giving an appropriate remedy. U.C.C. §§ 2-204(3); § 2-207(1); § 2-207(3). Thus, this approach gives the offeree some protection. While it is laudible for business persons to read the fine print and boilerplate provisions in exchanged forms, there is nothing in § 2-207 mandating such careful consideration. The provision seems drafted with a recognition of the reality that merchants seldom review exchanged forms with the scrutiny of lawyers. The "knock-out" rule is therefore the best approach. Even if a term eliminated by operation of the "knock-out" rule is reintroduced by operation of the U.C.C.'s gap-filler provisions, such a result does not indicate a weakness of the approach. On the contrary, at least the reintroduced term has the merit of being a term that the U.C.C. draftpersons regarded as fair.

We now address the question of reverse and remand regarding Counts I and II. The result of this court's holding is that the district court erred in granting summary judgment against Daitom on Counts I and II of its complaint. Operation of the "knock-out" rule to conflicting terms results in the instant case in the conflicting terms in the offer and acceptance regarding the period of limitations and applicable warranties cancelling. In the absence of any evidence of course of performance, course of dealing, or usage of trade providing the missing terms, §§ 2-725(1), 2-313, 2-314, 2-315 may operate to supply a four-year period of limitations, an express warranty,[7] an implied warranty of merchantability, and an implied warranty of fitness for a particular purpose, respectively. The ruling of the district court on Counts I and II does not invite this kind of a broad inquiry, and thus, we must recognize the superiority in terms of justice of the "knock-out" rule. Consequently, the ruling of the district court on Counts I and II must be reversed and the matter remanded for trial consistent with this court's ruling.

D. Unavailability of tort remedy

The district court correctly granted summary judgment against Daitom on Count III. It held that there is no cause of action in tort for a purely economic loss.

. . . .

Accordingly, the district court correctly concluded that Daitom's requested damages are not recoverable in tort. The court's summary judgment ruling against Daitom on Count III, therefore, should be affirmed. As explained above, we reverse the trial court with respect to Counts I and II. The cause is remanded for further proceedings consistent with this opinion.

BARRETT, Circuit Judge, dissenting:

I respectfully dissent. Insofar as the issue of contract formation is concerned in this case, we are confronted with a "battle of the forms" case involving the interpretation and application of U.C.C. § 2-207. I would affirm.

. . . .

The "knock-out" rule should not, in my view, be reached in this case. It can be applied only if, as Daitom argues and the majority agrees, the "conflicting terms" cancel each other out. The "knock-out" rule does have substantial support in the law, but I do not believe it is relevant in this case because the only conflicting terms relate to the scope of the warranty. In this case, it is not an important consideration because, pursuant to the express time limitations contained in Pennwalt's "offer," Daitom lost its right to assert any warranty claim. There was no term in Daitom's purchase order in conflict with the express one-year limitation within which to bring warranty actions. . . .

---

[7] Daitom alleges that several letters from Pennwalt expressly warrantied the performance of the rotary dryers. E.g., Pretrial Order, Record Volume II at 59, para. 12, 13, 14, 15.

Assignment 6: Contract Enforceability (Statute of Frauds)

§ 2-201

Even though a contract may have been created in compliance with the Article 2 provisions on contract formation (2-204, 2-205, 2-206, and 2-207(1)), a party may be prevented from enforcing that contract if it does not satisfy the dictates of the Article 2 statute of frauds, found in 2-201. If 2-201 renders the contract unenforceable, the court will not consider the merits of the contract claim. The statute of frauds thereby permits a party to end a breach of contract action early in litigation, based on the determination that a sufficient writing does not exist to satisfy 2-201.

Although we are addressing these issues as arising after formation to determine enforceability of an otherwise valid agreement, individuals entering contracts should more properly consider these questions before, at the time of, or shortly after contract formation so the proper steps can be taken at that time to ensure enforceability. From the perspective of a transactional lawyer, the issue is how to create an enforceable obligation. From the perspective of a litigator, the issue is whether a statute of frauds defense is available; if so, it must be raised as an affirmative defense in the earliest stages of the lawsuit and may result in dismissal of the suit before the court considers whether a contract existed.

In analyzing 2-201, there are three critical questions to be answered:

(1)   Is the contract the kind of agreement for which 2-201 requires a writing?

(2)   Does one of the exceptions in 2-201 apply to eliminate the requirement of a writing?

(3)   If a writing *is* required, what kind of writing does 2-201 mandate?

Reading the Code

Problem 6-1. Requirement of a Signed Writing: General Rule.

(A) "Except as otherwise provided" elsewhere in the section, for what kinds of contracts does 2-201(1) require a writing?[1]

2003 (B) Read the 2003 amended version of 2-201(1). What significant change is made in the scope of 2-201? Will this change increase or decrease the number of contracts enforceable without a writing?

Problem 6-2. Requirement of a Signed Writing: Exceptions.

(A) Read 2-201(3) and comment 7. Under what circumstances is a writing *not* required for a contract to be enforceable, even though 2-201(1) would otherwise require one? For each set of circumstances, is all or only part of the contract enforceable?

2003 (B) Read the 2003 amended version of 2-201(4) and comment 8. Will this provision increase or decrease the number of contracts enforceable without a writing?

2003 [1] The phrase "except as otherwise provided in this section" was deleted in the 2003 amendments. The reason for the deletion is considered in Problem 6-6 below.

Problem 6-3. Nature of the Required Writing.

(A)   What must a writing contain to satisfy the requirements of 2-201(1)? Be sure to read comments 1, 5, and 6[2] and to search out defined terms in preparing your answer.

(B)   Seller sends buyer a document on its letterhead saying "Thank you for your recent purchase order for 500 widgets at $5 each." Would this communication satisfy the requirements of 2-201(1) in an enforcement action by the seller? By the buyer?

(C)   Buyer sends seller a document on its letterhead saying "Confirmation of agreement for our purchase from you at $30 per bushel of all the apples produced in the next harvest from your Fairfax orchard."   The named orchard annually produces 5000 to 6000 bushels of apples. Would the buyer's document satisfy the requirements of 2-201(1) in an enforcement action by the seller? By the buyer?

Problem 6-4. Confirmations Between Merchants. Section 2-201(2) sets out a special rule for enforceability of a contract between merchants. If a plaintiff seeks to enforce a contract and must use 2-201(2) to prove the existence of a

---

2003   [2] Under the 2003 amended version, the relevant comments are 1 and 6.

sufficient writing, what facts must the plaintiff establish in order to satisfy the requirements of 2-201(2)? What does "sufficient against the sender" mean in 2-201(2)?

The Statute of Frauds Meets Electronic Commerce

As discussed in Assignment 4, both UETA and E-Sign ensure that a contract will not be denied validity or legal effect merely because it is in electronic form. Equally important, both acts ensure that a contract will not be denied legal enforceability solely because an electronic record or electronic signature was used in its formation. E-Sign § 101(a)(2); UETA § 7(b). UETA goes on to say that "[i]f a law requires a record to be in writing, an electronic record satisfies the law," and "[i]f a law requires a signature, an electronic signature satisfies the law." UETA § 7(c), (d) (footnotes added). In addition, the definition of "signing" is expanded to include sounds (such as audio recognition patterns) and processes (such as biometrics like retinal scans and fingerprints, as well as digital signatures).

The effect of UETA and E-Sign is to overlay these definitions and rules onto Article 2. Thus, if a writing and signature are required by 2-201, an electronic record and signature will be sufficient. For example, an e-mailed contract confirmation with a header accurately identifying the sender of the e-mail often will satisfy 2-201 if enforcement is sought against the sender. Thus, electronic contracts are reliably enforceable.

2003　　　The 2003 amended version of 2-201 directly incorporates the UETA and E-Sign vocabulary by substituting "record" for "writing."

Applying the Code

Note on solving statute of frauds problems: *To demonstrate that __no__ writing is required for enforcement, you must show that the contract is not one for which 2-201(1) requires a writing or that it fits any __one__ of the exceptions in 2-201(3). To demonstrate that a writing __is__ required, it is necessary to show that a writing is required by 2-201(1) and that __none__ of the exceptions in 2-201(3) applies. If* *a writing is required, the writing will be sufficient if it satisfies the requirements of 2-201(1) <u>or</u> 2-201(2). If it is arguable that a writing is required, you should determine whether a writing exists that satisfies that requirement.*

Problem 6-5. Early in August, Winona attends the Uptown Art Fair in search of a leather briefcase. She finds several she likes at the booth for Tom's Tannery but none are quite what she's looking for. Thomas Wright, the artist and proprietor, agrees to modify one of his designs to suit her and to sell the resulting briefcase to her for $600. (Each set of facts below is independent of the others.)

(A) Winona is buying the briefcase for personal use. She gives Thomas $60 towards the purchase price, paying by personal check without other notation on it. Thomas cashes the check and begins work on the briefcase, cutting leather pieces to fit the proposed style. A week later, Winona calls Thomas to cancel the order. Thomas goes to small claims court, seeking to enforce the contract. Winona raises 2-201 as a defense and seeks dismissal of the lawsuit. Will Winona be successful? Why or why not?

(B) Winona is buying the briefcase for personal use. She gives Thomas her business card and writes her home address and phone number and the word "briefcase" on the back. Thomas gives Winona a receipt marked "Modified design saddlebag $600, estimated delivery date: 6 weeks." The receipt has "Tom's Tannery" stamped at the top. At the end of the day, Winona decides she was too hasty in selecting the briefcase and calls Thomas to cancel the order. She leaves a message on his voicemail, which he receives when he returns to his workshop at the end of the Art Fair. Thomas goes to small claims court, seeking to enforce the contract. Winona raises 2-201 as a defense and seeks dismissal of the lawsuit. Will Winona be successful? Why or why not?

(C)   Winona agrees to buy the briefcase to resell it in her own crafts store. Thomas gives Winona his business card and marks it on the back "Agreement for modified design saddlebag, $600, delivery on 10/15." Five days later, Winona calls Thomas to tell him she is no longer interested in purchasing the briefcase. Thomas seeks enforcement of the contract in small claims court. Winona raises 2-201 as a defense and seeks dismissal of the lawsuit. Will Winona be successful? Why or why not?

(D)   Winona agrees to buy the briefcase to resell it in her own crafts store. She gives Thomas her business card, which contains her e-mail address. Thomas sends Winona an e-mail which, on its subject line and in the body of the e-mail, says "Briefcase order." The sender of the e-mail is identified as "Tom's Tannery." An attachment contains a confirmation of the purchase transaction, but Winona is on vacation for three weeks and does not open the e-mail until she returns, at which point she sends back an e-mail objecting to the confirmation. Thomas seeks enforcement of the contract, and Winona raises 2-201 as a defense. Will Winona be successful? Why or why not? Assume that UETA has been enacted in this jurisdiction.

(E)   Winona agrees to buy the briefcase to resell it in her crafts store. Thomas realizes the price he quoted to Winona is too low. Since she made no payment and he gave her no receipt, Thomas decides to cancel the contract. He writes Winona a letter in which he says "I am not able to supply the briefcase you ordered at the price quoted so will have to cancel our arrangement. If you would pay $100 more than the agreed price, I would reinstate the order." Winona seeks enforcement of the contract, and Thomas raises 2-201 as a defense. Will Thomas be successful? Why or why not?

(F)   Thomas seeks to enforce his agreement with Winona. Her answer says: "The parties' contract for sale of the briefcase is not enforceable because there is no writing to satisfy the statute of frauds." Will Winona be successful when she seeks dismissal on the basis of 2-201? Why or why not?

(G)   If Thomas seeks to enforce his agreement with Winona and is successful in meeting the requirements of 2-201, is he then entitled to summary judgment on his breach of contract claim?

Problem 6-6. Estoppel and the Statute of Frauds. Is it appropriate to use promissory estoppel to permit enforcement of an alleged contract that would otherwise be unenforceable because it is not in writing? On the one hand, promissory estoppel is designed to make a promise binding even though all the requirements for an enforceable contract are not met, as long as the elements of a promissory estoppel are established. If those elements can be proved with respect to an oral contract, perhaps the promise should be enforceable even though there is no writing that satisfies 2-201. On the other hand, permitting enforcement of an oral promise on this basis would allow parties to circumvent the writing requirement, sometimes facilitating a fraud, and would encourage parties to rely on oral promises rather than put their agreements in writing.

Most courts have permitted parties to invoke promissory estoppel to enforce unfulfilled promises to put agreements in writing or not to rely on the statute of frauds. But when faced with the broader question whether promissory estoppel should be available for enforcement of simple oral contracts that would otherwise be unenforceable under 2-201, the courts have reached conflicting conclusions.

(A)   Some of the arguments for and against permitting the use of promissory estoppel to overcome a statute of frauds defense can be derived from closely reading the relevant statutory text and comments. Read 1-103 and comment 1,[3] and review all of 2-201, paying particular attention to the opening clause. How do these provisions support

(1)   permitting as exceptions to 2-201(1) *only* those circumstances explicitly contained in 2-201(2) and (3)?

---

[3] Section 1-103(b) and comment 2 in the revised Article 1. The statutory text in revised Article 1 is identical to the prerevision version, but the comment is significantly modified and expanded. The language in the pre-revision comment suggesting that other bodies of law apply unless "explicitly displaced" by the UCC has been removed because it "did not accurately reflect the proper scope of Uniform Commercial Code preemption, which extends to displacement of other law that is inconsistent with the purposes and policies of the Uniform Commercial Code, as well as with its text." Comment 2 to revised 1-103.

(2)   permitting exceptions to 2-201(1) *other than* the ones explicitly contained in 2-201(2) and (3)?

2003   (B)   Read the 2003 amended version of 2-201(1) and comment 2. Does the absence of the pre-2003 opening clause mean that promissory estoppel can always be used to enforce a contract not otherwise enforceable because it does not satisfy the requirements of 2-201?

Assignment 7: The Definition of Merchant

§ 2-104(1), (3)

Although Articles 1 and 2 as a whole apply to both merchants and non-merchants, in some provisions merchants are held to different standards than non-merchants. We have already encountered two such provisions— 2-201(2) and 2-207(2). Determining who is and who is not a merchant therefore is sometimes critical in determining rights and obligations. The definition of merchant is contained in section 2-104, but the definition is written in a less-than-straightforward manner. Work your way through the following set of problems in order to help you analyze and understand 2-104.

Reading the Code

Problem 7-1. Goods Merchants vs. Practices Merchants. Under the definition contained in 2-104(1), a "person" (see 1-201(30)) may be either a merchant *with respect to goods involved in the transaction*, a merchant *with respect to practices involved in the transaction*, or both. Read carefully through 2-104(1) and list the three ways to be found a merchant with respect to goods and the two ways to be found a merchant with respect to practices:

A merchant with respect to goods is:

> a person who:

OR   a person who:

OR   a person who:

A merchant with respect to practices is:

> a person who:

OR   a person who:

Problem 7-2. "By His Occupation." Note the presence of this phrase in 2-104(1).

(A)   Does a professional musician become a merchant with respect to cars by loudly proclaiming she is an expert on them?

(B)   Does a computer programmer become a merchant with respect to cars by studying about automobiles and actually knowing more about cars than the average professional mechanic?

Problem 7-3. "Deals." A person who "deals in goods of the kind" is a merchant under 2-104(1). Read comments 1 and 2, and consider the phrase "otherwise by his occupation holds himself out as having knowledge or skill . . ." in 2-104(1). Consider also the reference in 2-312(3) to a merchant "regularly dealing in goods of the kind." Check a dictionary for the meaning of the word "deals." What do these sources suggest about the meaning of the word "deals"? What kinds of actions by a person might be considered "dealing" in goods?

Problem 7-4. Effect on Other Code Sections. As already indicated, being a merchant has certain consequences under the Code, but those consequences differ according to whether a party is considered a merchant with respect to the goods in the transaction or a merchant with respect to the business practices involved in the transaction. The following chart reflects the special standards for merchants, as further explored in (A) through (D) below.

UCC provision	Nature of special standard for merchant	Applies to merchant with respect to goods? practices? either?
2-312(3)	merchant seller who regularly deals in goods of the kind makes warranty against rightful claims of infringement	goods
2-314	merchant seller makes implied promises that goods will meet certain quality standards	goods
2-402(2)	buyer from a merchant seller is protected against certain claims by seller's creditors	goods
2-403(2)	buyer in ordinary course of business from a merchant to whom goods entrusted may receive entruster's ownership rights without approval of entruster	goods
2-201(2)	merchants may sometimes use own confirmation to satisfy the signature requirement for the statute of frauds	practices
2-205	offer in writing by merchant may become irrevocable for a time	practices
2-207(2), second sentence[1]	additional terms from merchant may become part of contract without affirmative agreement by other merchant	practices
2-209(2), final clause	merchant must obtain signature of non-merchant for certain modifications	practices
2-103(1)(b)[1]	merchant has higher standard for acting in good faith	either
2-327(1)(c)	merchant buyer has extra responsibility when returning goods	either
2-509(3)	merchant seller has increased responsibility for damage to goods prior to physical delivery	either
2-603(1)	merchant buyer has extra responsibility when returning goods	either

---

2003　　[1] This provision is deleted in the 2003 amended version.

UCC provision	Nature of special standard for merchant	Applies to merchant with respect to goods? practices? either?
2-605(1)(b)	merchant may have to more fully document product defects	either
2-609(2)	commercial standards apply to judging whether there are reasonable grounds for party to doubt performance of other party and whether assurances of performance are reasonable	either

(A)   Read 2-104 comment 2, paragraph 3, which indicates the special standards applied to merchants *with respect to goods* involved in their sales transactions. The first four rows in the chart above reflect these standards. (We have added one not mentioned in comment 2.) Why should these standards attach only to those parties who are merchants with respect to goods, but not attach to merchants with respect to practices? Note that all four standards apply only to *sellers* who are merchants with respect to goods.   Which special standards would apply to *buyers* who are merchants with respect to goods?

(B)   Read 2-104 comment 2, paragraph 2, which indicates the special standards applied to merchants *with respect to the practices* involved in the transaction. The fifth through eighth rows in the chart above reflect these special standards for merchants with respect to practices. Why should these standards attach to "almost every person in business," as stated in the comment?

(C)   Read 2-104 comment 2, paragraph 4, which indicates the special standards applied to *all merchants*, whether they are merchants with respect to goods or merchants with respect to practices involved in the transaction. The last six rows of the chart above reflect these special standards. Why should these standards attach to all merchants?

(D)   Consider "merchants with respect to goods" and "merchants with respect to practices." Draw a diagram indicating the approximate relative size of the two groups and how they likely overlap. If this question stumps you, return to it after you answer Problem 7-5.

Applying the Code

Problem 7-5. Are the following buyers and sellers (listed in italics) merchants with respect to these goods, merchants with respect to business practices, both, or neither, in the transactions described?

(A)   An *appliance and electronics store* sells a microwave oven to a *consumer*.

(B)   A *homeowner* sells a portable microwave oven to *a neighbor* in a garage sale.

(C)   A *stationery store* sells *Colonial Dry Cleaners* dry cleaning receipt pads for recording the list of clothes left by customers.

(D)   A *customer* buys a dress from *Shirley* at Shirley's Sportswear Boutique, which she operates at the local flea market every weekend.

(E)   An *office worker* becomes an expert crafter of fine wood sculptures which she makes in her garage workshop. She makes 2 or 3 sculptures a year, each of which takes about a month to craft, and sells one or two of them each year to *friends*. Would your answer be the same or different if she made a dozen each year and sold most of them?

(F)   The office manager of a *law firm* buys a photocopy machine for the law office from an *office equipment distributor*. The law firm has bought 14 photocopy machines over the last 9 years.

(G)   The *office manager of a law firm* buys stationery supplies for home use from a *stationery store*.

(H)   In a one-time sale, a *manufacturer* sells extra manufacturing machinery no longer needed in the business to other *companies* engaged in the same industry.

(I)   In a one-time sale, a *homeowner* hires an estate-sale firm to sell household goods left behind after his move to a retirement village. Some of the goods are bought by city *residents* who frequently buy at local garage sales; *Shirley* (see (E) above) buys a few items for resale in her flea market stall.

Problem 7-6. Chuck owns and manages a coffee shop. He also collects antique clocks as a hobby, and he sometimes displays a few of his clocks in the shop. He is known in the neighborhood as an expert on clocks, and customers sometimes talk with him about their own purchases.

(A)   When Chuck buys coffee beans for his shop, is he held to commercial standards of fair dealing in the trade? See 1-203, 2-103(1)(b), and 1-201(19).[2]

---

[2] Remember that under the 2003 amended version, good faith for both merchants and non-merchants includes both honesty in fact and the "observance of reasonable commercial standards of fair dealing." See 2-103(1)(j) and also 1-201(b)(20) in revised Article 1.

(B)   Chuck orally agrees to buy a clock from a dealer for $670, and the dealer sends him a signed confirmation. Will the confirmation satisfy the Statute of Frauds if the dealer seeks to enforce the contract against Chuck?

Problem 7-7. Betsy is on the staff of a newspaper and writes a regular column on antiques. She has an extensive collection of antique figurines.

(A)   If Betsy sells several of her figurines, is she a merchant with respect to the figurines? With respect to practices?

(B)   Betsy leaves her job with the newspaper and opens a store selling sports memorabilia. Is she a merchant with respect to baseball cards when she makes her first sale on grand opening day?

Problem 7-8. Sylvan Surplus Store regularly buys closeout inventories of goods for resale to customers. Its wares range from novelty key chains to plumbing supplies to metal scraps to cheap crystal ashtrays. Sylvan does not restock items once they are sold, but may occasionally find closeout inventories of the same or similar items, in which case it may purchase them for resale. Is Sylvan a merchant with respect to all of the kinds of goods it sells?

Note on Farmers as Merchants

Courts have reached differing conclusions regarding whether farmers are merchants under the definition in 2-104. Most cases involve application of the statute of frauds (2-201), but others relate to contract formation with conflicting forms (2-207) and the warranty of merchantability (2-314). Some courts have reasoned that farmers are merchants, because they make their livelihoods from the business of farming and regularly buy supplies and sell their crops. They therefore should be considered merchants with respect to normal business practices and also merchants with respect to the crops they sell. However, other courts have considered a farmer to be a "tiller of the soil" rather than a business person; others have concluded that a farmer is not a professional seller of the goods in question. Corporate farmers may be treated differently in this regard and are more likely to be considered merchants. Should the issue arise, it is wise to research the precedents in the particular jurisdiction in question.

2003   The comments to the 2003 amended version of Article 2 attempt to settle the controversy over whether farmers are merchants with respect to business practices (or at least as to 2-201(2)). Comment 4 to 2-201 declares that "a professional or a farmer should be considered a merchant [for the purposes of 2-201] because the practice of objecting to an improper confirmation ought to be familiar to any person in business." Whether all courts will follow this comment remains to be seen. The comments say nothing about whether farmers should be considered merchants with respect to other business practices or as to goods they sell or supplies they buy.

Assignment 8: Introduction to Warranties;
Creation of Implied Warranties

§§ 2-312, 2-314, 2-315

When goods sold to a buyer are defective, the buyer has a claim for breach of warranty, which raises the following questions, to be covered in the listed assignments:

Did the contract include
    (a) an implied warranty?   Assignment 8
    (b) an express warranty?   Assignment 9
    (c) a warranty obligation to a
          third-party beneficiary?   Assignment 11
If so, was that warranty excluded or limited
    (a) by a disclaimer
          or a conflicting warranty?   Assignment 10
    (b) by the parol evidence rule?   Assignment 12
Was any remaining warranty breached?   Assignments 16, 19
Did that breach cause the claimed injury? common law
What remedies are available for that injury? Assignments 17, 18,
                                                      20, 21

Were those remedies limited or barred
    (a) by a remedy limitation?   Assignment 22
    (b) by the statute of limitations?   Assignment 23

With the exception of the questions about including and disclaiming a warranty, these issues are common to the analysis of all contract-based claims by a buyer (or a third-party beneficiary) against the seller, whether or not the breach involves a warranty. For any breach-of-contract claim, a plaintiff would need to establish the pertinent term of the contract, the fact of its breach, the nature of plaintiff's loss, the fact that the breach actually caused that loss, the available remedies for that loss, and any limitations on those remedies.

This assignment concentrates on implied warranties (as distinguished from express warranties). Implied warranties are warranties furnished by

Article 2 as default terms. With one exception,[1] they are not "agreed upon" by the parties, so they can be disclaimed by agreement (as Assignment 10 will detail). Depending on the facts, a buyer might receive any of the following implied warranties: merchantability, fitness for a particular purpose, title, and non-infringement. For drafting convenience, Article 2 calls the warranties of merchantability and fitness for a particular purpose "implied warranties," but it does not include the warranties of title and non-infringement in that category. This textbook will call all of those warranties "implied warranties" but will alert you to the consequences of Article 2's different nomenclature.

Reading the Code

Problem 8-1. Introduction to Warranties.

(A)   The sections dealing with warranties appear at 2-312 through 2-318. Make a jot list (see page 5), identifying the subject matter of each section.

(B)   The warranty provisions appear in Part 3 (General Obligation and Construction of Contract). What other sections have you thus far studied that also appear in the same Part? What do they have in common with the warranty cluster?

---

[1] The implied warranties created by course of dealing or usage of trade under 2-314(3) are by "agreement" of the parties.

Problem 8-2. Introduction to Implied Warranties. Read the following implied warranties and reword each in one or more if/then paraphrases, using the form prescribed for each section number below:

(A)   2-312(1):[2] If _____, then there is a warranty that _____.

(B)   2-312(3):[3] If _____, then there is a warranty that _____except that _____.

(C)   2-314(1): If _____, there is a warranty that _____.

(D)   2-315 and the last sentence of comment 1: If _____, then there is a warranty that _____.

2003 [2] In the 2003 amended version, this subsection also includes a warranty against "unreasonably expos[ing] the buyer to litigation because of any colorable claim to or interest in the goods."

2003 [3] In the 2003 amended version, this subsection is moved to 2-312(2).

Problem 8-3. Relation Between Warranties and Other Provisions. Recall the hierarchy of contractual provisions discussed in Assignment 3.

(A)   The implied warranties in Problem 8-2 are (circle one):
          mandatory provisions
          express terms
          implied-in-fact terms
          default provisions

(B)   The implied warranties in 2-314(3) are (circle one):
          mandatory provisions
          express terms
          implied-in-fact terms
          default provisions

(C)   If a course of performance, course of dealing, or usage of trade runs contrary to one of the implied warranties in Problem 8-2, which will prevail?

Problem 8-4. Scope and Timing of Implied Warranties.

(A)   Does 2-314(2) fully define the warranty of merchantability? See also comment 6.

(B)   If a consumer product (say, a toaster) breaks down six months after purchase, is that a breach of the implied warranty of merchantability under 2-314(2)(a)-(f)? If you answered yes (or maybe), is it because the merchantability warranty has a duration of (at least) six months? Or does the warranty instead contain only a promise or affirmation about the goods as of the moment of delivery? If you answered yes to this latter question, how is the breakdown six months later a breach of that warranty?

Applying the Code

Problem 8-5. Your client proposes to put the following advertisement in the newspaper:

(A)   If Windy City Windshields delivers the promised steaks to the customer along with the repaired vehicle, are the steaks covered by a warranty of merchantability? Make sure that your answer analyzes the elements that you listed in your answer to Problem 8-2(C).

(B)   Are the steaks covered by a warranty of merchantability if Windy City gives the buyer a coupon for the steaks and the buyer then obtains the steaks at the grocery store specified on the coupon?

(C)   Read 1-201(17),[4] 2-314(2)(b), and 2-501 comment 5. In the contract between Windy City and its glass supplier, are the windshields fungible goods? In the contract between the grocery store and its meat supplier, are the boxes of steaks fungible goods?

Problem 8-6. Assume that a warranty under 2-314 has been created. Determine which particular parts of 2-314(2) have been breached in each set of facts. If more than one, determine which breach will be easier to establish. Consider comment 8.

---

[4] In revised Article 1, this definition appears in 1-201(b)(18) and is reworded but is essentially unchanged in substance.

(A)   A restaurant patron orders a glass of wine and is cut by a glass chip on the rim of the glass. (Assume the warranty is given by the restaurant, not the restaurant's supplier.)

(B)   The manager of a delicatessen orders four gallon-size bottles of colossal-size olives (this is a size specified in a federal regulation), containing 90 olives apiece. The label on each bottle says that a bottle contains "90 colossal-size olives." The four bottles delivered to the deli are gallon size and contain colossal olives only, but the bottles contain 110, 85, 90, and 80 olives, respectively.

Problem 8-7. Consider 2-315 comment 2 when analyzing the following facts, which are designed to expand your understanding of the difference between fitness for an ordinary purpose (2-314(2)(c)) and fitness for a particular purpose (2-315). Each scenario involves sale of house paint. Assume the paint was bought from a paint store. Also assume that most house paint is sold with a label that says it should be used when the temperature will remain above 40° F for six hours. For each set of facts below, was a warranty of merchantability (fitness for the ordinary purpose) created and, if so, was it breached? Was a warranty of fitness for a particular purpose created and, if so, was it breached?

(A)   Label on exterior house paint says to paint only when temperature remains above 40° for six hours. Buyer tells salesperson she wants to paint at 35-40°. Salesperson points to a specific paint and responds, "You can use this paint all the way down to 30°." Buyer paints when it is 35-40°, but the paint crystallizes and flakes off because the salesperson is wrong.

(B)   Label on exterior low-temperature paint says to apply paint only between 35° and 45°. Buyer applies it at 50°, and it dries almost immediately with streaks and brush marks.

Problem 8-8. These fact situations explore issues surrounding the meaning of the warranty in 2-314(2)(c). For each scenario, consider whether the goods "are fit for the ordinary purpose for which such goods are used." What are the best arguments for and against that conclusion? Assume the goods are bought from a merchant who deals in goods of this kind. Are there additional facts you would want to know?

(A)   A restaurant patron chips a tooth on a chicken bone in what the menu says is "homemade chicken salad." Would your analysis change if the restaurant is run by a sole proprietor who makes everything from fresh ingredients? if the chicken salad is very chunky? finely ground up? not billed as "homemade"?

(B)   A buyer of a new motor home develops asthma and can no longer use the vehicle because of formaldehyde fumes from the plywood paneling. Assume that the buyer can prove that this level of formaldehyde fumes is harmful to 8% of the population.

(C)   A cigarette lighter is taken out of a purse by the purchaser's child, who starts a serious fire while playing with the lighter. You represent the purchaser seeking recovery for injury from the manufacturer of the lighter. You discover that each year, fires started under similar circumstances cause an average of 120 deaths, 750 personal injuries, and $300 million in property damage.

Problem 8-9. A buyer approaches a seller who has advertised six horses for sale. The buyer tells the seller that it wants a "sound horse who can compete favorably in the racing circuit in our five-state region." The seller points out three of the horses and says, "You should look at those three." The buyer consults with its own trainer and veterinarian to select among those three horses. The horse he buys is and has been intermittently lame, so it is able to race in only 21 of 28 races during the first season. It wins three of those races. What implied warranties, if any, were created? Were any such warranties breached?

Assignment 9: Creation of Express Warranties

§ 2-313

This assignment continues to explore the first question raised at the beginning of the last assignment—determining what warranties are included in a contract. Assignment 8 focused on implied warranties. We now turn our attention to express warranties.

2003 Section 2-313 covers express warranties from the seller to the immediate buyer. The 2003 amendments add 2-313A and 2-313B, two new sections on seller's "obligations" (quasi-warranties) to "remote purchasers" (not direct buyers). Those sections are modeled on portions of 2-313 and therefore are covered in this Assignment. Also new in the 2003 amendments is coverage of "remedial promises," which are discussed in the assignments on remedies.

Reading the Code

Problem 9-1. Introduction to Express Warranties. Read § 2-313(1). An express warranty may be created in three possible ways. List the elements the buyer would have to establish to prove the existence of a warranty under

(A)   2-313(1)(a):

(B)   2-313(1)(b):

(C)   2-313(1)(c):

(D)   What is the content of the warranty created in each instance?

Problem 9-2. "Part of the Basis of the Bargain" and its Relationship to Reliance. Under the Uniform Sales Act, the predecessor statute to Article 2, a promise or an affirmation of fact created an express warranty "if the natural tendency of such affirmation or promise is to induce the buyer to purchase the goods, and if the buyer purchases them *relying thereon*." Article 2, as you have seen, requires instead that the affirmation of fact, promise, description, sample, or model be "part of the basis of the bargain." Courts have reached varying conclusions regarding the meaning of this phrase—in particular, whether reliance by the buyer is necessary for the creation of a warranty, as it was under the Uniform Sales Act.

Courts have adopted three different approaches as to how and when a representation[1] becomes part of the basis of the bargain. These approaches are summarized below, with a short-hand name for each for ease of reference:

> *Reliance approach:* This approach is based on the pre-UCC requirement of reliance. A seller's representation about the goods becomes part of the basis of the bargain and therefore becomes an express warranty if the buyer can prove, by a preponderance of the evidence, that it decided to buy the goods based, at least in part, on the seller's representation. Of course, the seller can prevent the buyer from sustaining its burden of proof by establishing the buyer's non-reliance on the representation, perhaps showing that the buyer knew nothing of the representation at the time of contract formation, or that the seller gave the buyer reason not to rely on the representation, or that the parties never agreed to the draft term.

> *Comment 3 approach:* This approach is based on 2-313 comment 3 (and to some extent, comment 8). Read those comments now. The buyer must show that the seller made a representation about the goods during the bargain[2] preceding the formation of the parties' contract. (Note that this element focuses on the seller's conduct in making a representation, not on the buyer's awareness of that conduct.) This showing creates a rebuttable presumption that the seller's representation was part of the

---

[1] Seller makes a "representation" about the goods when seller makes a promise or an affirmation of fact, provides a description about the goods, or shows a model or sample of the goods. This assignment will use "representation" to encompass all of those statements and actions by the seller.

[2] See the Code's use of "bargain" in the definition of "agreement" in 1-201.

basis of the bargain. The seller can rebut that presumption by clear affirmative proof that the buyer did not rely at all on the seller's representation in deciding to buy the goods.

Non-reliance approach (adopted in fewer than 10 jurisdictions): This approach is based on part of comment 3:

> In actual practice affirmations of fact made by the seller about the goods during a bargain are regarded as part of the description of those goods; hence no particular reliance on such statements need be shown in order to weave them into the fabric of the agreement. Rather, any fact which is to take such affirmations, once made, out of the agreement requires clear affirmative proof.

Under this approach, the mere fact that the seller made a statement in the process of marketing the goods is sufficient to make it part of the basis of the bargain in a subsequent sale transaction, regardless of buyer's non-reliance or even lack of knowledge of the representation. In the cases adopting this approach, the representations were made directly to the buyer, accompanied the goods in the packaging, or were part of a catalog or other public advertising issued prior to the contract being formed between buyer and seller.

(A)   In the chart below, for each specified approach, place checkmarks in the boxes showing which facts the buyer must prove to establish that a seller's representation was "part of the basis of the bargain." If the buyer gains a presumption by proving those facts, note the nature of the presumption and how the seller could rebut that presumption. Complete one vertical column at a time. Ignore the *Cipollone* column until Problem 9-3.

	Reliance approach	Comment 3 approach	Non-reliance approach	*Cipollone*
Seller made representation during the bargain, before entering into contract with buyer				

	Reliance approach	Comment 3 approach	Non-reliance approach	*Cipollone*
Buyer gained actual knowledge of represen-tation before entering into contract with seller				
Buyer relied on representation in entering into contract				
Seller's rebuttal (if any)				
Buyer's counter-rebuttal (if any)				

(B)   Order the three approaches from most favorable to the seller to most favorable to the buyer.

(C)   Look back at your list of elements of an express warranty in Problem 9-1. How is that list changed in a non-reliance jurisdiction?

(D)   Which statement is true in both a comment 3 jurisdiction and a reliance jurisdiction?
> 1. Buyer establishes a warranty merely by proving that it was aware of the seller's representation.
> 2. A representation cannot be part of the basis of the bargain if seller proves buyer's non-reliance.
> 3. A buyer will always be able to prove basis of the bargain by producing the packaging with which the goods were sold.
> 4. The seller's representation must be the sole reason motivating buyer to buy the goods.

Representations by Remote Sellers

Section 2-313 warranties for a buyer can be created only by the immediate seller, not by a seller further up the distribution chain. This is implicit in the requirement that the representation be made by "the seller" and be part of the basis of the bargain between the seller and the buyer. Comment 2 to 2-313 makes this point explicit by noting that "this section is limited in its scope and direct purpose to warranties made by the seller to the buyer as part of a contract for sale." However, comment 2 continues: "[W]arranties need not be confined either to sales contracts or to the direct parties to such a contract. . . . [T]he matter is left to the case law with the intention that the policies of this Act may offer useful guidance in dealing with further cases as they arise." In response, courts often have expanded warranty coverage beyond the direct seller-buyer relationship, especially when the remote seller has made representations knowing they would be passed on to later purchasers. Remote sellers thus may have obligations to remote buyers that are virtually identical with 2-313 warranties, though based on common law extension rather than direct application of 2-313. The representation must still satisfy the other aspects of 2-313 (be an affirmation of fact, promise, description, or sample or model, not be puffing, and be part of the basis of the bargain in the immediate sales transaction).

Representations Made after Contract Formation

The preceding descriptions of the three approaches for "part of basis of the bargain" indicated that a representation does not become an express warranty unless it is made before the contract is formed between seller and buyer. In fact, however, there is some flexibility in this requirement. Comment 7 to 2-313 states,

> The precise time when words of description or affirmation are made or samples are shown is not material. The sole question is whether the language or samples or models are fairly to be regarded as part of the contract. If language is used after the closing of the deal (as when the buyer when taking delivery asks and receives an additional assurance), the warranty becomes a modification, and need not be supported by consideration if it is otherwise reasonable and in order (Section 2-209).

Under 2-313 and comment 7, representations made after but close to the time of the sales transaction (e.g., a statement made as the buyer turns away after paying for the goods) are sometimes found to be part of the basis of the original bargain; representations made any time after the sales contract is made may be a modification of the agreement and hence part of the basis of the bargain.

Problem 9-3. Representations in Advertising. In *Cipollone v. Liggett Group, Inc.*, 893 F.2d 541 (3d Cir. 1990), a consumer injured by years of smoking cigarettes sued the manufacturers for breach of the express warranties in the manufacturers' advertisements. The Third Circuit applied 2-313 and formulated the following approach for express warranties in advertisements:

- To gain a presumption that the buyer relied on the representations in an advertisement and that they are part of the basis of the bargain, the buyer must show that, at the time of purchase, the buyer had read, heard, or seen the advertisement containing the representations.
- The seller may rebut that presumption with clear affirmative proof that the buyer knew the representation in the advertisement was untrue *or* that the buyer did not rely on the representation in deciding to buy the goods.

•   The buyer may counter the seller's rebuttal with proof that the buyer relied on the seller's representations without believing them.[3] (For example, buyer sees a late-night TV advertisement about kitchen knives that cut pop cans and does not believe the ad but orders the knives anyway, counting on the seller to take the knives back if they do not cut pop cans.)

The *Cipollone* approach has been adopted by a minority of jurisdictions, none of which has defined "advertisement," nor has any of the jurisdictions applied it beyond advertisements. In the jurisdictions adopting *Cipollone*, that approach takes the place of the jurisdiction's usual approach when the dispute involves an advertisement.

(A)   In the chart in Problem 9-2, place checkmarks in the boxes showing which facts the buyer must show, in a *Cipollone* jurisdiction, to establish that a seller's advertising representation was "part of the basis of the bargain." If the buyer gains a presumption by showing those facts, note the nature of the presumption, how the seller can rebut that presumption, and how the buyer can counter the rebuttal.

(B)   Because section 2-313 covers express warranties only between a seller and the immediate buyer of the goods, an advertisement creates warranty liability under 2-313 only if the advertiser is the immediate seller. However, as noted on pages 125-6, courts have applied 2-313 by analogy to create similar obligations when remote sellers make representations that they know will be communicated to remote buyers. The same is true with respect to representations made in advertisements. In *Cipollone* and other cases, courts have recognized liability if a remote seller (for example, the cigarette

---

[3] The question whether a buyer may successfully claim reliance on a representation while not believing it has arisen in warranty cases in comment 3 and reliance jurisdictions, as well as in warranty cases outside of the UCC, and the courts have reached inconsistent results. Some courts understand reliance to mean that the buyer is relying on the *truth* of the representation—that is, the buyer bought the goods in part because the buyer believed that the goods would be as the seller represented them to be. Other courts see the buyer as relying on the *existence* of the representation—that is, the buyer bought the goods believing only that the seller's statement means seller will be obligated to give a remedy to the buyer if the warranty turns out not to be true, but -the buyer need not believe in the truth of the representation. Under this latter line of cases (but not the former line of cases), a buyer who thinks the representation to be in error at the time of contract formation, but still enters into the contract on the strength of seller's guarantee, should be able to recover damages from the seller who made the erroneous representation.

manufacturer) advertised its products so as to reach ultimate consumers who bought with knowledge of the advertisement.

2003   In amended Article 2, 2-313 makes explicit that the section applies only to immediate buyers. New section 2-313B codifies and adds to evolving case law about liability for advertisements, establishing a warranty-like "obligation" to a remote purchaser created by means of advertising or similar communication to the public. This section does not apply to advertising to the immediate buyer, who is covered under 2-313. Read 2-313B(1) to (3) in the 2003 amended version of Article 2. What elements must be proven to establish an obligation under 2-313B?

Problem 9-4. Representations Made after Contract Formation (Including "Representations in a Box"). In Assignment 5, we considered the uncertainty created when a seller responds to a buyer's order by sending goods accompanied by documentation containing additional terms ("terms in the box"). As seen in the *ProCD/Hill* and *Step-Saver/Arizona Retail/Klocek* lines of cases, the courts have reached varying conclusions regarding how and when a contract is created under those circumstances, which leads to varying conclusions regarding whether the terms in the box become part of the contract. See Problem 5-10 and the text preceding it.

Even if a court concludes that a "term in the box" should be considered assented to as part of contract formation, if that term is a representation about the goods it must in addition satisfy the standards in 2-313 in order to qualify as an operative warranty. In particular, that means the term must be "part of the basis of the bargain." Whether a representation is part of the basis of the bargain is a distinct question from whether both parties agreed to include the representation in the contract, so a party seeking not to be bound by a "term in the box" may raise both lack of assent and "no basis of the bargain" as defenses. Problem 5-10 focused on the issue of agreement; this problem focuses on the "basis of the bargain" requirement.

As discussed in Problem 9-2, whether any representation becomes part of the basis of the bargain depends on when the representation was made, when the contract was formed, and whether the applicable jurisdiction has adopted a reliance, comment 3, or non-reliance test. The same is true for a "representation in the box." As discussed in the text following Problem 9-2, the representation may become part of the basis of the bargain even if the contract was formed before the representation was made. Representations made shortly after the moment of contract formation are sometimes considered part of the original bargain (perhaps because the buyer still retained the power to rescind the sale) and sometimes are considered agreed-upon modifications to the original bargain. To complicate matters, even unassented-to terms, including representations and other terms "in the box," are sometimes found to be binding through application of an equitable doctrine such as waiver or promissory estoppel. For instance, a buyer may have justifiably and foreseeably relied to its detriment on the seller's "promises in the box." Or a seller may have waived its right to object to the "terms in the box" being part of the contract, because it was the seller who intended the buyer to receive the "terms in the box" after the contract was formed, so seller should be estopped from raising defenses like buyer's lack of assent or the representation not being part of the basis of the bargain.

Determining whether "representations in the box" are part of a contract thus requires a highly fact-dependent consideration of when the contract was formed and whether the representation became part of the basis of the bargain, as well as whether an equitable doctrine applies. In amended Article 2, a new section, 2-313A, seeks to more reliably impose a warranty-like obligation on a seller who makes "terms in the box" representations to a remote purchaser. Comment 1 to 2-313A colloquially calls these representations "pass-through warranties" because they are transmitted with the goods from the seller to one or more intermediaries, who pass them through to the remote purchaser.

2003 (A)   Read 2-313A(1) to (3) in the 2003 amended version of Article 2. What elements must be proven to establish an obligation under 2-313A?

(B)   Charles visits Big Discounts, a local electronics store, to look at DVD players.   He asks the salesperson to show him which models play both commercially recorded and home-recorded DVDs.   The salesperson shows Charles several models and recommends one, manufactured by Electrolite, as providing the best value for the money.   Charles takes a box containing that model of DVD player to the counter to purchase it.   He signs the credit card receipt, and takes the player home.   The outside of the box (which Charles does not read until he gets the box home) says, "PLAYS ALL YOUR FAVORITE MOVIES AND MUSIC!"   Inside the box is a pamphlet that Charles saves but does not read.   The pamphlet contains the following text:

> Limited Six-Month Warranty: Electrolite warrants this product against all defects in material and workmanship for a period of six months from purchase. Normal wear and tear is excluded.

Assume that this jurisdiction has *not* enacted the 2003 amendments to Article 2. Is there an express warranty as to the DVD player between Charles and Deep Discounts? between Charles and Electrolite? In your answer, consider whether a contract was formed and whether the representation was part of the basis of the bargain.   If you think that the likely answer to either issue is no, determine whether other arguments from the discussion above favor the enforcement of the representation, even if no contract is formed or even if the representation is not part of the basis of the bargain.

2003 (C)   How does your answer to (B) change if the jurisdiction has enacted the 2003 amendments to Article 2?

Problem 9-5. Puffing. Read 2-313(2), which says no warranty is created by "an affirmation merely of the value of the goods or a statement purporting to be merely the seller's opinion or commendation of the goods."[4] These kinds of affirmations or statements are often known as "puffing" or "puffery." Also read comments 4 and 8 to unamended 2-313, and comment 10 to amended 2-313. Note that these provisions arguably furnish an additional element to 2-313, in addition to those you listed in Problem 9-1(A): the affirmation of fact or promise must not be a statement of value of seller's opinion or commendation of the goods. Alternatively, the provisions on puffing may be seen not as adding an element but as clarifying when a representation is not part of the basis of the bargain or identifying when no promise or affirmation of fact has been made, thus amplifying the elements established by 2-313(1)(a).

Courts have held that a seller's statement is puffing if a reasonable person would not take the representation seriously. Seller's statements of opinion or commendation of the goods also are puffing, because opinions are not measurable or objective and because their meaning varies from person to person. Seller's commendations often exaggerate the degree of quality of the product,

---

2003 [4] Words to the same effect also appear in 2-313A(4) and 2-313B(4) in the 2003 amended version.

and such exaggerations are reasonably to be expected of a seller.[5] Cases frequently use the following test for differentiating between warranty and opinion: "whether the seller asserts a fact of which the buyer is ignorant or merely states an opinion or judgment on a matter of which the seller has no special knowledge and on which the buyer may be expected also to have an opinion and to exercise his judgment."[6]

UCC case law on what is and is not puffing is fairly consistent at either end of the spectrum but very inconsistent in the middle. According to two leading commentators, "[A]nyone who says he can consistently tell a 'puff' from a warranty is a fool or a liar. . . ."[7] For instance, in sales of used goods between two consumers, the following statements have been held to be puffing and therefore not express warranties: that the car was "in good shape," was "in excellent condition," and that an outboard motor was in "perfect running condition" (in conjunction with a description of damage to the motor). In other sales of used goods between consumers, the following statements were held to be express warranties and not puffing: that the car was in "good mechanical shape or condition," was "a good reliable car," was in "A-1 shape" and "mechanically perfect," had "no problems," was "road ready" (after buyer said it wanted a car without mechanical problems).

The puffing defense arose in the mid-1800s, when caveat emptor ("buyer beware") ruled the marketplace, there often was just a single buyer and seller, and buyer often had the opportunity and the ability to inspect the goods before the contract was entered into. Accordingly, some courts have allowed the defense when the buyer is capable of checking the veracity of the seller's statement, because the buyer's loss is caused by the buyer's failure to check

---

[5] *See generally* Cullen Goretzke, *The Resurgence of Caveat Emptor: Puffery Undermines the Pro-Consumer Trend in Wisconsin's Misrepresentation Doctrine*, 2003 Wis. L. Rev. 171, 173-88. However, recent studies have shown that consumers give equal credence and equal importance to puffing and non-puffing statements and do not recognize the difference between them. Moreover, advertisers would not continue to use puffery if it did not influence consumer behavior. Thus, some commentators have argued that the puffing defense is too widely available to sellers, was created in an era of caveat emptor that no longer reflects societal values, and ought to be narrowed to prevent sellers from defrauding consumers. *Id.* at 173-74.

[6] *Royal Business Machines, Inc. v. Lorraine Corp.*, 633 F.2d 34, 41 (7th Cir. 1980).

[7] James J. White & Robert S. Summers, *Uniform Commercial Code* § 9-4 (5th ed. 2000).

rather than by the seller's faulty statement. However, other courts have refused to impose on buyer a duty to check the veracity of seller's statements and have not allowed the puffing defense on that basis.

The defense of puffing is not limited to claims of breach of warranty; it also is a defense to misrepresentation and false advertising. A recent case on false advertising set out the following guidelines on identifying puffing:

- Puffing is a vague, general exaggeration that no reasonable person would rely upon in making a purchasing decision, because it lacks specificity. Puffing may involve outrageous claims, boasting, or blustering. One commentator has opined that puffing is the seller's privilege to lie his head off, so long as he says nothing specific, on the theory that no reasonable man would believe him, or that no reasonable man would be influenced by such talk.
- The context in which a statement is made may add enough specificity to an otherwise vague statement to remove it from the category of puffing.
- A statement is not puffing if it is a specific and measurable claim, capable of being proved false or of being reasonably interpreted as a statement of objective fact. That means that it is capable of being adjudged true or false, perhaps by empirical verification.[8]

Thus, the following factors influence courts toward determining that a seller's statement is puffing:[9]

- general rather than specific statement
- hedged rather than unqualified statement
- phrased as opinion rather than fact
- medium of communication (oral rather than written, or in informal statement rather than in formal written contract)
- experimental rather than standard goods
- statement refers to a consequence of buying the goods, rather than to an aspect of the goods

---

[8] *Pizza Hut, Inc. v. Papa John's International, Inc.*, 227 F.3d 489, 494-95 (5th Cir. 2000).

[9] This list merges the factors in 2-313 comments 4 and 8; amended 2-313 comment 10; Barkley Clark & Christopher Smith, *The Law of Product Warranties* § 4:10 (2d ed. 2002 & Supp. 2003); James J. White & Robert S. Summers, *Uniform Commercial Code* § 9-4 (5th ed. 2000). These commentators also note that the courts seem to be more likely to hold that a statement is not puffing when the plaintiff has suffered a serious injury.

- defect is not a hidden or unexpected nonconformity
- claim is not capable of objective measurement or being adjudged true or false
- unreasonableness of buyer's reliance on the statement
- seller not significantly more sophisticated or knowledgeable than buyer
- bargain price rather than premium price for the goods
- usage of trade suggests buyer should not rely on statement

The following fact situations are drawn from real cases. Which of the above factors weigh in favor of the italicized statement being puffing, and which ones weigh against? Do enough of the factors tilt in one direction to allow you to determine that the statement is puffing or not?

(A)   An experienced dealer in racehorses tells a buyer (who owns and races standard-bred horses as an avocation) that *the horse can "leave like a deer, take a forward position, and if you brush him from the head of the stretch home, he would just jog home in preferred company every week."* In fact, the horse is later found to suffer from temporary tendinitis and thrombosis. At trial, the seller testifies that among horse traders it is "not a common thing" to guarantee a horse and that he has never guaranteed a horse unless he had an "understanding" that an ignorant buyer was relying totally on a knowledgeable seller not "to make a mean deal." The buyer does not contradict this testimony.

(B)   In a non-reliance jurisdiction, seller shows buyer a diamond bracelet and says that *the bracelet is worth a lot more than $15,000 but the shop needs to "move the bracelet,"* so the sale price is $15,000. Buyer later phones seller to say he wants to buy the bracelet and will stop by the next day to complete the purchase. Seller fills out and signs a form with the following language: *"This is our estimate, for insurance purposes only, of the present retail replacement cost of identical items, and not necessarily the amounts that might be obtained if the articles were offered for sale. Estimated value: $25,000.00."* When Buyer comes the next day, Seller shows Buyer the estimate form and then puts it in the box. Buyer pays Seller and leaves with the bracelet. The diamonds are later found to be worth $13,000.

(C)   Buyer tells the salesperson at a used-car business that she needs a reliable car to drive 700 miles and back home again, with her seven-month-old daughter, to visit her husband at the army base at which he is serving. She wants to spend less than $1000. The salesperson points to a car on the lot and says that it is in "good condition," that he has driven the car and can recommend it, and that the car is in "A-1 shape." Buyer purchases the car, which breaks down after seventy-five miles and leaves the buyer and her daughter stranded in a very small town for two days while the repairs are being made.

Applying the Code

Problem 9-6. Among your own purchases of "goods," locate packaging or enclosed material that contains an affirmation of fact, a promise, a description, and puffing.

(A)   Bring the packaging or enclosed material to class, and be prepared to identify which language fits into each category and defend your conclusions.

(B)   If you didn't buy the goods directly from the manufacturer (or other person who packaged the goods), did the seller from whom you bought make any warranties (express or implied) to you based on the packaging? (Assume that you are in a non-reliance jurisdiction.)

2003 (C)   Under 2-313A in the 2003 amended version, does the manufacturer (or other person who packaged and sold the goods earlier in the distribution chain) owe any obligations to you as a remote purchaser?

Problem 9-7. In (A) through (C) below, does the immediate seller's representation become part of the basis of the bargain under any of the approaches to "part of the basis of the bargain"? Consider them in the order of most to least favorable to the buyer: non-reliance, comment 3, *Cipollone* (if applicable), reliance.

(A)   Buyer shows that she told the sales agent she wanted a van that has anti-lock brakes and that the agent told her the van she was looking at has such brakes. Buyer also shows that the van does not actually have anti-lock brakes. The owner's manual, which was delivered in the glove box of the van a week later, says that the van has an "anti-skid feature that's particularly well suited to front-wheel drive vans" but that the van does not have anti-lock brakes.

(B)   Buyer, a hospital, shows that its purchasing agent received a brochure listing the characteristics of an MRI machine before she ordered the machine for the hospital. Unfortunately, she left her job and moved away soon after, so neither party can depose her about whether she actually read or relied on the brochure in making the purchase.

(C)   Buyer shows that she saw Seller's TV infomercial that showed the paint remover could strip four layers of paint off a radiator overnight. Buyer admitted on cross-examination that she did not believe the infomercial's demonstration but bought the paint remover anyway, because she figured that Seller would stand behind its word.

Problem 9-8. Beverly is a purchasing manager for a company that runs a catalog business for consumer garden tools and projects. Devon, a vendor's representative for a garden tool company, visits Beverly's company and shows Beverly a new line of specially hardened steel tools. Devon takes Beverly to a remote section of the parking lot and says, "Watch what these tools can do," as he uses the hoe and the shovel to pry and break up the edge of the asphalt pavement. He makes no oral or written representations as to the tools' strength. Beverly is very impressed and orders 200 of each for the next season. Unfortunately, the tools break easily when they are used to pry stones out of the ground (a frequent task in some gardens). The customers who bought the tools from Beverly's company return the broken tools in droves, and her company cheerfully refunds the price, to keep goodwill. She is then astonished when the vendor refuses to reimburse her company for those returned tools. The vendor says that the tools were not covered by an express warranty, and even if they were, that warranty was not breached. See 2-313 comment 6.

(A)   Has Devon's company made any express warranties to Beverly's company? If so, what are they, and have they been breached? (Assume that the jurisdiction's case law is confused as to whether this is a reliance, comment 3, or non-reliance jurisdiction, so your answer needs to consider all three possibilities.)

(B)   Would your answer to (A) be any different if Devon tells Beverly that the hoe and shovel he is demonstrating are prototypes of the products that will be available next month, but that the factory has not yet geared up to make those particular hoes and shovels?

Assignment 10: Warranty Disclaimers and Conflicts

§§ 2-312, 2-316, 2-317

Assignments 8 and 9 showed how implied and express warranties are created. This assignment shows how to resolve conflicts among warranties and how those warranties may be disclaimed by seller's language or action.

A note on vocabulary: Although 2-316 is titled "Exclusion or Modification of Warranties," a common synonym is "disclaimer of warranties." This textbook uses "disclaimer" to describe either an exclusion or a modification of a warranty.

Reading the Code

Problem 10-1. Disclaiming Express Warranties. Section 2-316(1) contains two rules of law dealing with disclaimer of express warranties. Rewrite those rules in if/then paraphrases. How do those two rules relate to each other?

Problem 10-2. Disclaiming Implied Warranties.[1]

(A) Section 2-316(2) contains three rules of law pertaining to warranty disclaimer. Section 2-316(3) contains three additional means of warranty disclaimer. Fill in the chart below listing the ways a seller may disclaim each of the implied warranties. Jot down the subsection number and letter as well. As you fill in the chart, consider the relationship between subsections 2 and 3, as indicated by subsection 2 being "subject to subsection (3)" and subsection 3 applying "Notwithstanding subsection (2)." Consider using a dictionary if you are uncertain about the meaning.

---

[1] Thirteen states have enacted statutes that forbid the disclaimer of one or both implied warranties as to consumer goods. *See* 1 Barkley Clark & Christopher Smith, *The Law of Product Warranties* § 8:34 (2d ed. 2002); 1 William D. Hawkland, *Uniform Commercial Code Series* § 2-316:1, at 2-703 n.5 (2001).

How to disclaim an implied warranty of merchantability	How to disclaim an implied warranty of fitness for a particular purpose

(B)   Locate the definition of "conspicuous." If you were the deciding judge, would you think that boxed or colored text was conspicuous? What about the first or last clause in a three-page agreement? What about a disclaimer in all capital letters, when the rest of the agreement was also in all capital letters? What about a disclaimer in the middle of a long clause labeled with the heading "Warranty"?

(C)   Read 2-316 comment 8.   What does comment 8 add to your understanding of 2-316(3)(b)? Under 2-316(3)(b), if seller demands and buyer examines or refuses to examine, which warranties are disclaimed?

2003 (D)   Read the 2003 amended version of 2-316. Aside from the changes of "writing" to "record," how does the amended version alter the chart above in (C)?

(E)   Read 2-312(2) and (3) and comment 6. Does 2-316 provide a means of disclaiming the warranties in 2-312? How is the warranty of title disclaimed? How is the warranty of non-infringement disclaimed?

2003 (F)   What effect does the 2003 amended version of 2-312 have on your answer to the last two questions in (E)?

Applying the Code

Problem 10-3. Note that 2-316(4) refers to 2-719, the section on remedy limitations and exclusions. Sellers can use warranty disclaimers or remedy limitations (or both) to limit their liability. A warranty disclaimer is designed to limit a warranty by restricting the scope of the representations about the nature of the goods being sold. In contrast, a remedy limitation leaves the scope of the warranty untouched but restricts what remedies the buyer may obtain, once a breach of warranty is established.

You have a client who wants to know the validity and effect of its standard warranty and disclaimer provisions. For the statement below:

(1)   Label in the margin which sentence or phrase is

     (a)   a warranty or language clarifying the scope of that warranty,

     (b)   a warranty disclaimer, or

     (c)   a remedy or a remedy limitation.

(2)   Which warranties does the disclaimer language successfully disclaim, under 2-316?

(3)   Is any language invalid under 2-316(1)?

AUDIO CORNER LIMITED WARRANTY

This product is warranted against defects for 1 year from date of purchase from Audio Corner's company-owned stores and authorized Audio Corner franchisees and dealers. Within this period, we will repair it without charge for parts and labor. Simply bring your Audio Corner sales slip as proof of purchase date to any Audio Corner store. Warranty does not cover transportation costs. Nor does it cover a product subjected to misuse or accidental damage. EXCEPT AS PROVIDED HEREIN, AUDIO CORNER MAKES NO WARRANTIES, EXPRESS OR IMPLIED, INCLUDING WARRANTIES OF MERCHANTABILITY AND FITNESS FOR A PARTICULAR PURPOSE. AUDIO CORNER HAS NO LIABILITY FOR ANY INCIDENTAL OR CONSEQUENTIAL DAMAGES, SUCH AS DATA LOSS. Some states do not permit limitation or exclusion of implied warranties; therefore, the aforesaid limitation(s) or exclusion(s) may not apply to the purchaser. This warranty gives you specific legal rights and you may also have other rights which vary from state to state.

Problem 10-4. In each of the fact situations below, what express and implied warranties have been created? Which, if any, have been effectively disclaimed?

(A)   Sarah is shopping for a campstove from a store that sells outdoor recreational equipment. She is concerned about her friends' stories about campstoves flaring up with large flames while being lit. She tells the store employee that she wants a stove that lights without producing large flames. The employee helps her to select a model with a butane tank, which avoids the flare-up problem of stoves with white gas. The particular stove that Sarah later buys is on display, out of its package, and assembled. The salesperson suggests that Sarah carefully look over the stove because it is a floor sample and to see if it has all the features Sarah wants. Sarah glances at the stove to make sure it is the model recommended to her, then takes it to the register and pays for it.

(B)   Sarah is shopping for a sleeping bag from a store that sells outdoor recreational equipment. The label sewn onto the bottom of one of the sleeping bags says that the bag is "machine washable in warm water with a mild soap and an extra rinse cycle." Sarah reads the label, then asks a salesperson whether the bag is really machine washable. The salesperson says that machine washing shortens the life of the bag by weakening stitching and decreasing the insulating quality so he'd recommend dry cleaning. Sarah buys the sleeping bag. When Sarah washes the bag according to the label instructions, the insulation bunches up into lumps that can't be completely separated.

Problem 10-5. True story. The following letter to the editor appeared in 315 New Eng. J. Med. 1234 (Nov. 6, 1986):

IF YOU SNIP, DON'T ZIP!

To the Editor: We are a manufacturer of zippers. It has recently come to our attention that at least one physician is using our zippers to close surgical incisions.

Our products are not designed or manufactured for medical purposes and were never intended for such use. In addition, our product is not sterile or packaged or manufactured in a medically sterile environment. During the manufacturing process our zippers are in contact with or made with oils, lubricants, detergents, dyestuff, and other common chemicals. The finished product is not hazardous if used as it is intended to be used. Therefore, illness or injury may result if this product is used for surgical purposes.

We urge *Journal* readers not to use zippers for medical purposes. We cannot be responsible for any injury caused by such use, and we disclaim any warranty, expressed or implied, in connection with medical use of our products.

Bernard J. Rubin

Macon, GA 31297   YKK (U.S.A.)

The above letter prompted the following reply:

To the Editor: The use of the Zipper has greatly facilitated reexploration of the abdomen when it is required on an almost daily basis. We have tried many different zippers over the past few years. Our initial studies used the YKK, but at the present we prefer the Talon, since it is less likely to disengage spontaneously and lead to evisceration.

H. Harlan Stone, M.D.

Baltimore, MD 21202   University of Maryland

You are corporate counsel for a competing zipper company. Explain how your client may be making an implied warranty covering surgical use of its zippers even though such a use is not intended by the manufacturer. What courses of action might you recommend that your company take to eliminate any such warranty for medical use of your company's ordinary zippers? (Assume that physicians and hospitals are buying the zippers directly from the manufacturer.)

Problem 10-6. Disclaimers Packaged with or Accompanying the Goods.
Problem 9-4 explored the issues raised when considering whether
"representations in the box" are binding as express warranties. The issues
include whether the buyer assented to the alleged term, whether the
representations became part of the basis of the bargain, and whether an equitable
doctrine like waiver or promissory estoppel can successfully be invoked by the
buyer.

Whether "warranty disclaimers in the box" become part of the contract
depends upon only the first of these questions: whether the buyer assented to the
term. Disclaimers are not governed by 2-313, so the disclaimer does not have
to be part of the basis of the bargain. And the equitable doctrines of waiver and
promissory estoppel prevent a party (here, the seller) from withdrawing a
promised benefit (here, the express warranty), so they are irrelevant to whether
the seller gets the benefit of a disclaimer term.

Even though assent is an issue for both warranties and disclaimers, that
requirement may be understood differently when the question is whether a buyer
assented to a largely favorable warranty term than when the issue is buyer's
assent to a generally unfavorable disclaimer term (and differently again if the
disclaimer is packaged with a favorable warranty). For example, the buyer may
argue that evidence sufficient to show that buyer agreed to a favorable term (e.g.,
by the inaction of not sending back delivered goods) may not be sufficient to
show that buyer agreed to an unfavorable term. On the other hand, a seller may
argue that fairness dictates that all "terms in the box" be treated the same, no
matter who benefits from the term, and that seller's warranty and disclaimer
terms are a package to which buyer assents (or doesn't assent) as a whole.

Review the facts in Problem 9-4(B) and (C) and your answers to those
problems. Assume the same facts and that the Limited Six-Month Warranty also
contains the following language in bold type: **"The seller undertakes no
responsibility for the quality of the goods except as provided in this
contract. The seller assumes no responsibility that the goods will be fit for
any particular purpose for which you may be buying these goods, except as
otherwise provided in the contract. These goods are not covered by
warranties of merchantability or fitness."**

(A)   Does the quoted language above disclaim the implied warranties between Charles and Big Discounts?

2003 (B)   Same question as in (A) above, but under the amended version of Article 2.

2003 (C)   Note that there are no implied or express warranties between a seller and a remote purchaser, so, as between Charles and Electrolite, the disclaimer language quoted above can disclaim—at the most—Electrolite's obligation under 2-313A. Reread new 2-313A and comment 5 in the 2003 amendments. Also read the amended version of 2-316. Assume that the front of the pamphlet inside the DVD box says that the DVD player "plays all formats, both home-recorded and commercially recorded." The inside of the pamphlet says that the DVD player "may not be able to play all formats, depending on the age of buyer's recording hardware and the version of the recording software. In particular, recordings made on MusicStash software will not play on this player unless they were made with an upgrade to the 8.1 version of the software." What is Electrolite's obligation to Charles under new 2-313A? Can Electrolite claim the benefit of the limiting language? If so, under what specific provisions of 2-313A?

Magnuson-Moss Warranty Act

Article 2 is supplemented by a federal statute called the Magnuson-Moss Warranty Act, 15 U.S.C. § 2301 et seq.; the accompanying regulations appear in 16 C.F.R. Parts 700-703. Although the statute and its regulations may appear in your statutory supplement, they are not easily understood in several readings (even by an experienced UCC reader), so the most salient provisions are summarized here.[2]

Background: Congress enacted the Magnuson-Moss Warranty Act in the 1970s at the height of the consumer protection movement so that consumers would have additional warranty protection beyond the UCC's warranty provisions, which have several default warranties but no mandatory warranties. Although the Act and its regulations impose many rules beyond the scope of this course, some of the Act's provisions supplement and even change UCC Article 2's provisions on contracts for sale of goods. In particular, Magnuson-Moss

---

[2] For detailed coverage of the Act and its regulations, see 2 Barkley Clark & Christopher Smith, *The Law of Product Warranties* chs. 14-21 (2d ed. 2002).

- mandates clearer labeling of warranties, to provide a quick guide to consumer buyers;
- restricts the extent to which the Article 2 implied warranties can be disclaimed, and in what format;
- restricts remedy limitations (to be covered in Assignment 22); and
- makes consumer lawsuits against warrantors more feasible.

Scope: The Act does not require any seller to give a warranty. However, when a "warrantor" (a seller, manufacturer, or supplier) offers a "written warranty" on a "consumer product," the Act requires that the warranty satisfy certain disclosure requirements and minimum federal standards. The same requirements apply when a warrantor enters into a "service contract" as to a consumer product, either at time of sale or within ninety days.

- A "consumer product" is goods normally used for personal, family, or household purposes, whether or not, in the particular contract at issue, the goods were bought for such a use. The Act protects a business buying a consumer product such as an automobile or a typewriter. See 16 C.F.R. § 700.1(a).
- A "written warranty" is (1) a written affirmation of fact or promise by a supplier (direct or indirect) that affirms or promises that the material or workmanship of the goods is defect-free or will meet a specified level of performance over a specified period of time, or (2) a supplier's written undertaking to refund, repair, replace, or take other remedial action as to the goods upon the failure of the goods to meet contract specifications, so long as (1) or (2) is contained in a writing that becomes part of the basis of the bargain between the supplier and the buyer.
- A "service contract" is a written contract to perform maintenance or repair services over a fixed period of time.

An express warranty created orally or by conduct (based on a sample or model) is covered by UCC § 2-313, but not by Magnuson-Moss. On the other hand, Magnuson-Moss covers some "service contracts," which often are outside the scope of UCC Article 2 unless they are within a contract whose predominant purpose is the sale of goods.

Terms in a written warranty: Magnuson-Moss requires that any written warranty given to the buyer "fully and conspicuously" disclose all the "terms and conditions of such warranty." If the goods cost more than $15, certain specified terms (see 16 C.F.R. § 701.3) must be clearly and conspicuously disclosed in a single document in simple and readily understood language, including, for example, the following:

> Some states do not allow the exclusion or limitation of incidental or consequential damages, so the above limitation or exclusion may not apply to you. This warranty gives you specific legal rights, and you may also have other rights which may vary from state to state.

Mandatory two-tier system of warranty labeling: The Act sets up a choice between two labels to be attached to "written warranties": Full [duration] Warranty, or Limited Warranty. (If a "written warranty" is not so labeled, a small line of cases has held that it becomes a Limited Warranty by default.) If the warranty is labeled a "Full [duration] Warranty," the warrantor cannot exclude[3] or modify any UCC implied warranty, including limiting its duration. If the warranty is labeled a "Limited Warranty" or becomes one by default:

*   the supplier cannot exclude any UCC implied warranty and cannot limit its duration to a period shorter than the supplier's written warranty of reasonable duration;
*   such limitation must be conscionable, must be in clear and unmistakable language, and must appear prominently on the face of the written warranty.

If a warrantor gives a full warranty, the regulations forbid the warrantor from requiring the buyer of a consumer product to return a warranty registration card as a condition precedent to warranty coverage and performance, unless the warrantor can prove that the duty is a reasonable one. See 16 C.F.R. § 700.7. The Act also restricts a warrantor's ability to limit remedies and provides some additional remedy provisions. Those aspects of the Act will be covered in Assignment 22 on remedy limitations.

---

[3] Magnuson-Moss uses "disclaimer" to mean only an exclusion of a warranty, not other modifications of a warranty. As noted at the beginning of this assignment, this textbook uses "disclaimer" to mean either an exclusion or a modification of a warranty.

Problem 10-7. Effect of the Magnuson-Moss Warranty Act.

(A)   Draw a diagram of overlapping or inclusionary circles to show the relationship between a 2-313 "express warranty" and a "written warranty" under Magnuson-Moss, or use some other method to show their relationship.

(B)   Must a supplier make a written warranty? If a supplier gives no written warranty, do the provisions governing Full and Limited Warranties apply to the transaction?

(C)   Which UCC Article 2 rules does Magnuson-Moss actually change (rather than supplement)?

(D)   Refer back to your answer to Problem 8-4(B). Notice that Magnuson-Moss restrictions on seller's ability to limit the duration of an implied warranty seem to suggest that an implied warranty *has* a duration. How can UCC Article 2 and Magnuson-Moss be reconciled in this respect? What is the most reasonable result of applying both statutes?

(E)   Does Magnuson-Moss have any effect on the warranties in 2-312?

Problem 10-8. What effect does Magnuson-Moss have on the following warranty provision that you analyzed in Problem 10-3, assuming that the product is a "consumer product"?

AUDIO CORNER LIMITED WARRANTY

This product is warranted against defects for 1 year from date of purchase from Audio Corner's company-owned stores and authorized Audio Corner's franchisees and dealers. Within this period, we will repair it without charge for parts and labor. Simply bring your Audio Corner sales slip as proof of purchase date to any Audio Corner store. Warranty does not cover transportation costs. Nor does it cover a product subjected to misuse or accidental damage. EXCEPT AS PROVIDED HEREIN, AUDIO CORNER MAKES NO WARRANTIES, EXPRESS OR IMPLIED, INCLUDING WARRANTIES OF MERCHANTABILITY AND FITNESS FOR A PARTICULAR PURPOSE. AUDIO CORNER HAS NO LIABILITY FOR ANY INCIDENTAL OR CONSEQUENTIAL DAMAGES, SUCH AS DATA LOSS. Some states do not permit limitation or exclusion of implied warranties; therefore, the aforesaid limitation(s) or exclusion(s) may not apply to the purchaser. This warranty gives you specific legal rights and you may also have other rights which vary from state to state.

Problem 10-9. Cumulation and Conflict of Warranties. What happens when the parties' various writings and oral assurances contain conflicting warranties, even after any disclaimers are applied? Read 2-317 and consider the following scenario: Katie has bought a powerful new gas stove for her kitchen. She is having problems getting the stovetop burners to simmer liquids at a low enough temperature to prepare particularly delicate sauces like Hollandaise, even though the burners are adjusted correctly. Assume that the seller made the following express warranties to Katie before the contract was entered into:

•   The seller's salesperson simmered a small pan of Hollandaise sauce on the same model stove at the store.

- The seller's salesperson said that the 15,000 BTU burners "have the power to stir fry and sear meat at very high temperatures, but also to simmer delicate sauces at very low temperatures."
- The seller's brochure about the stove, given to Katie by the seller, says that the lowest burner setting heats at 180° F. (The stove meets these latter specs, but to properly prepare some sauces requires the burners to heat at 150° F.)

Assume that the contract also contains an implied warranty of merchantability but not fitness for a particular purpose. Which of the warranties can't reasonably be construed consistently with each other? How does 2-317 resolve the conflict(s)?

Assignment 11: Extending Warranties to Third-Party Beneficiaries

§ 2-318

In Assignments 8 and 9, we explored express and implied warranties made by a seller to the immediate buyer in sales transactions. We also saw that warranty liability may be created for a remote seller by written warranty language packaged with the goods and passed on to a remote buyer, and by the seller's advertisements seen by a remote buyer. But what about other third parties to a sales transaction? For example, when a seller creates a warranty with respect to goods, is the buyer's spouse or other family member protected by that warranty if the goods fail to conform while the goods are in their hands? What about the buyer's friend? Or a bystander? If warranties are made by a manufacturer to a wholesaler, is the retailer who buys from the wholesaler covered by the original warranty? What about the retailer's customer? Are any of these "third parties" (those not part of the original contract) beneficiaries of the warranty provisions made in the sale by the original warrantor?

Under older common law rules, the answer to all these questions was "no." Only persons in "privity of contract"—the direct parties to the sale—were permitted to sue for relief under a contract, which meant that only the immediate buyer in a sales transaction was protected by a seller's warranty. As already noted in Assignment 9, some courts have concluded that sellers are liable to remote buyers for written representations passed through to those buyers and made part of the basis of the bargain, e.g., warranty booklets in new cars or warranty provisions appearing on the outside of packaged goods. Liability for such "pass-through warranties" is supported by comment 2 to 2-313 (and is made mandatory in the 2003 amendments). But these rules protect only buyers, not others who may be injured by a breach of warranty. Moreover, under the pre-2003 version of Article 2, a remote buyer is protected only if the written warranty was made part of the basis of the bargain in the sale to the remote buyer.

The common law offered one other way for an injured person to circumvent the privity obstacle to liability. A seller/warrantor might be held "indirectly" liable to customers or others not in privity under a combination of tort and contract principles. For example, if a car dealer warrants a car against defects and a third party is injured in an accident when the steering mechanism fails while the buyer is driving, the third party would not be in privity with the seller and therefore could not collect directly from the seller for breach of warranty. However, the third party might sue the driver (buyer) for tortious injury and the buyer might then seek recovery from the car dealer (seller) for any tort damages the buyer owed to the third party as a result of the dealer's warranty breach. Similarly, assume AC/DC, Inc. manufactures and sells batteries to Ford, warranting their quality, and Ford installs those batteries in some of its cars and then sells those cars to dealers with an implied warranty of merchantability, and a dealer sells the cars to consumers with an implied warranty of merchantability. If one of the batteries caused an engine fire, the consumer could seek relief from the car dealer for breach of the dealer's warranty, the dealer could seek reimbursement by claiming against Ford for breach of Ford's warranty to the dealer, and Ford could seek relief against AC/DC under AC/DC's warranty made to Ford. Liability of AC/DC or Ford for injury to ultimate purchasers would thus depend upon a series of contractual warranty provisions (AC/DC to Ford, Ford to the dealer, dealer to the consumer). The procedural obstacles are evident, and liabilities up the "warranty chain" depend on the nature of the warranty given (or disclaimed or excluded) in each contract.

To respond to problems created by such privity rules, courts during the twentieth century gradually relaxed the rules requiring privity of contract, and Article 2 followed that trend. Moreover, because states have had differing attitudes about how much to relax the requirement of privity, 2-318 offers three alternative versions of third-party warranty liability, and some states have created their own variations. By a recent count, 30 jurisdictions have adopted Alternative A, 10 use Alternative B, and approximately a dozen have adopted Alternative C, though a number of states adopting each alternative have modified the UCC text to suit local preferences.[1]

Reading the Code

Problem 11-1. Differentiating Among the 2-318 Alternatives. Read carefully all three alternatives for section 2-318, then find and read your own state's version of the section. Note that each version indicates *the category of persons* to whom the seller's warranty extends (beyond the immediate buyer) and *the*

---

[1] The count includes the District of Columbia and the Virgin Islands. Gary L. Monserud, *Blending the Law of Sales with the Common Law of Third Party Beneficiaries*, 39 Duq. L. Rev. 110, 129-34 (2000). Although the majority of jurisdictions have adopted Alternative A, in many of those states the courts have adopted common law liability rules approximating the broader coverage in Alternatives B and C. See Problem 11-3.

nature of the injury included in such warranty protection. In the final sentence of each version, the section *restricts the ability of sellers to modify the effect of the section.* Based on your reading of the four alternatives, fill in the following chart and note the differences among the versions:

	Who else is protected by seller's warranty besides the immediate buyer?	For what kind of injury?	Limits on seller's power to restrict 2-318 protection
Alternative A (see Note below)			
Alternative B			
Alternative C			
Your state's version			

Note: In construing Alternative A, consider whether the "his" in "his buyer" and "in his home" refer to the same party to the transaction.

Applying the Code

Problem 11-2. Applying 2-318. Consider the following scenario:

• Elektron, Inc. sells 10,000 portable CD players (with earphone sets) and 500 stereo mini-systems to Audio Products, Inc. a regional wholesale distributor of Elektron products. Elektron expressly warrants to Audio Products that the goods have no defects in materials or workmanship.

Because Elektron is a merchant with respect to goods of the kind, the goods are also covered by an implied warranty of merchantability.

- Audio Products sells 1000 Elektron portable CD players and 100 stereo mini-systems to Better Buy Discounts, making no express warranties,[2] and disclaiming all implied warranties.
- Better Buy sells one portable CD player and one stereo mini-system to Vicki Quesada and provides a one-year warranty against defects, but disclaims the implied warranty of merchantability.
- The day after her purchase, Quesada gives the portable CD player to her friend, Hawo Abukar, as a birthday present.
- For the purposes of this question, assume Elektron made *no* warranty directly to Quesada in any package inserts, brochures, or manuals, or on the package.

The warranties made from each seller to the immediate buyer in this series of transactions may be represented in the following manner:

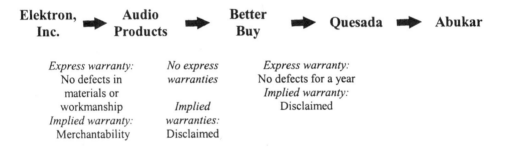

The following occurs within a month of Quesada's purchase:

- The electrical connections in Quesada's mini-system short out, resulting in a house fire that causes considerable damage.
- The portable CD player given to Abukar has a button that is supposed to prevent the unit from playing too loudly but the button fails suddenly and the resulting extremely loud blast of music damages Abukar's ears permanently.

---

[2] Of course, even if Audio Products tries to avoid making any express warranties, it will almost certainly have at least made a warranty of description (e.g., that the thing sold is an Elektron portable CD player). Such warranties are not relevant for this problem so, for the sake of simplicity, we will assume no express warranty was made.

•   When the defect in Quesada's mini-system is publicized, neither Audio Products nor Better Buy is able to sell any more Elektron mini-systems from their inventory.

(A)   Complete the following chart, indicating for each of the three sellers in the distribution chain (Elektron, Audio Products, Better Buy), which of the injured parties (Audio Products, Better Buy, Quesada, Abukar) would be covered by that seller's warranty (and for which injury) under the three 2-318 Alternatives. Note whether the warranty coverage is direct (under 2-313 or 2-314) or indirect (through the operation of 2-318). (You will probably find it easier to fill in the chart one row at a time.)

Which parties would be covered by a warranty from the indicated seller under the three 2-318 alternatives?

	Elektron	Audio Products	Better Buy
Alternative A			
Alternative B			
Alternative C			

(B)   Would the result under any of the 2-318 alternatives change if Quesada gave Abukar her present at a birthday party Quesada held in her home? Read comment 3 to the unamended version of 2-318, as well as comment 2 to the 2003 amended version.

(C)   Does the Magnuson-Moss Warranty Act operate to change any of the warranties in operation in this scenario?

Problem 11-3. Extending Warranty Coverage Beyond 2-318.   You have seen that 2-318 Alternative A does not mandate warranty coverage for affected individuals unless they are in the family or household of the buyer or are a guest in the buyer's home. Similarly, 2-318 Alternatives A and B do not mandate warranty coverage for affected individuals who suffer property damage rather than personal injury. Read 2-318 comment 3 and 2-313 comment 2. May a court extend warranty coverage to include individuals or injuries not granted warranty protection by the state legislature through its adoption of Alternative A or B? In view of the text of the comments, is there a difference between extending coverage for personal injury to an otherwise excluded individual and extending coverage for property damage to someone already protected against personal injury?

Problem 11-4. The 2-318 Limit on Seller's Power to Disclaim. As we have seen in earlier assignments, a seller may disclaim or limit warranties given to an immediate buyer as long as the seller does so in accordance with the provisions of 2-316 and within the limits of the Magnuson-Moss Warranty Act. We know as well that, under the first sentence of each version of 2-318, whatever warranties are given to the immediate buyer—whether full or more limited—will extend to some additional persons. Thus, if the seller includes in its initial sale an effective warranty disclaimer, that disclaimer will be effective as well against any person who makes a claim pursuant to 2-318.

But can the seller distinguish between the immediate buyer and others in the "distributive chain" by contracting for a greater degree of warranty protection for the immediate buyer than for others? That is, can the seller specify that its warranty protections extend *only* to the immediate buyer, thereby altering the extension of warranty protection granted by 2-318?

(A)   Read the last sentence of 2-318 Alternative B and all of 2-318 comment 1. What effect, if any, would the last sentence of Alternative B have on the following clauses, if included in a sales contract? (Assume the sale does not involve consumer products, so no issues are raised under the Magnuson-Moss Warranty Act.)

1. Seller expressly disclaims the implied warranty of merchantability.

2. Seller and Buyer expressly agree that in the event of a breach of warranty, Buyer's sole remedy shall be to return the item to Seller for repair or replacement, and in no event shall Seller be liable for any consequential damages.

3. The muffler you are buying for your car is guaranteed for as long as you own your car.

(B)　　The last sentence of Alternative C differs from the last sentences of Alternatives A and B. Write a clause for a seller that makes use of the additional power sellers are given in Alternative C to restrict warranty coverage.

(C)　　How does your own state's version of 2-318 compare to Alternatives A, B, and C with respect to the limit on the seller's power to disclaim?

2003 **Problem 11-5. The 2003 Amended Version.**

(A)　　Read the 2003 amended version of 2-318. What additional obligations are placed on sellers as a result of the amendment?

(B)　　Under the 2003 amended version of 2-318 Alternative A, *"a seller's warranty to an immediate buyer*, . . . a seller's remedial promise to an immediate buyer, or a seller's obligation to a remote purchaser under Section 2-313A or 2-313B . . . *extends to any natural person who is in the family or household of* the immediate buyer or *the remote purchaser* . . . ." Do the italicized words mean that a manufacturer's warranty to its wholesale distributor covers a family member of a consumer purchaser who buys the goods from the retailer, who bought the goods from the wholesale distributor? Consider comments 3 and 4 to the 2003 amendments as you answer.

Assignment 12: Parol Evidence Rule: Suppression of Evidence of Express Warranties

§ 2-202

Reading the Code

As we have seen, 2-316(2) and (3) provide a mechanism for completely disclaiming implied warranties. That is, even though the circumstances under which the parties reached agreement might, by operation of law, make an implied warranty part of the contract, the seller can nonetheless remove that warranty by using the correct words of disclaimer. On the other hand, once an express warranty exists, it is nearly impossible for a party to disclaim that warranty. A seller is not permitted to make promises about the goods being sold and then retract those promises. More precisely, section 2-316(1) provides that "words or conduct relevant to the creation of an express warranty and words or conduct tending to negate or limit warranty shall be construed wherever reasonable as consistent with each other," but if they cannot be read as consistent with one another, the express warranty prevails.

According to 2-316(1), however, the rule that the warranty prevails over the warranty limitation is "subject to the provisions of this Article on parol or extrinsic evidence (Section 2-202)." The parol evidence rule, codified in 2-202, specifies whether terms may be part of a contract when those terms appear elsewhere than in the parties' written document that memorializes their agreement. When words of warranty are written or spoken outside of such a contract document and the contract document contains words disclaiming warranties, the parol evidence rule privileges the contract document and sometimes successfully defeats an otherwise valid express warranty by simply excluding it from evidence. The parol evidence rule has a similar effect on other terms spoken or written outside of such a contract document.

But just when will the contract document be privileged in this fashion? And what kinds of evidence will be excluded? The answers to these questions are hidden in an awkwardly worded section that must be pulled apart and reconstructed carefully to create a workable strategy for solving problems. As you work through the materials in this assignment, you should recognize that terminology used by 2-202 differs somewhat from the terminology used in the parol evidence rule as articulated in the common law or Restatement of Contracts. You should concentrate on learning the vocabulary of the Code, but realize that the concepts you learn here will help you understand the common law and Restatement rules as well.

First, some context. When parties to a contract seek to prove the content of their contract, any evidence showing to what terms they agreed is relevant. Examples of relevant evidence might include details of the negotiations leading up to the adoption of a written contract document, including an alleged oral agreement to terms not in the written document; notes written on documents exchanged during the negotiation; conversations that might help to explain ambiguous words in the contract document; and discussions held after the signing of the contract document.

In order to be considered by the fact-finder, evidence that is relevant to prove the content of a contract must also satisfy—or not violate—other evidentiary standards on admissibility. For example, evidence tending to show that the parties agreed to a particular term might be excludable as hearsay, and documents containing relevant evidence regarding contract terms might be excludable under the best evidence rule.

Section 2-202 establishes an additional set of rules explicitly forbidding the use of certain evidence to prove contract terms, but explicitly permitting the use of other kinds of evidence for that same purpose. Although 2-202 is not, strictly speaking, a rule of evidence, it operates like such a rule by forbidding the fact-finder from using certain evidence to determine the content of a contract. To understand the effect of 2-202, it is important to remember that evidence *is admissible* if neither 2-202 nor any other rule of law forbids its use.

We will start by considering how 2-202 applies when the parties have exchanged written confirmations and then see how the rule extends to other written memorializations of contract terms.

Problem 12-1. Operation of the Parol Evidence Rule With Respect to Confirmations. Read 2-202, including (a) and (b), but ignore for now the last clause of (b) (starting with "unless the court finds . . .").[1] Assume the parties to

---

[1] As you read 2-202, you should note whether you are using the version that reflects conforming amendments to Article 2 adopted with the 2001 revisions to Article 1. The text of 2-202(a) is modified by the 2001 conforming amendments, although the substance remains unchanged.

an oral agreement have exchanged written confirmations that both contain some terms that are the same in both confirmations.

(A)   After the confirmations are entered into evidence, one party seeks to introduce other evidence to contradict a term in both confirmations by showing that during negotiations the parties actually agreed to something different. What does 2-202 say about the use of such evidence? Does the application of the rule depend on whether the alleged prior agreement was written or oral, or when it took place?

(B)   One party seeks to introduce evidence to supplement the agreement by showing that during negotiations they agreed to something not mentioned in the confirmations. What does 2-202 say about the use of such evidence? Does it matter what the source of the evidence is?

(C)   Read 2-202 comment 2. One party seeks to introduce evidence to supplement the agreement by proving the existence of an additional term arising from course of dealing, usage of trade, or course of performance. What does 2-202 say about the use of such evidence?

(D)   Assume that one week after exchanging their confirmations, the parties orally agreed to change one of the terms contained in both confirmations. What does 2-202 say about the use of such evidence to convince the fact-finder that the term was changed? May such evidence be used in that fashion? What about evidence that the course of performance changed a term appearing in the contract document?

(E)   What does 2-202 say about the use of evidence from the negotiations, or from course of dealing, usage of trade, or course of performance, to explain a written term in the confirmations? May such evidence be used in that fashion? If so, is there an explicit requirement that the written term be vague, ambiguous, or otherwise uncertain in meaning in order to use parol evidence to explain the meaning?

(F)   Assume that a party claims an alleged contract is invalid or avoidable on one of the following grounds: fraudulent inducement, mutual mistake, duress, undue influence, absence of consideration, lack of assent, or nonoccurrence of a condition to contract formation. What does 2-202 say about the use of evidence to support such a claim? May such evidence be used in that fashion?

Problem 12-2. "Final Expression." The rules you articulated in answering Problem 12-1 apply to "[t]erms with respect to which the confirmatory memoranda of the parties agree." According to the express language of 2-202, what *other* kind of writing is subject to the same rules? Why is this kind of writing given the same protection as confirmatory memoranda?

Problem 12-3. "Complete and Exclusive Statement." Section 2-202 refers in its first paragraph to "a writing intended by the parties as a final expression of their agreement with respect to such terms as are included therein." For ease of reference, we'll call this a "final expression." Section 2-202(b)—all of which you should read now—refers to "writing . . . intended also as a complete and exclusive statement of the terms of the agreement." (We'll call this a "complete and exclusive statement.")

(A)   What is the difference between these two kinds of contractual writings? See comment 1(a). Could a writing be both? Could it be a "final expression" but not a "complete and exclusive statement"? Could it be a "complete and exclusive statement" but not a "final expression"? Could a writing relevant to prove the terms of a contract be neither a "final expression" nor a "complete and exclusive statement"?

(B)   Section 2-202 does not indicate how a court should decide whether a particular contract document is a final expression, a complete and exclusive statement, or neither. What facts or circumstances would help a court to decide among these alternatives? Consider the nature of the document as well as the surrounding circumstances.

(C)   If the judge finds a writing to be a "complete and exclusive statement," what is the effect as mandated by 2-202(b)?

Problem 12-4. Parol Evidence and the Complete and Exclusive Statement. If a writing is "intended also as a complete and exclusive statement of the terms of the agreement," what does 2-202 say about:

(A)   the use of evidence from a prior agreement or contemporaneous oral agreement to contradict terms in the writing?

(B)   the use of evidence from a prior agreement or contemporaneous oral agreement to supplement the written agreement by adding a term not appearing in the writing?

(C)   the use of evidence of a course of dealing, usage of trade, or course of performance between the parties to supplement the written agreement?

(D)   the use of evidence of an agreement from conversations held subsequent to the parties' adoption of the written agreement?

(E)   the use of evidence from the negotiations or from course of dealing, usage of trade, or course of performance to explain a written term?

(F)   the use of evidence from the negotiations to show that the contract was invalid or avoidable because of fraudulent inducement, mistake, duress, undue influence, lack of assent, or nonoccurrence of a condition to contract formation?

Problem 12-5. Admissibility and Effect of Evidence of Course of Dealing, Usage of Trade, and Course of Performance.

(A)   Under 2-202, may a party introduce evidence of course of dealing, usage of trade, or course of performance that is inconsistent with a term contained in a writing found to be a final expression or a complete and exclusive statement?

(B)   If 2-202 allows the fact finder to consider both a written term and inconsistent evidence from usage of trade to determine the meaning of a contract, which meaning will prevail?

(C)   Read *Nanakuli Paving & Rock Co. v. Shell Oil Co.*, at page 176, and 2-202 comment 2. For what purpose was the evidence of usage of trade admitted in *Nanakuli Paving*? Was it to explain, to supplement, or to vary a written term of the agreement? How does *Nanakuli Paving* change your understanding of the admissibility and use of evidence of trade usage to vary a written term?

Problem 12-6. "Prior Agreement" and "Contemporaneous Oral Agreement." Section 2-202 says terms set forth in a final expression may not be contradicted by evidence of *any agreement* entered prior to the parties' adoption of the writing.

(A)   Section 2-202 also bars contradiction by evidence of a *contemporaneous oral agreement*. May a party contradict a term in a final expression from evidence of a contemporaneous *written* agreement?

(B)   Section 2-202 also says terms with respect to which the confirmatory
        memoranda of the parties agree may not be contradicted by evidence of
        any prior agreement. Does this rule bar use of evidence prior to the date
        of the first of the confirmatory memoranda, or prior to the date of the
        second confirmation? (Neither the Code nor the comments answer this
        question expressly. You will have to reason out a plausible answer
        based on your understanding of 2-202 and the policies underlying it.)

Problem 12-7. Putting All the Pieces Together. Based on your answers to the
previous questions, you should be able to fill in the following chart, answering
YES or NO to the question, "If the contract document is as described (top row),
is the particular evidence specified (left column) admissible for the purpose
indicated?"

Parol Evidence Chart: Is the Evidence Offered Admissible?

	Document is not final expression	Document is final expression	Document is complete and exclusive statement
Evidence is from prior agreement, contemporaneous oral agreement, offered to contradict			
Evidence is from prior agreement, contemporaneous oral agreement, offered to supplement with additional term			

	Document is not final expression	Document is final expression	Document is complete and exclusive statement
Evidence is from usage of trade, course of dealing, or course of performance, offered to supplement			
Evidence is from subsequent oral or written agreement			
Evidence is offered to explain a written term			
Evidence is offered to show fraudulent inducement, mistake, duress, absence of consideration, lack of assent, condition to contract formation			
Evidence offered from usage of trade, course of dealing, course of performance appears inconsistent with written terms			

Problem 12-8. Comment 3 Restriction. Read comment 3. The first sentence of comment 3 paraphrases the rule expressed in 2-202(b): "[C]onsistent additional terms . . . may be proved unless the court finds that the writing was intended by both parties as a complete and exclusive statement of all the terms."[2] The second sentence adds a separate constraint on the admissibility of evidence

---

[2] The comment actually says "consistent additional terms *not reduced to writing*" may be used in this fashion. Because 2-202 clearly allows evidence of written terms to be used to supplement the written terms in a final expression, the italicized language must instead mean that evidence of consistent additional terms, written or oral, may be used even though they were *not written into the final expression.*

of "the additional terms" referred to in the first sentence. What kind of evidence is barred in the second sentence? Does the rule found there apply to final expressions? to complete and exclusive statements?

Problem 12-9. Implied Warranties and the Parol Evidence Rule. In order to establish a 2-315 implied warranty, a buyer seeks to introduce evidence that the seller recommended the buyer purchase a particular brand. May the seller suppress that evidence if the written agreement was a complete and exclusive statement under 2-202? More generally, can 2-202 be used to suppress evidence that would create an implied warranty? You can answer this question by reading 2-202 very carefully and then determining the section's proper reach. Keep in mind that key words used in 2-202 may be defined elsewhere in the Code.

Problem 12-10. Interaction Between 2-316 and 2-202. Consider the following far-from-unusual scenario: A prospective seller and buyer negotiate over purchase of an item, and during the course of the negotiations the seller makes oral or written representations about the goods. The parties then sign a written contract that contains a clause disclaiming all express warranties not appearing on the face of the contract. Under 2-316(1), the disclaimer should be inoperative to the extent it is inconsistent with oral or written representations that constitute warranties under 2-313. Under 2-202, however, if the written contract is a final expression of the parties' agreement, the representations made by the seller cannot be used to contradict the written term disclaiming all express warranties. Which of these two seemingly conflicting rules prevails and why? Reread 2-316(1) for assistance in answering.

2003   **Problem 12-11. The 2003 Amended Version.** Read the 2003 amended version
of 2-202. What is the effect of the omission of "explained" in newly numbered
2-202(1)? What is the effect of the addition of 2-202(2)?

Applying the Code

As you can see from the previous set of questions, when analyzing
whether the parol evidence rule bars admission of certain evidence, the result is
controlled by the answer to three questions:

* What kind of document memorializes the contract (final, complete and
  exclusive, neither)?
* What is the source of the evidence offered (prior agreement,
  contemporaneous oral agreement, contemporaneous written agreement,
  subsequent events)?
* For what purpose is the evidence offered (to add a term, to contradict,
  to resolve an ambiguity, to supplement, to show that no contract or an
  avoidable contract exists)?

Consider each of these three questions as you solve the problems below.

Problem 12-12. Section 2-202 draws a distinction between *contradicting* and
supplementing the terms of an agreement with evidence of consistent additional
terms. This distinction may appear clear on the surface, but the determination
whether a particular piece of evidence supplements or contradicts an agreement
may sometimes be difficult. Consider the following contract:

Ben and Sasha agree to the sale of a 1996 Buick LeSabre, identification number 123456789, for $1800, as is, sale to include the spare tire, the two extra snow tires, tire-changing tools in the trunk, and the stereo equipment installed in the car.

Assume that the writing is found to be a "final expression." Ben wants to prove that Sasha had agreed orally to six additional terms before or during contract formation:

1. That the exchange of car for money would be made on September 12.
2. That the car would be washed and waxed before delivery.
3. That the sale includes the Minnesota Winter Safety Kit in the trunk (candles, matches, blankets, sand, shovel, chocolate bar, etc.).
4. That Ben would receive the portable Yakima equipment rack and luggage compartment that Sasha used for long car trips.
5. That the price would be reduced by $100 if paid in cash.
6. That Ben would be excused from performing if he fails his upcoming driver's license examination.

Do these items contradict or supplement the written terms? Will 2-202 permit Ben to testify about their oral conversations with respect to each of these alleged terms? As you answer this question, consider also the second sentence of comment 3.

Problem 12-13. Beverage Distributors enters an agreement to deliver to Cal's Grocery 20 cases of soda pop each month for the next two years at a designated price per case. The parties use a two-page form contract, filling in appropriate blanks for quantity and price. The blank for delivery date is marked "monthly." The parties add to the form contract a clause specifying the following:

> Beverage mix in each monthly shipment will be as follows:
> > 5 cases cola
> > 5 cases diet cola
> > 5 cases lemon-lime
> > 5 cases root beer

(A)   Cal claims that when she spoke with the Beverage Distributors sales agent before the contract was signed, she was told that (1) deliveries would be made on the first Thursday of each month; (2) she could change the mix of beverages up to 3 days before the delivery date; and (3) Cal would have the option of renewing the contract for an additional two years, with all other terms remaining the same. Does 2-202 permit Cal to present these three statements as evidence of the alleged terms?

(B)   Cal would also like to introduce evidence that in contracts with beverage wholesalers, only the overall quantity of beverages is considered set by the contract and the mix of particular soda pops ordered is typically subject to change at any time during the life of the contract. Does 2-202 permit Cal to present that evidence?

Problem 12-14.

(A)   Assume that the written contract between Beverage Distributors and Cal's Grocery in Problem 12-13 contained any of the following clauses (often called "integration" or "merger" clauses):

*   This Agreement supersedes all prior agreements and representations, written or oral, concerning the subject matter herein.
*   The parties agree that all past representations and agreements are merged into this writing.
*   This agreement sets forth the entire understanding of the parties.
*   There are no contract terms beyond the four corners of this document.
*   This contract integrates all previous oral or written agreements, if any, between the parties, and constitutes the entire agreement between the parties.

What additional arguments could Beverage Distributors make to prevent consideration of the statements Cal wishes to introduce? What arguments might Cal make to prevent the merger clause from having the effect of excluding her evidence?

(B)   Instead, assume that the contract between Beverage Distributors and Cal's Grocery contains the following additional clause:

This agreement contains the entire agreement of the parties with respect to mix of beverages, and no other representations, commitments, or agreements have any effect.

How is this clause different from the clauses listed in Problem 12-14(A)? How is it similar? What effect would this clause have on the admission of the evidence Cal wishes to introduce?

Problem 12-15. Same facts as Problem 12-13. Write a clause for Beverage Distributors to insert in its contract to bar as much extrinsic evidence as possible, including the kind of evidence permitted in *Nanakuli Paving*, should a dispute arise about the contract. Of the kinds of evidence listed in the chart in Problem 12-7, which can the parties not effectively exclude with such a clause?

Problem 12-16. Jerry Johnson, owner of Jerry's Jalopies, a used car dealer, has come to you for legal advice. In each of the sales entered by his company, Jerry's Jalopies includes in the written sales agreement a minimal express warranty in compliance with state statutes regulating used car sales. He does not wish to make any additional express or any implied warranties. He knows, however, that no matter what he tells his sales force, some of the sales representatives will make assorted promises and representations about the cars when they talk with prospective customers. Jerry wants to be sure that when the customer signs the sales agreement, the only warranties will be the ones mandated by the state law, as already included in the written sales agreement. What alternatives will you suggest to him, taking into account 2-313, 2-314, 2-315, 2-316, 2-317, and 2-202? For each alternative you suggest, how could a customer ensure that an oral promise made during the negotiations nonetheless becomes part of the contract?

Nanakuli Paving and Rock Company, Plaintiff-Appellant,

v.

Shell Oil Company, Inc., Defendant-Appellee.

664 F.2d 772 (9th Cir. 1981)

HOFFMAN, District Judge:

Appellant Nanakuli Paving and Rock Company (Nanakuli) initially filed this breach of contract action against appellee Shell Oil Company (Shell) in Hawaiian State Court in February, 1976.] Nanakuli, the second largest asphaltic paving contractor in Hawaii, had bought all its asphalt requirements from 1963 to 1974 from Shell under two long-term supply contracts; its suit charged Shell with breach of the later 1969 contract. The jury returned a verdict of $220,800 for Nanakuli on its first claim, which is that Shell breached the 1969 contract in January, 1974, by failing to price protect Nanakuli on 7200 tons of asphalt at the time Shell raised the price for asphalt from $44 to $76. Nanakuli's theory is that price-protection, as a usage of the asphaltic paving trade in Hawaii, was incorporated into the 1969 agreement between the parties, as demonstrated by the routine use of price protection by suppliers to that trade, and reinforced by the way in which Shell actually performed the 1969 contract up until 1974. Price protection, appellant claims, required that Shell hold the price on the tonnage Nanakuli had already committed because Nanakuli had incorporated that price into bids put out to or contracts awarded by general contractors and government agencies. The District Judge set aside the verdict and granted Shell's motion for judgment n. o. v., which decision we vacate. We reinstate the jury verdict because we find that, viewing the evidence as a whole, there was substantial evidence to support a finding by reasonable jurors that Shell breached its contract by failing to provide protection for Nanakuli in 1974. Quichocho v. Kelvinator Corp., 546 F.2d 812, 813 (9th Cir. 1976). We do not believe the evidence in this case was such that, giving Nanakuli the benefit of all inferences fairly supported by the evidence and without weighing the credibility of the witnesses, only one reasonable conclusion could have been reached by the jury. Cockrum v. Whitney, 479 F.2d 84, 85-86 (9th Cir. 1973).

Nanakuli offers two theories for why Shell's failure to offer price protection in 1974 was a breach of the 1969 contract. First, it argues, all material suppliers to the asphaltic paving trade in Hawaii followed the trade usage of price protection and thus it should be assumed, under the U.C.C., that the parties intended to incorporate price protection into their 1969 agreement. This is so, Nanakuli continues, even though the written contract provided for price to be "Shell's Posted Price at time of delivery," F.O.B. Honolulu. Its proof of a usage that was incorporated into the contract is reinforced by evidence of the commercial context, which under the U.C.C. should form the background for viewing a particular contract. The full agreement must be examined in light of the close, almost symbiotic relations between Shell and Nanakuli on the island of Oahu, whereby the expansion of Shell on the island was intimately connected to the business growth of Nanakuli. The U.C.C. looks to the actual performance of a contract as the best indication of what the parties intended those terms to mean. Nanakuli points out that Shell had price protected it on the two occasions of price increases under the 1969 contract other than the 1974 increase. In 1970 and 1971 Shell extended the old price for four and three months, respectively, after an announced increase. This was done, in the words of Shell's agent in Hawaii, in order to permit Nanakuli's to "chew up" tonnage already committed at Shell's old price.[1]

Nanakuli's second theory for price protection is that Shell was obliged to price protect Nanakuli, even if price protection was not incorporated into their contract, because price protection was the commercially reasonable standard for fair dealing in the asphaltic paving trade in Hawaii in 1974. Observance of those standards is part of the good-faith requirement that the Code imposes on merchants in performing a sales contract. Shell was obliged to price protect Nanakuli in order to act in good faith, Nanakuli argues, because such a practice was universal in that trade in that locality.

Shell presents three arguments for upholding the judgment n. o. v. or, on cross appeal, urging that the District Judge erred in admitting certain evidence. First, it says, the District Court should not have denied Shell's motion in limine to define trade, for purposes of trade usage evidence, as the sale and purchase of asphalt in Hawaii, rather than expanding the definition of trade to include other suppliers of materials to the asphaltic paving trade. Asphalt, its argument runs, was the subject matter of the disputed contract and the only product Shell supplied to the asphaltic paving trade.[2]

---

[1] Price protection was practiced in the asphaltic paving trade by either extending the old price for a period of time after a new one went into effect or charging the old price for a specified tonnage, which represented work committed at the old price. In addition, several months' advance notice was given of price increases.

[2] Shell's argument would, in effect, eliminate all trade usage evidence. First, it argues that its own acts were irrelevant as mere waivers, not acts in the course of the performance of the contract. Second, it contends that all acts of price protection by the only other asphalt supplier in Hawaii, Chevron, the marketing division of Standard Oil Company, were

Shell protests that the judge, by expanding the definition of trade to include the other major suppliers to the asphaltic paving trade, allowed the admission of highly prejudicial evidence of routine price protection by all suppliers of aggregate.[3] Asphaltic concrete paving is formed by mixing paving asphalt with crushed rock, or aggregate, in a "hot-mix" plant and then pouring the mixture onto the surface to be paved. Shell's second complaint is that the two prior occasions on which it price protected Nanakuli, although representing the only other instances of price increases under the 1969 contract, constituted mere waivers of the contract's price term, not a course of performance of the contract. A course of performance of the contract, in contrast to a waiver, demonstrates how the parties understand the terms of their agreement. Shell cites two U.C.C. Comments in support of that argument: (1) that, when the meaning of acts is ambiguous, the preference is for the

irrelevant to prove trade usage because Chevron at one time owned all or part of the paving company it supplied and routinely price protected Hawaiian Bitumuls (H.B.). The court correctly refused to bar that evidence since the one-time relationship between the two went to the weight, not the admissibility, of the evidence. Nanakuli was given permission to offer evidence in rebuttal that Chevron price protected other customers in California with whom it had no such relationship in the event Shell tried to impeach that evidence.

[3] The judge excluded evidence of price protection usage by suppliers of cement because cement was too infrequently used in the production of asphaltic paving and, when used, formed too small a percentage of the finished product.

waiver interpretation, and (2) that one act alone does not constitute a relevant course of performance. Shell's final argument is that, even assuming its prior price protection constituted a course of performance and that the broad trade definition was correct and evidence of trade usages by aggregate suppliers was admissible, price protection could not be construed as reasonably consistent with the express price term in the contract, in which case the Code provides that the express term controls.

We hold that the judge did not abuse his discretion in defining the applicable trade, for purposes of trade usages, as the asphaltic paving trade in Hawaii. . . . We base our holding on the reading of the Code Comments as defining trade more broadly than transaction and as binding parties not only to usages of their particular trade but also to usages of trade in general in a given locality. This latter seems an equitable application of usage evidence where the usage is almost universally practiced in a small market such as was Oahu in the 1960's before Shell signed its 1969 contract with Nanakuli. Additionally, we hold that, under the facts of this case, a jury could reasonably have found that Shell's acts on two occasions to price protect Nanakuli were not ambiguous and therefore indicated Shell's understanding of the terms of the agreement with Nanakuli rather than being a waiver by Shell of those terms.[4]

[4] In addition, Shell's Bohner volunteered on direct for Shell that Shell price protected Nanakuli again after 1974 on the only two occasions of later price increases in 1977 and 1978. Although not constituting a course of performance, since the

Lastly we hold that, although the express price terms of Shell's posted price of delivery may seem, at first glance, inconsistent with a trade usage of price protection at time of increases in price, a closer reading shows that the jury could have reasonably construed price protection as consistent with the express term. We reach this holding for several reasons. First, we are persuaded by a careful reading of the U.C.C., one of whose underlying purposes is to promote flexibility in the expansion of commercial practices and which rather drastically overhauls this particular area of the law. The Code would have us look beyond the printed pages of the contract to usages and the entire commercial context of the agreement in order to reach the "true understanding" of the parties. Second, decisions of other courts in similar situations have managed to reconcile such trade usages with seemingly contradictory express terms where the prior course of dealings between the parties, trade usages, and the actual performance of the contract by the parties showed a clear intent by the parties to incorporate those usages into the agreement or to give to the express term the particular meaning provided by those usages, even at times varying the apparent meaning of the express terms. Third, the delineation by thoughtful commentators of the degree of consistency demanded between express terms and usage is that a usage should be allowed to modify the apparent

---

occasions took place under different contracts, these two additional instances of price protection could have reinforced the jury's impression that Shell's earlier actions were a carrying out of the price term.

agreement, as seen in the written terms, as long as it does not totally negate it. We believe the usage here falls within the limits set forth by commentators and generally followed in the better reasoned decisions. The manner in which price protection was actually practiced in Hawaii was that it only came into play at times of price increases and only for work committed prior to those increases on non-escalating contracts. Thus, it formed an exception to, rather than a total negation of, the express price term of "Shell's Posted Price at time of delivery." Our decision is reinforced by the overwhelming nature of the evidence that price protection was routinely practiced by all suppliers in the small Oahu market of the asphaltic paving trade and therefore was known to Shell; that it was a realistic necessity to operate in that market and thus vital to Nanakuli's ability to get large government contracts and to Shell's continued business growth on Oahu; and that it therefore constituted an intended part of the agreement, as that term is broadly defined by the Code, between Shell and Nanakuli.

I.

History Of Nanakuli-Shell Relations
Before 1973

. . . .

Lennox' [Nanakuli's president's] testimony, which was partially stricken by the court as inadmissible, was that Shell's agreement with Nanakuli in 1969 included a commitment by Shell never to charge Nanakuli more than Chevron charged H.B., in order to carry out the underlying purpose of the agreement to make Nanakuli competitive with H.B. and thus expand its and Shell's respective businesses on Oahu. This testimony was ruled inadmissible as parol evidence.[5]

────────────

[5] The judge ruled evidence of prior dealings and additional terms inadmissible at several points. At one point he said, "Well, unless it refers to the trade usage, I don't think I'm going to allow anything prior to the date of the contract," and at another he asked, "Why don't you start with the 1969 contract? Why do you have to go before that?" One exclusionary ruling relied on paragraph H, a boilerplate clause in Shell's printed-form contract in the "Remedies/Waivers" section that evidence of dealings or waivers was disallowed as affecting "Shell's right to require specific performance of buyer's obligations." That limited exclusion should not have operated to exclude all dealings evidence for any purpose, unless the parties had evidenced a clear intent to contract with no reference whatsoever to such evidence. "Writings are to be read on the assumption that the course of prior dealing between the parties . . . (was) taken for granted when the document was phrased. Unless carefully negated they become an element of the meaning of the words used." Haw.Rev.Stat. § 490:2-202, Comment 2 (emphasis supplied). In our opinion paragraph H did not carefully negate all uses of evidence of prior dealings. The court also relied on paragraph E, a classic integration or merger clause, but such a clause at most might show that the agreement was "a complete and exclusive statement of the terms of the agreement," in which case evidence of additional terms would be excluded but not evidence of prior dealings, which is admitted under subsection (a) and not excluded, even if the court makes a finding of completeness and exclusivity. Accord, White & Summers, Uniform Commercial Code, § 2-5 at 67, § 2-10 at 73, §§2- 12 at 77 (1972). Even though additional terms evidence is excluded if such a finding is made, a boilerplate merger clause is not enough. The drafters directed the court to look to whether the additional terms are "such that, if agreed upon, they would

. . . . He said Nanakuli understood the price term to mean that Shell would not increase prices without advance notice and would hold the price on work bid for enough time to allow Nanakuli to use up the tonnage bid at the old price. Smith's testimony backed up that of Lennox: the price was to be "posted price as bid as was understood between the parties," further explaining that it was to be Shell's price at time and place of delivery, except for price increases, at which point the price was time and place

────────────

certainly have been included in the document. . . ." Haw.Rev.Stat. § 490:2-202, Comment 3 (emphasis supplied). The only indication that the court was aware of this test was a rhetorical query: "(I)f that point (price protection) is so important, at the time the contract was entered into, why wasn't it stated in the contract?" In fact, however, "the Code presumption seems to be that unless proven otherwise the writing does not include all the terms," White & Summers, supra, § 21-10 at 69-70, and price protection might well not be written into a contract between parties with a long and close relationship. Certainly Shell would not be likely to put its agreement never to charge more than Chevron charged H.B. into writing. The judge also excluded the offer of proof by Lennox that Shell agreed to price protect Nanakuli because, when voir dired by Shell as to the basis of that understanding, he cited Chevron's price protection of H.B., later specifying Chevron's actions in 1970 and 1971, after the 1969 contract was signed. Had his testimony not been cut short, he might have cited earlier acts of price protection by Chevron. In addition, the judge's ruling ignored the second basis he stated for his understanding: "and the general principle of price protection."

of bid for a period of time or a specified tonnage.[6]

. . . .

III

Shell's Course Of Performance Of The 1969 Contract

The Code considers actual performance of a contract as the most relevant evidence of how the parties interpreted the terms of that contract. In 1970 and 1971, the only points at which Shell raised prices between 1969 and 1974, it price protected Nanakuli by holding its old price for four and three

---

[6] The principal reason the judge initially refused to allow any such testimony and one major reason for his inclination to grant the defendant's motion for a directed verdict, see note 20 infra, was his belief that there was no ambiguity in the express price term of "posted price at time of delivery." He was reluctantly persuaded to allow the evidence because of Shell's answer to interrogatory 11, asking its understanding of the contract term, that it had never had a posted price although it did have a list price. The court stated its doubts about Nanakuli's case at the time it denied Shell's directed verdict motion: lack of ambiguity in the express term and inconsistency between the trade usage of that term. When first requested to allow evidence of prior dealings the judge asked, "Can you point out what terms (in the written contract) are supposed to be ambiguous?" However, the Code lets in evidence of prior dealings, usage, and performance under 2-202(a) even if the contract terms are clear: "This section definitely rejects: . . . . (c) The requirement that a condition precedent to the admissibility of the type of evidence specified in paragraph (a) is an original determination by the court that the language used is ambiguous." Haw.Rev.Stat. § 490:2-202, Comment 1.

months, respectively, after announcing a price increase.

. . . .

IV

Shell-Nanakuli Relations, 1973-74

. . . .

We conclude that the decision to deny Nanakuli price protection was made by new Houston management without a full understanding of Shell's 1969 agreement with Nanakuli or any knowledge of its past pricing practices toward Nanakuli. If Shell did commit itself in 1969 to price protect Nanakuli, the Shell officials who made the decisions affecting Nanakuli in 1974 knew nothing about that commitment. Nor did they make any effective effort to find out. They acted instead solely in reliance on the 1969 contract's express price term, devoid of the commercial context that the Code says is necessary to an understanding of the meaning of the written word. Whatever the legal enforceability of Nanakuli's right, Nanakuli officials seem to have acted in good faith reliance on its right, as they understood it, to price protection and rightfully felt betrayed by Shell's failure to act with any understanding of its past practices toward Nanakuli.

V

Scope Of Trade Usage

The validity of the jury verdict in this case depends on four legal questions. First, how broad was the trade to whose usages Shell was bound under its 1969 agreement with Nanakuli: did it extend to the Hawaiian asphaltic paving trade or was it limited merely to the purchase and sale of asphalt, which would only include evidence of practices by Shell and Chevron? Second, were the two instances of price protection of Nanakuli by Shell in 1970 and 1971 waivers of the 1969 contract as a matter of law or was the jury entitled to find that they constituted a course of performance of the contract? Third, could the jury have construed an express contract term of Shell's posted price at delivery as reasonably consistent with a trade usage and Shell's course of performance of the 1969 contract of price protection, which consisted of charging the old price at times of price increases, either for a period of time or for specific tonnage committed at a fixed price in non- escalating contracts? Fourth, could the jury have found that good faith obliged Shell to at least give advance notice of a $32 increase in 1974, that is, could they have found that the commercially reasonable standards of fair dealing in the trade in Hawaii in 1974 were to give some form of price protection?

. . . .

The Code defines usage of trade as "any practice or method of dealing having such regularity of observance in a place, vocation or trade as to justify an expectation that it will be observed with respect to the transaction in question." Id. § 490:1-205(2) (emphasis supplied). We understand the use of the word "or" to mean that parties can be bound by a usage common to the place they are in business, even if it is not the usage of their particular vocation or trade. That reading is borne out by the repetition of the disjunctive "or" in subsection 3, which provides that usages "in the vocation or trade in which they are engaged or of which they are or should be aware give particular meaning to and

supplement or qualify terms of an agreement." Id. § 490:1-205(3). The drafters' Comments say that trade usage is to be used to reach the ". . . . commercial meaning of the agreement. . . ." by interpreting the language "as meaning what it may fairly be expected to mean to parties involved in the particular transaction in a given locality or in a given vocation or trade." Id., Comment 4 (emphasis supplied). The inference of the two subsections and the Comment, read together, is that a usage need not necessarily be one practiced by members of the party's own trade or vocation to be binding if it is so commonly practiced in a locality that a party should be aware of it. Subsection 5 also shows the importance of the place where the usage is practiced: "An applicable usage of trade in the place where any part of performance is to occur shall be used in interpreting the agreement as to that part of the performance." The validity of this interpretation is additionally demonstrated by the Comment of the drafters: "Subsection (3), giving the prescribed effect to usages of which the parties 'are or should be aware', reinforces the provision of subsection (2) requiring not universality but only the described 'regularity of observance' of the practice or method. This subsection also reinforces the point of subsection (2) that such usages may be either general to trade or particular to a special branch of trade." Id., Comment 7 (emphasis supplied). This language indicates that Shell would be bound not only by usages of sellers of asphalt but by more general usages on Oahu, as long as those usages were so regular in their observance that Shell should have been aware of them. This reading of the Code, in our opinion, achieves an equitable result. A party is always held to conduct generally observed by members of his chosen trade because the other party is justified in so assuming unless he indicates otherwise. He is held to more general business practices to the extent of his actual knowledge of those practices or to the degree his ignorance of those practices is not excusable: they were so generally practiced he should have been aware of them.

. . . .

Shell argued not only that the definition of trade was too broad, but also that the practice itself was not sufficiently regular to reach the level of a usage and that Nanakuli failed to show with enough precision how the usage was carried out in order for a jury to calculate damages. The extent of a usage is ultimately a jury question. The Code provides, "The existence and scope of such a usage are to be proved as facts." Haw.Rev.Stat. § 490:1-205(2).[7] The practice must have "such regularity of observance . . . as to justify an expectation that it will be observed. . . ." Id. The Comment explains:

> The ancient English tests for "custom" are abandoned in this connection. Therefore, it is not required that a usage of trade be "ancient or immemorial," "universal" or the like. . . . (F)ull recognition is thus available for new usages and for usages currently observed by the great majority of decent dealers, even though

dissidents ready to cut corners do not agree.

Id., Comment 5. The Comment's demand that "not universality but only the described 'regularity of observance' " is required reinforces the provision only giving "effect to usages of which the parties 'are or should be aware' . . . ." Id., Comment 7. A "regularly observed" practice of protection, of which Shell "should have been aware," was enough to constitute a usage that Nanakuli had reason to believe was incorporated into the agreement.

. . . .

VI

Waiver Or Course Of Performance

Course of performance under the Code is the action of the parties in carrying out the contract at issue, whereas course of dealing consists of relations between the parties prior to signing that contract. Evidence of the latter was excluded by the District Judge; evidence of the former consisted of Shell's price protection of Nanakuli in 1970 and 1971. Shell protested that the jury could not have found that those two instances of price protection amounted to a course of performance of its 1969 contract, relying on two Code comments. First, one instance does not constitute a course of performance. "A single occasion of conduct does not fall within the language of this section. . . ." Haw.Rev.Stat. § 490:2-208, Comment 4. Although the Comment rules out one instance, it does not further delineate how many acts are needed to form a course of performance. The prior occasions here were only two, but they constituted the only occasions

---

[7] Written trade codes, however, are left to the court to interpret. Id.

before 1974 that would call for such conduct.

. . . .

Shell's second defense is that the Comment expresses a preference for an interpretation of waiver. . . . The preference for waiver only applies, however, where acts are ambiguous. It was within the province of the jury to determine whether those acts were ambiguous, and if not, whether they constituted waivers or a course of performance of the contract. The jury's interpretation of those acts as a course of performance was bolstered by evidence offered by Shell that it again price protected Nanakuli on the only two occasions of post-1974 price increases, in 1977 and 1978.

VII

Express Terms As Reasonably Consistent With Usage In Course of Performance

Perhaps one of the most fundamental departures of the Code from prior contract law is found in the parol evidence rule and the definition of an agreement between two parties. Under the U.C.C., an agreement goes beyond the written words on a piece of paper. " 'Agreement' means the bargain of the parties in fact as found in their language or by implication from other circumstances including course of dealing or usage of trade or course of performance as provided in this chapter (sections 490:1-205 and 490:2-208)." Id. § 490:1-201(3). Express terms, then, do not constitute the entire agreement, which must be sought also in evidence of usages, dealings, and performance of the contract itself. The purpose of evidence

of usages, which are defined in the previous section, is to help to understand the entire agreement.

(Usages are) a factor in reaching the commercial meaning of the agreement which the parties have made. The language used is to be interpreted as meaning what it may fairly be expected to mean to parties involved in the particular commercial transaction in a given locality or in a given vocation or trade. . . . Part of the agreement of the parties . . . is to be sought for in the usages of trade which furnish the background and give particular meaning to the language used, and are the framework of common understanding controlling any general rules of law which hold only when there is no such understanding.

Id. § 490:1-205, Comment 4. Course of dealings is more important than usages of the trade, being specific usages between the two parties to the contract. "(C)ourse of dealing controls usage of trade." Id. § 490:1- 205(4). It "is a sequence of previous conduct between the parties to a particular transaction which is fairly to be regarded as establishing a common basis of understanding for interpreting their expressions and other conduct." Id. § 490:1-205(1). Much of the evidence of prior dealings between Shell and Nanakuli in negotiating the 1963 contract and in carrying out similar earlier contracts was excluded by the court.

A commercial agreement, then, is broader than the written paper and its meaning is to be determined not just by the language used by them in the written contract but "by their action, read and interpreted in the light of commercial practices and other surrounding circumstances. The measure and background for interpretation are set by the commercial context, which may explain and supplement even the language of a formal or final writing." Id., Comment 1. Performance, usages, and prior dealings are important enough to be admitted always, even for a final and complete agreement; only if they cannot be reasonably reconciled with the express terms of the contract are they not binding on the parties. "The express terms of an agreement and an applicable course of dealing or usage of trade shall be construed wherever reasonable as consistent with each other; but when such construction is unreasonable express terms control both course of dealing and usage of trade and course of dealing controls usage of trade." Id. § 490:1-205(4).

Of these three, then, the most important evidence of the agreement of the parties is their actual performance of the contract. Id. The operative definition of course of performance is as follows: "Where the contract for sale involves repeated occasions for performance by either party with knowledge of the nature of the performance and opportunity for objection to it by the other, any course of performance accepted or acquiesced in without objection shall be relevant to determine the meaning of the agreement." Id. § 490:2-208(1). "Course of dealing . . . is restricted, literally, to a sequence of conduct between the parties previous to the agreement. However, the provisions of the Act on course of performance make it clear that a sequence of conduct after or under the agreement may have equivalent meaning (Section 2-208)." Id. 490:1-205, Comment 2. The importance

of evidence of course of performance is explained: "The parties themselves know best what they have meant by their words of agreement and their action under that agreement is the best indication of what that meaning was. This section thus rounds out the set of factors which determines the meaning of the 'agreement' . . ." Id. § 490:2-208, Comment 1. "Under this section a course of performance is always relevant to determine the meaning of the agreement." Id., Comment 2.

Our study of the Code provisions and Comments, then, form the first basis of our holding that a trade usage to price protect pavers at times of price increases for work committed on nonescalating contracts could reasonably be construed as consistent with an express term of seller's posted price at delivery. Since the agreement of the parties is broader than the express terms and includes usages, which may even add terms to the agreement,[8] and since the commercial background provided by those usages is vital to an understanding of the agreement, we follow the Code's mandate to proceed on the assumption that the parties have included those usages unless they cannot reasonably be

---

[8] "The agreement of the parties includes that part of their bargain found in course of dealing, usage of trade, or course of performance. These sources are relevant not only to the interpretation of express contract terms, but may themselves constitute contract terms." White & Summers, supra, § 3-3 at 84.

construed as consistent with the express terms.

Federal courts usually have been lenient in not ruling out consistent additional terms or trade usage for apparent inconsistency with express terms. The leading case on the subject is Columbia Nitrogen Corp. v. Royster Co., 451 F.2d 3 (4th Cir. 1971). Columbia, the buyer, had in the past primarily produced and sold nitrogen to Royster. When Royster opened a new plant that produced more phosphate than it needed, the parties reversed roles and signed a sales contract for Royster to sell excess phosphate to Columbia. The contract terms set out the price that would be charged by Royster and the amount to be sold. It provided for the price to go up if certain events occurred but did not provide for price declines. When the price of nitrogen fell precipitously, Columbia refused to accept the full amount of nitrogen specified in the contract after Royster refused to renegotiate the contract price. The District Judge's exclusion of usage of the trade and course of dealing to explain the express quantity term in the contract was reversed. Columbia had offered to prove that the quantity set out in the contract was a mere projection to be adjusted according to market forces. Ambiguity was not necessary for the admission of evidence of usage and prior dealings.[9]

Even though the lengthy contract was the result of long and careful negotiations and apparently covered every contingency, the appellate court ruled that "the test of admissibility is not whether the contract appears on its face to be complete in every detail, but whether the proffered evidence of course of dealing and trade usage reasonably can be construed as consistent with the express terms of the agreement." Id. at 9. The express quantity term could be reasonably construed as consistent with a usage that such terms would be mere projections for several reasons:[10] (1) the

---

[9] As discussed earlier, the District Judge here mistakenly equated ambiguity with admissibility. He said, "I think this is a close case. On the face of the contract it would seem to be unambiguous," although acknowledging that liberal commentators on the Code would let in evidence of usage and performance even without ambiguity. He

only let in usage evidence because Shell's answer to interrogatory 11 provided some ambiguity, see note 16 supra, saying "I think if these can be consistently used to explain the apparently unambiguous terms, they should be allowed in." In fact, this court has ruled that ambiguity is not necessary to admit usage evidence. Board of Trade of San Francisco v. Swiss Credit Bank, 597 F.2d 146, 148 (9th Cir. 1979).

[10] State court cases have interpreted express quantity as mere projections in similar circumstances. E. g., Campbell v. Hofstetter Farms, Inc., 251 Pa.Super. 232, 380 A.2d 463, 466-67 (1977). (Express agreement to sell a specified number of bushels of corn, wheat, and soy beans was not, as a matter of law, inconsistent with a usage of the trade that amounts specified in contracts are only estimates of a seller-farmer's farms); Loeb & Co. v. Martin, 295 Ala. 262, 327 So.2d 711, 714-15 (Ala. 1976) (It was a jury question whether, in light of trade usage, "all cotton produced on 400 acres" called for all cotton seller produced on 400 acres or for 400 acres of cotton.); Heggblade-Marguleas-Tenneco, Inc. v. Sunshine Biscuit, Inc., 59 Cal.App.3d 948, 131 Cal. Rptr. 183, 188-89 (1976) (Usage in the potato-processing trade that the amount specified in the contract was merely

contract did not expressly state that usage and dealings evidence would be excluded; (2) the contract was silent on the adjustment of price or quantities in a declining market; (3) the minimum tonnage was expressed in the contract as Products Supplied, not Products Purchased; (4) the default clause of the contract did not state a penalty for failure to take delivery; and (5) apparently most important in the court's view, the parties had deviated from similar express terms in earlier contracts in times of declining market. Id. at 9-10. As here, the contract's merger clause said that there were no oral agreements. The court explained that its ruling "reflects the reality of the marketplace and avoids the overly legalistic interpretations which the Code seeks to abolish." Id. at 10. The Code assigns dealing and usage evidence "unique and important roles" and therefore "overly simplistic and overly legalistic interpretation of a contract should be shunned." Id. at 11.

. . . .

Numerous state courts have interpreted their own state's versions of the Code in line with the weight of federal authority on the U.C.C. to admit freely evidence of additional terms, usages, and prior dealings and harmonize them in most instances with apparently contradictory express terms.

. . . .

---

an estimate of buyer's requirements was admissible); Paymaster Oil Mill Co. v. Mitchell, 319 So.2d 652, 657-58 (Miss.1975) (Additional term that the seller was not obliged to deliver the full 4000 bushels of soy beans called for in the contract was admissible).

The district judge, "in his refusal to bar evidence of the circumstances surrounding the transaction, was applying this modern principle," which was the "same view adopted" in a law review article cited by the court:

> As between immediate parties, however, all evidence whether written or oral, whether of conditions precedent or subsequent, should be admitted to determine what the parties understood the true contractual relationship to be. Any inherent improbability, such as a contradiction between what allegedly was agreed upon and what was signed will naturally affect the weight to be accorded such evidence, but procedural wrangles can be avoided by allowing the fact finder to hear all the evidence which either party wishes to bring to bear.

Id. at 396 (citing E. R. Jordan, "Just Sign Here-It's Only a Formality": Parol Evidence in the Law of Commercial Paper, 13 Ga.L.Rev. 53, 95 (1978)).

. . . .

[The court rejects as misreadings of the Code the results in "the two leading cases that have rejected usage evidence as inconsistent with express terms. . . ." One of the courts held] that only consistent usages are admissible, which is an incorrect reading of the Code. Usage is always admissible, even though the express term controls in the event of inconsistency, which is a jury question.

. . . .

Some guidelines can be offered as to how usage evidence can be allowed to modify a contract.[11] First, the court must allow a check on usage evidence by demanding that it be sufficiently definite and widespread to prevent unilateral post-hoc revision of contract terms by one party. The Code's intent is to put usage evidence on an objective basis. J. H. Levie, Trade Usage and Custom Under the Common Law and the Uniform Commercial Code, 40 N.Y.U.L.Rev. 1101 (1965), states:

> When trade usage adds new terms to cover matters on which the agreement is silent the court is really making a contract for the parties, even though it says it only consulted trade usage to find the parties' probable intent. There is nothing wrong or even unusual about this practice, which really is no different from reading constructive conditions into a contract. Nevertheless the court does create new obligations, and perhaps that is why the courts often say that usage . . . must be proved by clear and convincing evidence.
>
> . . . .

Id. at 1102. Although the Code abandoned the traditional common law test of nonconsensual custom and views usage as a way of determining the parties' probable intent, id. at 1106-07, thus abolishing the requirement that common law custom be universally practiced, trade usages still must be well settled, id. at 1113.

> . . . .

Levie, supra, at 1112, writes, "Astonishing as it will seem to most practicing attorneys, under the Code it will be possible in some cases to use custom to contradict the written agreement. . . . Therefore usage may be used to 'qualify' the agreement, which presumably means to 'cut down' express terms although not to negate them entirely." Here, the express price term was "Shell's Posted Price at time of delivery." A total negation of that term

---

[11] White and Summers write that usage and dealings evidence "may not only supplement or qualify express terms, but in appropriate circumstances may even override express terms." White & Summers, supra, § 3-3 at 84. "(T)he provision that express terms control inconsistent course of dealing and (usages and performance evidence) really cannot be taken at face value." Id. at 86. That reading, although at odds with the actual wording of the Code, is a realistic reading of what some of the cases allow. A better formulation of the Code's mandate is offered by R. W. Kirst, Usage of Trade and Course of Dealing: Subversion of the UCC Theory, 1977 Law Forum 811:
The need to determine whether the parties intended a usage . . . to be part of the contract does not end if the court finds that the commercial practice is inconsistent with or contradicts the express language of the writing. If an inconsistency exists, the intention of the parties remains unclear. The parties may have intended either to include or exclude the practice. Determining the intent of the parties requires that the court attempt to construe the written term consistently with the commercial practice, if that is reasonable. If consistent construction is unreasonable the Code directs that the written term be taken as expressing the parties' intent. Before concluding that a jury could not reasonably find a consistent construction, the judge must understand the commercial background of the dispute.
Id. at 824.

would be that the buyer was to set the price. It is a less than complete negation of the term that an unstated exception exists at times of price increases, at which times the old price is to be charged, for a certain period or for a specified tonnage, on work already committed at the lower price on nonescalating contracts. Such a usage forms a broad and important exception to the express term, but does not swallow it entirely. Therefore, we hold that, under these particular facts, a reasonable jury could have found that price protection was incorporated into the 1969 agreement between Nanakuli and Shell and that price protection was reasonably consistent with the express term of seller's posted price at delivery.

. . . .

Because the jury could have found for Nanakuli on its price protection claim under either theory, we reverse the judgment of the District Court and reinstate the jury verdict for Nanakuli in the amount of $220,800, plus interest according to law.

REVERSED AND REMANDED WITH DIRECTIONS TO ENTER FINAL JUDGMENT.

KENNEDY, Circuit Judge, concurring specially:

The case involves specific pricing practices, not an allegation of unfair dealing generally. Our opinion should not be interpreted to permit juries to import price protection or a similarly specific contract term from a concept of good faith that is not based on well-established custom and usage or other objective standards of which the parties had clear notice. Here, evidence of custom and usage regarding price protection in the asphaltic paving trade was not contradicted in major respects, and the jury could find that the parties knew or should have known of the practice at the time of making the contract. In my view, these are necessary predicates for either theory of the case, namely, interpretation of the contract based on the course of its performance or a finding that good faith required the seller to hold the price. With these observations, I concur.

Assignment 13: Identification, Tender of Delivery, Risk of Loss, and Passage of Title

§§ 2-319, 2-320, 2-401, 2-501, 2-503, 2-504, 2-509

Reading the Code

Understanding the Diminished Role of Title in Article 2

In real property law, title is a "bundle of sticks," each stick representing a different aspect of property ownership. Unless the buyer and seller agree otherwise, the entire bundle of sticks usually is passed at one instant from buyer to seller. As a result, the moment of title passage for real property has enormous significance for a wide range of legal sub-issues, like risk of loss, responsibility for real estate taxes, right to exclude trespassers, right to convey security interests attached to the real estate, and so on. Predictably, because so much of realty law depends on title, the cases deciding when title to land passes have sometimes been inconsistent, varying in result by which underlying ownership right was at issue. (For instance, risk-of-loss cases might determine that title passes at different times than do cases on real estate taxes.)

Article 2 does not subscribe to this "unitary title" concept often applied to real property. Karl Llewellyn, the reporter for the Article 2 drafting committee in the 1940s and 1950s, persuaded the committee to abandon the unitary-title convention and instead "unbundle" the sticks, so that each right or obligation of ownership is transferred at the most sensible time, but not necessarily the same time that other rights and obligations are transferred. As the comment to 2-101 states, "the purpose is [1] to avoid making practical issues between practical [people] turn upon the location of an intangible something, the passing of which no [one] can prove by evidence and [2] to substitute for such abstractions proof of words and actions of a tangible character." This change was a radical innovation that has worked quite well, freeing Article 2 from the inconsistent case law results that have occurred in real property cases determining the moment of title passage. And it has meant that 2-401 on title passage has a very small role in determining the parties' rights and obligations under Article 2. That is, the Code allocates most rights and obligations to the buyer or the seller according to the common sense determination of who should have the particular right or bear the particular burden, regardless of who has title to the goods at that time. Thus, the actual passage of title becomes just one possible time for buyer and seller to acquire some of the unbundled sticks. In reality, the other moments in time are more important.

This assignment covers the following aspects of ownership and events that affect ownership:

> identification of goods (2-501)
> tender of delivery (2-503)
> risk of loss (2-509)
> receipt of goods (2-103(1)(c))
> responsibility to pay for transport/freight
> passing of title (2-401)

Identification of Goods

After contract formation, identification is often the next (or concurrent) event that affects rights and duties between the parties. As you learned in Assignment 1, identification is the process of designating which particular items are the goods that buyer will receive. Once identification occurs, the following consequences (among others) follow:

- The buyer obtains an insurable interest in the goods (2-501).
- The buyer acquires the right to inspect the goods at any reasonable place and time and in any reasonable manner, except in a few situations (2-513(1)).
- The buyer obtains a "special property" in the goods (2-501), which allows the buyer to recover the goods from an insolvent seller under certain limited circumstances (2-502).
- If the goods are identified when the contract is made and those identified goods are necessary for performance of the contract, under certain circumstances the damage or loss of those goods will excuse the seller from performance rather than causing a breach (2-613).
- If seller fails or refuses to deliver the goods and buyer is unable to locate a reasonable substitute for those goods, buyer can replevy the goods (2-716(3)).
- If the buyer refuses to take goods that have been identified to the contract, the seller will still be able to recover the purchase price of those goods if the seller is unable to resell them (2-709(1)(b), (2)).

- If the buyer repudiates or otherwise breaches while the risk of loss to the goods otherwise remains on the seller, the risk of loss nonetheless may be considered to be on the buyer to the extent that seller has under-insured the conforming goods (2-510(3)).

Problem 13-1. Timing of Identification. When does identification occur in each of the following scenarios?

(A)   Customer takes an apple from the produce section of a grocery store, brings it to the cash register, and pays for it.

(B)   Customer at SportsPlace selects a canoe from those on the display floor. She takes the product designation slip for that model of canoe to the cash register and pays for the canoe. After Customer drives around to Customer Pick-up, a warehouse worker takes a canoe of the correct model from storage, carries it to the loading dock, and lashes it to the top of the Customer's car.

(C)   Buyer, an appliance manufacturer, orders 300 electrical motors of a certain model from Seller. When the order arrives at Seller's warehouse by computer, the Seller's employee promptly locates the motors in the warehouse, wraps 300 of them in plastic on several pallets, labels them with Buyer's address and account information, and uses a fork lift to move the pallets to the loading dock of the warehouse. Seller's truck driver picks up the pallets at the loading dock and delivers them to Buyer's factory as directed by Buyer.

(D)   Lois visits a restaurant at which she orders lobster and then, at the invitation of the waiter, she goes over to the restaurant's tank to select a live lobster. The kitchen prepares it for her dinner. (Recall the second sentence of 2-314, if you are wondering about the scope issue.)

(E)   In February, a farmer contracts to sell the wheat crop that he will harvest the upcoming September. Planting will be in May. Will your answer differ if he enters into the contract in June, after the crop is planted?

Problem 13-2. Early Identification. Tina is her own contractor for her kitchen modeling. She visits a stone supply company to select the granite for her countertop from among 33 representative slabs of different granites. Each type of granite is displayed vertically with only the top one of several similar slabs visible. She signs an agreement to purchase the granite, to have it cut to fit her kitchen, and to have it installed. The cost of cutting and installation is $585, while the retail cost of the granite is $1900. The agreement reserves to the stone supply company the right to select the particular granite slabs to be used from among the slabs of the same type of granite. Tina makes a downpayment of $1500 and arranges dates for measuring and for installation.

A company employee comes to Tina's house and measures the kitchen precisely. He selects two slabs for Tina's kitchen and places her name on masking tape on the back of each slab. He cuts, polishes, and "edges" the granite to fit the measurements. Two employees come to Tina's house and install the granite. Tina pays the remaining amount due. When are the goods identified to the contract? Consider 2-501 and comments 1, 2, and 4, as well as 2-704, which allows the seller to take certain actions after buyer breaches by refusing to take the goods.

Tender of Delivery

Once the goods have been identified, the next event often is the seller's tender of delivery. Goods can be "delivered" in a variety of ways. The buyer can take possession of the goods at the time of sale. Or the seller's truck can deliver the goods to the buyer. Or the seller can enter into a contract with a third party (a "bailee") to deliver the goods, either by holding them at a warehouse for buyer to pick them up or by transporting them from seller to buyer. Which delivery method is used will depend upon the terms of the agreement and the provisions of Article 2.

The buyer and seller are acutely interested in determining when the seller has completed its delivery obligations, because that determination is relevant for allocating responsibility for accidental loss to the goods (e.g., from fire or theft) and for determining whether seller or buyer is responsible for pursuing remedies for problems caused by the carrier or the warehouse (e.g., delivery to the wrong location, late delivery, damage to goods, or refusal to hand the goods over to the buyer). In the absence of credit terms, seller's delivery probably also triggers buyer's obligation to pay. See 2-301.

It is tempting to imagine that seller's completion of delivery triggers shifting risk of loss from seller to buyer and also causes title to pass. Sometimes that is true, and sometimes it is not. You have to "unbundle" these items from each other and consider them as separate legal concepts.

Problem 13-3. Introduction to Tender of Delivery. Section 2-503 is the umbrella section dealing with "tender of delivery." Read 2-503(1)-(3), and skim (4) and (5). Subsection (1) sets out the basic rules governing tender of delivery, which apply regardless whether the goods are to be shipped, delivered at a warehouse, or handed over directly from seller to buyer. What must a seller do to comply with the basic requirements for tender of delivery in 2-503(1)?

Tender of Delivery via Carrier or Warehouse

The remaining subsections of 2-503 deal with particular types of tender of delivery—by carrier, by warehouse, and with delivery documents. A carrier is a person engaged in the business of transporting or forwarding goods for others and who enters into a contract with a buyer or seller to transport the goods.[1] A warehouse is a person engaged in the business of storing goods for hire. See 7-102(a)(13). Deliveries by carrier or warehouse may be accomplished using documents of title (often called simply "documents").

---

[1] This definition is derived from amended 7-102(a)(2), which defines "carrier" as "a person that issues a bill of lading." Under 1-201(6) (1-201(b)(6) in revised Article 1), a bill of lading is "a document evidencing the receipt of goods for shipment issued by a person engaged in the business of transporting or forwarding goods." The mechanics of issuing bills of lading are covered in Assignment 14.

Assignment 14 covers the meaning and use of documents of title. For the purpose of this assignment, think of these documents as simply receipts that may be presented to claim the goods from the carrier or warehouse.

If the seller is tendering the goods to the buyer by way of a carrier, tender of delivery may occur by what the trade calls a "shipment contract" or by what the trade calls a "destination contract." Subsection (2) of 2-503 refers to 2-504, which establishes the requirements for "shipment contracts." Subsection (3) of 2-503 establishes the requirements for "destination contracts." Subsection (4) sets forth the requirements for tender of delivery if the seller is storing the goods in or delivering the goods to a third-party warehouse, where the buyer is to retrieve them. The next two problems explore differences among these types of tender of delivery.

Problem 13-4. Fulfilling Tender Obligations. Fill in the chart below, adding what the seller has to do to satisfy its tender obligations for each type of delivery.

Section or subsection	Delivery type	Seller's obligations
2-503(1)	Buyer picks up goods at seller's business	
2-503(2), which refers to 2-504	Shipment contract, by carrier	
2-503(3)	Destination contract, by carrier or seller's vehicle	
2-503(4)	Warehouse	(Do not fill in this square; tender obligations will be treated in Assignment 14)

In this assignment, "tender" means tender of delivery of conforming goods, as detailed in Problems 13-3 and 13-4. However, Article 2 occasionally uses "tender" to mean a tender of nonconforming goods or a tender of documents. Consider the context in order to determine which meaning governs. See 2-503 comment 1.

Risk of Loss in Absence of Breach[2]

Now that we have examined identification and tender of delivery, we need to explore the links between those two events and risk of loss. The shifting of risk of loss has important consequences:

If the seller still has the risk of loss when the goods are lost, damaged, or delayed (whether the seller still has the goods or they are already in the possession of a carrier or warehouse), the seller usually is still contractually responsible for delivering conforming goods to the buyer in a timely manner or paying the buyer damages for the loss, damage, or delay. In an appropriate case, seller may be able to recover some of its losses by pursuing remedies against a carrier or warehouse or under its own insurance coverage.

On the other hand, if the buyer has the risk of loss when the goods are lost, damaged, or destroyed, the buyer is still contractually obligated to pay the seller for the goods. In an appropriate case, buyer may be able to recover some of its losses by pursuing remedies against a carrier or warehouse or under its own insurance coverage. In other words, the parties' contractual obligations are not modified by damage to or loss of the goods.[3]

Read 2-509(1), which establishes the risk of loss when the goods are to be transported by a carrier.[4] Note that it contains similar phrases to those you already read in 2-504 on shipment contracts and in 2-503(3) on destination contracts. In particular, subsection (1)(a) of 2-509 establishes the risk of loss for deliveries that do "not require [seller] to deliver [the goods] at a particular destination"—a Code phrase that refers to shipment contracts. Subsection (1)(b) establishes the risk of loss for deliveries that do "require [seller] to deliver [the goods] at a particular destination"—a Code phrase that refers to destination contracts.

---

[2] Assignment 18 covers risk of loss when buyer or seller has breached.

[3] There are a few exceptions to this rule, including common law excuse doctrines (e.g., impossibility) and provisions appearing in 2-613 (casualty to identified goods), 2-614 (substituted performance), and 2-615 (excuse by failure of presupposed conditions). We will cover these sections in Assignment 16.

[4] The seller cannot be its own third-party bailee and hence cannot be a "carrier," so delivery in seller's vehicle is not within the scope of 2-509(1).

Read 2-509(2), which covers contracts "where the goods are held by a bailee to be delivered without being moved"—a Code phrase that refers to seller's delivery by way of a third-party warehouse. This same phrase appears in 2-503(4) on tender in warehouse deliveries.

Read 2-509(3), a catch-all provision that covers all other types of deliveries, including when the buyer picks up the goods from the seller's business or residence or the seller delivers the goods in its own vehicle. Also read 2-509(4), which emphasizes that the parties' agreement can displace these default provisions on risk of loss.

Problem 13-5. Introduction to Risk of Loss. Fill in the remainder of the chart below, adding when 2-509 says that the risk of loss shifts for each type of delivery. What are the crucial differences?

Subsection	Delivery type	When risk of loss passes
2-509(1)(a)	Shipment contract, by carrier	
2-509(1)(b)	Destination contract, by carrier[5]	
2-509(2)	Warehouse	(Do not fill in this square; risk of loss for warehouse contracts will be treated in Assignment 14)
2-509(3)	Buyer picks up goods from seller, or seller's vehicle delivers goods	

In the bottom row, consider whether it makes any difference whether seller is a merchant as to goods or as to practices.[6]

---

[5] Note that 2-509(1)(b) applies only when a carrier is used for delivery. The tender requirements of 2-503(3) do not mandate use of a carrier for a destination contract.

2003   [6] The 2003 amended version of 2-509(3) does not differentiate between whether the seller is a merchant or not, so risk of loss always passes upon buyer's receipt of goods.

Problem 13-6. Moment of Risk-of-Loss Passage. Read comment 1 to 2-503, if you have not done so already. The questions below ask about the meaning of four important phrases in 2-509 that describe the actions that seller must take to pass the risk of loss in particular kinds of deliveries. What portions of 2-503, 2-504, and the definitions in Articles 1 and 2 assist you in discerning the meaning of those phrases?

(A)   What does it mean to "duly deliver" the goods to the carrier, in 2-509(1)(a)? Must the seller satisfy all or only some of the requirements of 2-504, in order to "duly deliver"? Consider comment 2 to 2-509.

(B)   What does it mean to "duly tender" the goods at a particular destination, in 2-509(1)(b)?

(C)   What does "receipt" mean in 2-509(3)?

(D)   What does "tender of delivery" mean in 2-509(3)?

Problem 13-7. Implications of Risk of Loss. Based on your understanding of risk of loss so far:

(A)   Would seller prefer a shipment contract or a destination contract?

(B)   Would buyer prefer a shipment contract or a destination contract?

(C)   Should buyer or seller carry insurance on the goods during a shipment contract?

(D)   Should buyer or seller carry insurance on the goods during a destination contract?

(E)   If the agreement calls for a shipment contract, may seller use its own vehicle?

(F)   If the agreement calls for a destination contract, may seller use its own vehicle? If seller does, are there any risk-of-loss consequences for that choice?

(G)   If the parties agree that the goods be sent by carrier, but they fail to agree on whether it is a shipment or destination contract, what is the default provision? See 2-503 comment 5. What does that default provision mean in terms of when tender occurs and who has the risk of loss while the carrier has the goods?

Problem 13-8. Specific Delivery Terms. Carrier contracts are referred to in acronyms that create a daunting alphabet soup, but the UCC fortunately deals with a limited set of carrier contracts. We will consider only some of the UCC carrier contracts:[7]

> F.O.B.[8] place of shipment (2-319(1)(a))
> F.O.B. place of destination (2-319(1)(b))
> C.I.F. (2-320 and comments 1 and 2)
> C. & F. or C.F. (2-320 (1), (3))

Read the sections and comments listed above, and decide whether the seller's obligations end upon delivery to a carrier ("shipment contract") or delivery at the destination ("destination contract"). Place each kind of carrier contract in the proper column below, creating a handy reference chart.

Shipment contracts   Destination contracts

---

[7] This assignment will ignore the additional shipping provisions in 2-322 to 2-325.

[8] Even if you know that F.O.B. originally meant "free on board," ignore that meaning and instead focus on the content of the Code.

Paying for the Freight

Yet to be discussed is the separate question of who is responsible for paying the cost of transporting the goods from the seller to the buyer. This cost of transport is known as "freight." The contract price does not always include freight; in fact, the norm is that it usually does not. Nor is it reliable to assume that the party with the risk of loss during transport is the party paying the freight. Nor does the distinction between shipment and destination contracts always dictate who pays the freight. Instead, one must know which particular shipping term is involved.

When this textbook asks who pays the freight, it is asking who has the *ultimate* legal responsibility to pay the freight. With respect to the actual mechanics of payment, many possible arrangements abound. Either party may choose a carrier with whom it has a regular account or has negotiated a flat fee for local deliveries; in that case, that party may both make the initial payment and take on the ultimate responsibility for the cost of the freight. Or the seller may pay the freight to the carrier, and then bill the buyer for it. Or the buyer may pay the carrier at the end of the trip, and then offset that cost against the cost of the goods when buyer pays the seller.

Problem 13-9. Introduction to Freight. To figure out who ultimately pays the freight, we need to read the shipping provisions and associated Code definitions with particular care. We know that, in each case, the goods must move from wherever they are to the buyer's location. Read the sections listed below and determine what part of the transportation the seller must *ultimately* furnish or pay for, and what part of the transportation the buyer must *ultimately* pay for. Note that these sections say what the seller must pay for; *by implication*, the rest of the cost of delivery is the buyer's cost.

F.O.B. place of shipment (2-319(1)(a))

F.O.B. place of destination (2-319(1)(b))

C.I.F. (2-320)

C. & F. or C.F. (2-320)

Domestic Shipping Terms Without the UCC

2003

The 2003 amended version of Article 2 repeals all of the specific delivery term provisions (sections 2-319 through 2-324). One rationale for this repeal was that the trade meanings of shipping terms change more frequently than the rest of Article 2 needs to be amended, so codified meanings tend to lag behind trade meanings. Another rationale for the repeal was that some shipping terms, like FOB, are defined differently in UCC Article 2, the 1941 Revised American Foreign Trade Definitions,[9] and the Incoterms 2000 from the International Chamber of Commerce (ICC).[10] Repealing the UCC shipping terms eliminated one source of definitional inconsistency. The comment to the repeal states that the "effect of a party's use of shipping terms such as 'FOB,' 'CIF,' or the like, absent any express agreement to the meaning of the terms, must be interpreted in light of any applicable usage of trade and any course of performance or course of dealing between the parties."

With the Article 2 provisions no longer in effect, the parties who ship goods within the U.S. will have the following options for drafting shipping terms: (1) copy the repealed Article 2 language directly into the contract, as needed; (2) use incorporation-by-reference techniques to make the repealed Article 2 language part of the contract; (3) use altered versions of international shipping terms like the 1941 Standard Revised Foreign Trade Definitions or ICC Incoterms 2000; (4) draft a shipping clause from scratch; or (5) rely on course of performance, course of dealing, and usage of trade. Whichever method is used, the drafter will need to understand how the chosen shipping terms affect the parties' tender responsibilities, risk of loss, and payment of freight.

---

[9] National Foreign Trade Council, *Revised American Foreign Trade Definitions* (1941).

[10] The ICC website is at www.iccwbo.org.

Passage of Title

As you can see from the preceding sections on identification, tender of delivery, risk of loss, and freight, many of the traditional indicia and consequences of holding title are passed separately from title in Article 2. Title is still important for some purposes, but most of them are outside of the UCC (for example, the timing of a "sale" for purposes of sales tax liability, whether the buyer or the seller can enforce tort liability for damage to or interference with the goods, whether certain actions interfering with the goods amount to criminal theft or other crimes, and insurance coverage of "owner's goods").

Read 2-401(2) and (3). The parties may pass title at any time agreed upon, subject to the limitations in 1-102(3). The default rule is that title passes when the seller completes its performance with regard to physical delivery of the goods.[11] Subsections (2) and (3) elaborate on that rule in particular delivery settings, using some phrases that parallel those used in 2-503 and 2-509.

Problem 13-10. Introduction to Title. Fill in the chart below.

Delivery type	Applicable portion of 2-401	When and where title passes
Shipment contract		
Destination contract		
Warehouse		
Buyer picks up goods at seller's location		

2003   [11] The 2003 amended version of 2-401 omits the word "physical."

Problem 13-11. Tying It All Together. Using your answers from many of the previous problems, fill in the following charts by recording the pertinent section number and the answer it gives to the question in the top row for the type of delivery in the left column. If more than one provision is needed to fully answer the question, jot down each provision in order of analysis.

(A)   Tender of delivery and payment of freight

	How does seller complete "tender of delivery"?	Who pays freight?
Buyer picks up goods at seller's location		no freight paid
Shipment contract, by carrier		
Destination contract, by carrier or seller's truck		
Warehouse (fill in only # of section or subsection)		no freight paid

(B)   Passage of risk of loss and title

	When does risk of loss pass to buyer (if no breach)?	When does title pass to buyer?
Buyer picks up goods at seller's location	If seller is merchant: If seller is not merchant:	If goods identified at time of contracting: If not:
Shipment contract, by carrier		
Destination contract, by carrier or seller's truck	If carrier: If no carrier:	
Warehouse (fill in only # of section or subsection)		

Applying the Code

Problem 13-12. Seller proposes to sell specified goods for "$500, F.O.B. seller's loading dock, ship to buyer's plant."

(A)   Buyer instead seeks "F.O.B. buyer's plant." Will the buyer's proposal cause the seller to want a change in the price?

(B)   Buyer instead seeks "F.O.B. buyer's plant, buyer to pay freight." Will the buyer's proposal cause the seller to want a change in the price?

Problem 13-13. Agreement between fish merchant in Duluth and a seafood restaurant in New Orleans calling for the sale of "500 lbs. No. 1 Quality Walleye, F.O.B. Duluth, ship to port of New Orleans. Payment due five days after goods arrive in New Orleans." The goods are shipped via a refrigerated container and loaded on a boat that travels the Mississippi River. Seller gets a bill of lading and forwards it to buyer. During shipment, the container malfunctions, and the fish spoil.

(A)   Who has the risk of loss for the spoilage of the fish, and why?

(B)   Will your answer in (A) differ if the agreement instead specifies "C.I.F. New Orleans"?

Problem 13-14. Bianca orders $180 worth of clothes for her school-age children on a web site run by Terra Children, Inc., a company with high quality clothing and particularly good prices. The web site says in its posted terms and conditions that purchased clothes will be sent by United Parcel Service (U.P.S.) within fourteen days. Terra Children gives the clothes to U.P.S. for shipment and sends Bianca a postcard saying that her clothes have been shipped and providing the U.P.S. tracking number. No additional documents are necessary for Bianca to obtain delivery. Thirty days after her order, Bianca contacts Terra Children to say that the clothes have not yet arrived. Terra Children says that U.P.S. picked up the clothes three days after her order. (Assume, for purposes of this problem, that U.P.S. is within the meaning of "carrier" in the UCC. Also assume that Bianca's credit card payment may be rightfully suspended only for defective goods or missing goods that are the seller's responsibility.)

(A)   Bianca asks Terra Children to track the order for her with U.P.S., but Terra Children refuses, saying that Bianca bears the responsibility of tracking things down with (or making a claim against) U.P.S. once Terra Children gives Bianca the U.P.S. tracking number. Is Terra Children correct?

(B)   Terra Children also tells Bianca that she still must pay Terra Children for the clothing (so she cannot rightfully suspend payment on her credit card). Is Terra Children correct?

(C)   If Bianca's homeowner's insurance policy covers the loss of goods that she "owns," regardless of where they are, will her policy cover the loss of this clothing if she never receives it?

Assignment 14: Documentary Transactions

§§ 2-310, 2-503, 2-504, 2-505, 2-512,
2-513, 7-102, 7-104, 7-501, 7-502

Reading the Code

A documentary transaction is a sale of goods in which control over the goods is passed through the transfer of documents that "represent" the goods rather than through immediate transfer of the goods themselves. Merchants developed the practice of using documents to represent goods and payment because it helped them to move goods through commerce effectively and with reduced risk. UCC Articles 2, 3, 4, 7, and 9 all contain provisions that relate to documentary transactions.[1] The materials in this assignment provide only a brief introduction to documentary transactions under the UCC, with an emphasis on how they operate in Article 2.

In this assignment, you will learn:

- why buyers and sellers might choose to engage in a documentary transaction and how it would be conducted;
- how to determine whether a contract permits or mandates that it be conducted as a documentary transaction; and
- how the buyer and seller perform their tender obligations in a documentary transaction.

Conducting a Documentary Transaction

Central to documentary transactions is the "document of title," a document that identifies particular goods in the possession or control of a bailee (typically a warehouse or carrier) and gives the person possessing the piece of paper the right to "receive, hold and dispose of the document and the goods it

---

[1] In addition, liabilities of the parties to a documentary transaction (including a carrier or warehouse) may also be governed by federal statutes such as the Carriage of Goods by Sea Act, 46 U.S.C. app. §§ 1300-1315, the Pomerene Act, 49 U.S.C. app. §§ 81-124, and the Harter Act, 46 U.S.C. app. §§ 190-196, as well as various international commercial conventions and customs.

covers" (1-201(15)).[2] A document of title may be a "bill of lading" issued by a carrier (1-201(6)), a "warehouse receipt" issued by a person in the business of storing goods for hire (1-201(45))[3], a dock receipt, an order for delivery of the goods, or any other document which, in the regular course of business or financing, gives the possessor of the document the right to receive the goods or direct their delivery. A document of title also contains the terms of the bailment contract (e.g., shipping or storage charges, instructions for delivery) between the bailee and the party arranging for shipment or storage of the goods (which may be either the buyer or seller). An example of a document of title—in this case, a simplified bill of lading—appears on the next page. By its nature, a document of title is used *only* in a transaction in which the goods are placed in possession of a third-party warehouse or shipper, not when goods are delivered directly from seller to buyer.

       UCC Article 7 defines the essential characteristics of documents of title, as well as the rights and responsibilities they create. A revised version of Article 7 was adopted by NCCUSL and the ALI in 2003, and the materials that follow refer to both pre- and post-revision versions of Article 7, as necessary.

Problem 14-1. Understanding Basic Terminology. Read 7-102(1)(a)-(c).[4] If Rivet Source, Inc. contracts to sell rivets to ABC Manufacturing Corp., then delivers to Careful Carriers a shipment of rivets to be sent to the buyer using a document of title that specifies ABC as the recipient of the rivets,

(A)   Who would issue the bill of lading?

(B)   Which of the parties is the bailee?

(C)   Which of the parties is the consignee?

(D)   Which of the parties is the consignor?

---

[2] Section 1-201(b)(16) in revised Article 1.

[3] Section 1-201(b)(42) in revised Article 1.

[4] The definitions in pre-revision 7-102(1)(a)-(c) appear at 7-102(a)(1), (3), and (4) in revised Article 7.

Bill of Lading
ORIGINAL—NOT NEGOTIABLE

RECEIVED, subject to the classifications and tariffs in effect on the date of the issue of this Bill of Lading

DATE: _____

FROM: _____
ADDRESS: _____

the property described below, in apparent good order, except as noted

CONSIGNED TO: _____
ADDRESS: _____
ROUTING: _____
DELIVERING CARRIER: _____

Remit C.O.D.
TO: _____   C.O.D. Amount $_____
ADDRESS: _____

Number of Packages	Kind of Package, Description of Articles, Special Marks, and Exceptions	Weight	Rate	Charges

Note–Where the rate is dependent on value, shippers are required to state specifically in writing the agreed or declared value of the property.

The agreed or declared value of the property is hereby specifically stated by the shipper to be not exceeding $_____ per _____.

SHIPPER   CARRIER
_____   _____
Per _____   Per _____

Negotiability

Documents of title come in two varieties: negotiable and non-negotiable (and, under the 2003 version of Article 7, may be in electronic form). If a bill of lading or warehouse receipt is *negotiable*, the document itself *must* be delivered to the carrier or warehouse in order to retrieve the goods held by the bailee. As a result, if a buyer receives a negotiable document of title in a sales transaction, the buyer can be certain that no one else has the power to retrieve the goods, and that the seller no longer has the ability to retain or reroute them. Similarly, if a bank or other financial institution holds in its possession a negotiable document of title for goods that serve as collateral for a loan, the bank can be sure that the borrower cannot transfer the collateralized goods without the bank's knowledge. In essence, the negotiable document of title serves as a substitute for the goods in financing and sales transactions and offers a high degree of certainty that the goods will remain available to the person in possession of the document.

A *non-negotiable* document of title gives the person named in it the right to take possession of the goods or redirect their delivery, but the document itself need not (although it may) be delivered to the carrier or warehouse in order to do so. The non-negotiable document of title thus offers more flexibility than does a negotiable document of title in transferring the goods in commerce because there is no need to deliver the document itself in order to transfer ownership rights in the goods. For example, the person named in the document of title may simply instruct the bailee in writing to deliver the goods to another person. Parties to a sales transaction may prefer using non-negotiable documents because the parties could be hampered if delivery of the goods cannot occur until the document itself is delivered, especially because negotiable documents of title often are transferred using banking channels, which sometimes are slower than direct delivery of the goods. What is lost by using non-negotiable documents of title, however, is certainty. Having possession of a non-negotiable bill of lading or warehouse receipt offers no guarantee to the buyer or bank that the seller has not resold the goods and ordered delivery to someone else.

Using either a negotiable or a non-negotiable document of title in a sales transaction offers the seller a mechanism for controlling disposition of the goods even after the seller deposits the goods with a carrier or warehouse. Rather than giving delivery instructions to the warehouse or carrier immediately, the seller instead obtains a document of title and the warehouse or carrier stores or transports the goods but awaits further instructions for delivery to the buyer. If payment from the buyer is due before or upon delivery of the goods, the seller can refuse to deliver to the buyer a negotiable document of title or refrain from ordering delivery to the buyer under a non-negotiable document of title until the buyer has paid. For the buyer, delivery to her of the bill of lading at the time of payment offers some assurance (more in the case of a negotiable bill of lading) that the goods are available to her.

Whether a document of title is negotiable or non-negotiable depends on how the instructions for delivery are given. Use of particular words is required to create a negotiable document of title, and they must be visible on the document itself so that buyers, sellers, financers, and carriers will know their rights and responsibilities under the document. (In addition, tangible negotiable bills of lading are customarily printed on yellow paper, while non-negotiable or "straight" bills of lading are on white paper, making it easier to distinguish whether any particular document is negotiable.)

Problem 14-2. Negotiability.

(A)   Read 7-104(1)(a),[5] which identifies the only two ways of specifying the delivery term in order to make a document of title negotiable. What are those two ways?

(B)   Read 7-104(2) and the second paragraph of the comment. Considering each one separately, do the following delivery terms satisfy the requirements specified for creating a negotiable document of title? (Be sure you can cite to the Code or comment statement that supports each answer.)

    (1) DELIVER GOODS TO: ABC Mfg. Corp.

    (2) DELIVER GOODS TO: Bearer

---

[5] The definition of negotiability in 7-104(1)(a) appears in revised Article 7 in 7-104(a). The reference in pre-revision 7-104(1)(b) to negotiability in overseas trade has been deleted in revised Article 7 as "not necessary in light of current commercial practice." Comment 1 to revised Article 7.

(3) DELIVER GOODS TO: ABC Mfg. Corp.
Goods deliverable on proper indorsement and surrender of this receipt

(4) DELIVER GOODS TO: the order of ABC Mfg. Corp.

(5) DELIVER GOODS TO: Bearer on receipt of proper instructions from Seller.

(6) DELIVER GOODS TO: the order of ABC Mfg. Corp., upon proper written instructions from ABC Mfg. Corp.

Problem 14-3. Negotiating a Tangible Document of Title. To see how a tangible negotiable document is "negotiated" so that the recipient obtains all the rights of a negotiable document of title, read 7-501(1), (2), and (3).[6] Note that "indorsement" is not defined, but, by analogy to the definition in 3-204, indorsement occurs when the consignee signs the document of title and does not unambiguously indicate the signature is not meant to negotiate the document of title.

(A)   If the carrier gave Frank's Furniture, Inc. (FFI) a bill of lading marked "DELIVER GOODS TO: Bearer," what does FFI have to do to negotiate the bill of lading to Discount Retailers?

(B)   If the carrier gave FFI a bill of lading marked "DELIVER GOODS TO: the order of FFI," what are three ways for FFI to negotiate the bill of lading to Discount Retailers?

---

[6] The same rules appear in 7-501(a)(1)-(4) in revised Article 7.

Note on Negotiating an Electronic Document of Title

As seen in the pages above, the use of negotiable documents of title provides special protections for the buyer because the document itself must be physically delivered to negotiate the document or to obtain the goods from the bailee. In order to facilitate the use of electronic documents of title, a primary aim of the 2003 Article 7 revision, it was necessary to establish a way to offer the same protections while allowing electronic rather than physical delivery. The Article 7 revision accomplishes that goal by providing that delivery of an electronic document of title can be effectuated by a "voluntary transfer of control" over that document, as long as:

- a single authoritative copy of the document of title is created, and non-authoritative copies are readily identifiable as such, and
- the person transferring control can reliably establish that it is the person to whom the electronic document was issued or transferred (i.e., that it has control of the document).[7]

Under the identified circumstances, an electronic document of title may be negotiated by delivery (that is, by voluntary transfer of control) without indorsement. In particular,

- if the document runs to "bearer," it is negotiated by voluntary transfer of control to another person;
- if the document runs "to the order of" a named person, the named person may negotiate the document by voluntarily transferring control to another person, without indorsing the document.

Problem 14-4. Duly Negotiating a Document of Title. "Due negotiation" of a negotiable document of title provides an additional level of protection to the transferee, giving her title to the document and the goods free of certain defenses otherwise available. (See 7-502.) Read 7-501(4) and 1-201(20) (second sentence)[8]. What are the additional requirements that make "negotiation" of a document of title into "due negotiation"?

---

[7] See revised 7-106 and the 2003 conforming amendments to 1-201(14).

[8] Section 1-201(b)(21)(B) in revised Article 1.

Using Negotiable Instruments (Drafts) in Sales Transactions

We have seen that in a sales transaction, using documents of title gives the seller the ability to direct and redirect transfer of the *goods* through manipulation of the documents. In similar fashion, documents may be useful in allowing the seller to direct and redirect disposition of the *buyer's payment* in advance of the payment due date. For example, if the purchase price is due only after delivery of the goods but the seller has an immediate need for cash to finance the sales transaction, the seller may transfer to a bank the right to collect the purchase price when the price becomes due, in exchange for the bank's immediate payment to seller of a smaller sum.

Under the Uniform Commercial Code, the piece of paper that is used to represent the buyer's obligation to pay is called a "draft." It is an order for the buyer to pay a sum of money to the bearer (possessor) of the draft or "to the order of" a named person. A draft accompanying a sale of goods might look like this:

To: Buyer	Date: _____

On _____
      ("sight" or specified date)

PAY to the order of _____ the
sum of _____ dollars

                        Signed: _____
                                    (Seller)

The seller signs the draft, filling in the amount of money owed by the buyer pursuant to the contract terms and specifying that the draft be paid either "on sight" (immediately) or on a specified date, depending on the agreed payment date under the contract. Because the buyer owes the seller the purchase price under the terms of the sales contract, the seller can order that the money owed be paid to the person holding the draft, and the buyer should be willing to pay that money at the specified time, assuming that the seller has by then fulfilled its contract obligations, probably by delivering to the buyer either the goods or the bill of lading representing the buyer's right to collect the goods. (We will return below to considering just when the buyer must pay; for now, concentrate on the way a draft works.)

Note the similarity between a draft and a check. A check, in fact, *is* a draft, but a special kind: one that is drawn on a bank. When you write a check, you are telling your bank—which owes you money, because you deposited funds with the bank or the bank agreed to make a loan to you—to pay the money it owes you to the named person (the phone company, or a magazine publisher, or a restaurant, etc.). Similarly, when the seller writes a draft, it is telling the buyer to pay the purchase price—which the buyer owes to the seller under the contract—to the bearer or a person named in the draft.

Just as was true with documents of title, drafts are negotiable or non-negotiable. To be negotiable (3-104), a draft

•   must be an unconditional order to pay a fixed amount of money;
•   must be payable "to bearer" or "to order";
•   must be payable on demand or at a definite stated time; and
•   must not state any other undertaking or instruction by the person ordering payment (with certain limited exceptions unimportant for our purposes).

Using Both Documents of Title and Drafts

Using *both* a document of title *and* a draft, the seller can provide for transfer of both the goods to the buyer (directly or indirectly) *and* the money to the seller's bank or agent or to a middleman in the transaction, simply by moving paper (or electronic documents) through commercial channels. Statutes and regulations outside Article 2 facilitate this set of transactions by creating obligations for both the carrier and the banks to handle the documents of title and the drafts in the manner that seller and buyer expect. The bank and the carrier would be liable to seller or buyer for failing to fulfill these duties, so both parties can reliably assume that the transaction will proceed as planned.

Why *would* a seller and buyer want to use such a seemingly complicated series of transactions to accomplish a "simple" sale of goods? Among the possibilities:

(1)   *Seller's need to reroute the goods:* When the seller first ships the goods, it may know what market it plans to use for the sale, but not who the buyer will be. The seller can ship the goods to that market under a bill of lading; when the seller finds a buyer, it can indorse the bill and create the draft.

(2)   *Seller's desire to sell to third party the right to payment for a discounted price:* After shipping or warehousing the goods, the seller may wish to sell to someone else the right to collect payment from the buyer before the goods are actually delivered. By creating both a document of title and a draft, the seller can transfer to that third party both the document that will allow the buyer to obtain the goods and the documentary manifestation of the right to demand payment from the buyer, so the third party can complete the sales transaction.

(3)   *The security of "cash on the barrelhead":* The seller does not want to give the buyer a right to get the goods without being paid, and the buyer does not want to pay without having the goods—or at least the right to demand the goods from a carrier or warehouse that is required to deliver them. (From the buyer's perspective, having the right to demand the goods from the *seller* may not be quite as good as having the right to demand them from a *carrier* or *warehouse*. If the goods are already in the hands of a carrier or a warehouse with instructions to deliver the goods to the buyer upon payment, the buyer is better protected from a default by seller and may feel more secure in making payment.)

It is this last scenario that probably occurs most frequently. Typically, the seller ships the goods, then sends the bill of lading and the draft, through banking channels, to the buyer's location, where the buyer receives the bill of lading when it authorizes transfer of funds to pay the draft. This is represented in the diagram on pages 218-219.

Article 2 and Documents of Title

What, you may ask, does all this have to do with Article 2? Article 2 provisions determine when a parties' agreement permits or requires the use of documents of title, establish the requirements for proper tender using documents of title, and determine the relationship between the seller's delivery of the documents of title and the buyer's right to inspect the goods and responsibility to pay for them. With respect to any particular contract for sale of goods, you need to be able to determine:

- Does the contract permit or require the seller to use documents of title, and what kind?
- What are the seller's responsibilities for tender of delivery if documents of title are used?
- At what point in the transaction does the buyer have to pay for the goods? Does this change if documents of title are used?
- If the buyer has to pay when the documents are delivered, does the buyer have the right to inspect the goods before paying? Are the buyer's rights to inspection different if documents of title are used?

Although the Code provisions often combine these aspects, we will address them separately in order to help sort through this complicated portion of Article 2.

Determining Whether Documents of Title May Be Used

As is true with respect to most contract terms, whether documents of title may be used is controlled by the language of the parties and the default provisions set forth in the Code.

- The contract may contain explicit language saying documents of title may or must be used, or specifying exactly what kind of documents of title are permitted or mandated (e.g., "delivery by bill of lading," "negotiable bill of lading required").
- Course of performance, course of dealing, or usage of trade may mandate or permit use of documents of title.
- If the contract specifies delivery "C.I.F."or "C. & F.", section 2-320(2)(a) mandates the use of a negotiable bill of lading.
- If the goods are held in a warehouse and are to be delivered without being moved, 2-503(4) indicates a seller may use documents of title.
- Section 2-310(b) says that if a seller is authorized to send the goods, he may ship them "under reservation." When a seller ships "under reservation," that means the seller uses a certain kind of document of title to reserve a security interest in the goods, obtaining a right under Article 9 of the Uniform Commercial Code to repossess the goods under certain circumstances if the buyer does not deliver the full purchase price.

Using Documents of Title and Drafts in a Sales Transaction

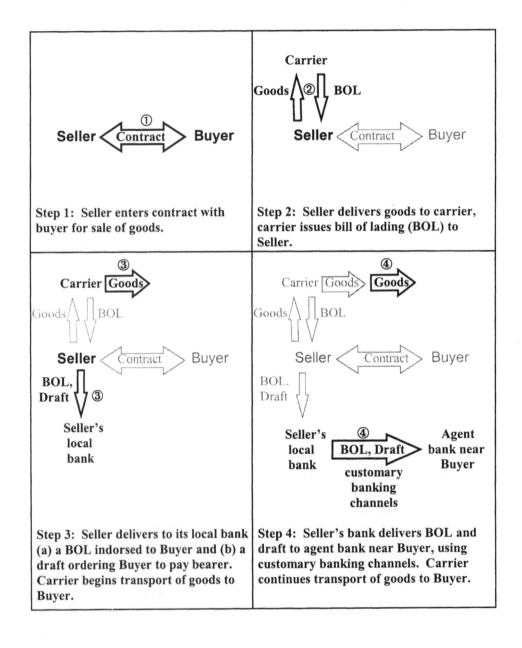

Step 1: Seller enters contract with buyer for sale of goods.

Step 2: Seller delivers goods to carrier, carrier issues bill of lading (BOL) to Seller.

Step 3: Seller delivers to its local bank (a) a BOL indorsed to Buyer and (b) a draft ordering Buyer to pay bearer. Carrier begins transport of goods to Buyer.

Step 4: Seller's bank delivers BOL and draft to agent bank near Buyer, using customary banking channels. Carrier continues transport of goods to Buyer.

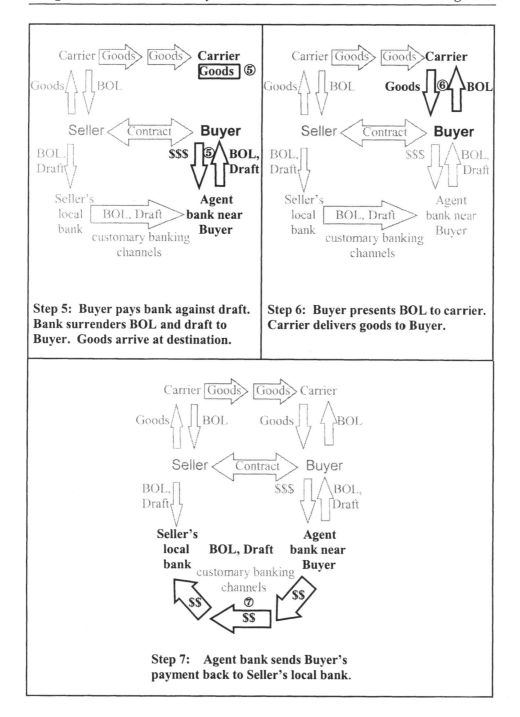

Step 5: Buyer pays bank against draft. Bank surrenders BOL and draft to Buyer. Goods arrive at destination.

Step 6: Buyer presents BOL to carrier. Carrier delivers goods to Buyer.

Step 7:   Agent bank sends Buyer's payment back to Seller's local bank.

Problem 14-5. Shipment Under Reservation.

(A)   Read 2-505(1), which specifies the two forms a document of title may take to reserve a security interest in the seller. What are those two forms?

(B)   Does each of the following notations on a bill of lading result in a shipment "under reservation"? Read comment 2.

   (1) Consigned to Seller

   (2) Consigned to order of Seller

   (3) Consigned to Buyer

   (4) Consigned to order of Buyer

   (5) Consigned to Bearer

Seller's Delivery Responsibilities When Using Documents of Title

Problem 14-6. Tendering Documents. Complete the following chart, reading the specified Article 2 subsections and recording seller's delivery responsibilities with respect to documents of title when documents of title are used.

Type of delivery term	Article 2 subsection	Seller's tender responsibilities with respect to documents of title
C.I.F., C. & F.	2-320(2)(e)	
Warehouse pickup	2-503(4)(a) and (b)	

Type of delivery term	Article 2 subsection	Seller's tender responsibilities with respect to documents of title
Shipment contract	2-504(b)	
Destination contract	2-503(1), comment 2, ¶ 3	
Documents of title required	2-503(5), comment 7 ¶ 1	

Risk of Loss and Documents of Title

Problem 14-7. Shifting Risk of Loss. Re-read 2-509 with documents of title in mind. When does risk of loss pass

(A)   if the seller ships the goods under a bill of lading?

(B)   if the goods are in a warehouse and delivered by document of title without being moved?

Buyer's Obligation to Pay When Documents of Title Are Used

Now we know what the seller is allowed and required to do with respect to documents of title in order to fulfill delivery obligations. As might be expected, if the seller uses documents of title, the buyer must be given whatever documents are required for the buyer to get delivery of the goods from the carrier or warehouse that has possession of the goods. But when those documents are presented to the buyer, must the buyer pay the contract price? Or can the buyer wait to pay until the buyer gets the goods themselves? The parties to the contract may specify explicitly when payment is required (e.g., "Payment by sight draft against bill of lading"), but what happens in the absence of such express terms?

Problem 14-8. When and Where Buyer is Obligated to Pay: Default Provisions. Complete the chart below, reading the specified Article 2 subsections.

Type of delivery term	Article 2 subsection	When and where is payment due?
C.I.F. & C. & F.	2-320(4) & comment 1	
Goods to be shipped; seller ships under reservation	2-310(b) & comment 2	
Goods to be shipped; parties agree delivery to be made by using documents of title	2-310(c)[9]	

---

[9] Section 2-310(c) applies if delivery is "authorized and made by way of documents of title *otherwise* than by subsection (b)." Section 2-310(b) permits a seller who is authorized to ship the goods to choose to use documents of title to ship under reservation. Delivery by way of documents of title is "otherwise" authorized only if there is an agreement (through language, usage of trade, course of performance, and course of dealing) that documents will be used *for delivery*. (Using documents of title to ship the goods is different from using documents of title to fulfill delivery responsibilities.) The 2003 amended version makes this explicit by applying the rule in 2-310(c) only "if tender of delivery is agreed to be made by way of documents of title otherwise than by paragraph (b)."

Type of delivery term	Article 2 subsection	When and where is payment due?
Goods to be held at warehouse; parties agree delivery to be made by using documents of title	2-310(c)	
All deliveries not described in 2-310(b) or 2-310(c)	2-310(a)	

Buyer's Right to Inspect the Goods

Section 2-513(1) specifies that "unless otherwise agreed and subject to subsection (3), where goods are tendered or delivered or identified to the contract for sale, the buyer has a right before payment . . . to inspect them at any reasonable place and time and in any reasonable manner." Inspection before payment is thus the default—unless the parties otherwise agree or subsection (3) says otherwise.

Problem 14-9. Buyer's Right to Inspect. Complete the chart below, reading the indicated Article 2 subsections and comments. Be sure you can identify the statutory language that provides the answers.

Type of delivery term	Article 2 subsection	Does buyer have right to inspect before payment?
C.O.D.[10]	2-513(3)(a)	
C.I.F. & C. & F.	2-513(3)(b) 2-320(4) & comment 1	

2003 [10] The 2003 amended version removes the reference to "C.O.D. or other like terms" and replaces it with a more general reference to "terms that under course of performance, course of dealing, or usage of trade are interpreted to preclude inspection before payment."

Type of delivery term	Article 2 subsection	Does buyer have right to inspect before payment?
Goods to be shipped; seller ships under reservation	2-310(b) & comments 2 and 3	
Goods to be shipped; parties agree delivery to be made by using documents of title	2-513(3)(b) 2-310(c)	
Same, but contract says "hold documents until arrival of goods"	2-513 comment 5	
Goods to be held at warehouse; parties agree delivery to be made by using documents of title	2-513(3)(b) 2-310(c) 2-513 comment 5 ¶ 3	
All deliveries not described in 2-310(b) or 2-310(c)	2-310(a)	

Problem 14-10. Excusing Payment Before Inspection. Read 2-512(1)(a) and comments 1 through 3 and 2-513 comment 1. If the buyer is required to pay before inspection, may the buyer refuse to pay because the goods are defective? If so, under what circumstances?

Applying the Code

You now have the tools to determine what the seller's obligations are with respect to tendering goods *and* documents, to determine when and where the buyer is required to make payment upon the seller's proper tender, and to determine whether the buyer has a right to demand inspection before paying. The problems below will test your understanding by asking you to determine whether the buyer has breached by demanding delivery or inspection of the goods before paying.

Problem 14-11. Agreement between High Seas, a fish merchant in Boston, and Sea Coast, a restaurant in Minneapolis, calling for the sale of "300 lobsters, each 1 to 2 pounds, ship to Sea Coast Restaurant, lobsters to be alive at delivery." (Each problem below is independent of the others unless otherwise noted.)

(A)   High Seas ships the lobsters, obtaining a bill of lading "to order of High Seas." When the lobsters arrive at the carrier's facility in Minneapolis, Sea Coast inspects the lobsters and finds them conforming. The agent for High Seas in Minneapolis demands payment before indorsing and releasing the bill of lading. Sea Coast refuses, claiming that payment is due only upon delivery of the lobsters to the restaurant, which the carrier refuses to do without an indorsed bill of lading. Has Sea Coast breached by refusing to pay until the lobsters are delivered?

(B)   High Seas ships the lobsters, obtaining a bill of lading "to order of High Seas." While the lobsters are en route, the agent for High Seas in Minneapolis presents the sight draft to Sea Coast and demands payment, promising an indorsed bill of lading in return. Sea Coast refuses, claiming the right to inspect the lobsters upon delivery to make sure they are still alive. Has Sea Coast breached by refusing to pay?

(C)   Same as (B), but agreement says "Delivery: C.I.F. Minneapolis." When Sea Coast demands inspection before paying against the sight draft, has Sea Coast breached?

Problem 14-12. Agreement on October 1 between Commodities Corp. and Cereals Deluxe for sale of $50,000 worth of grain owned by Commodities Corp. and stored in a grain warehouse owned by Great Silos, Inc. (Each problem below is independent of the other.)

(A)   On October 2, Commodities Corp. sends to Great Silos a letter authorizing delivery of the grain to Cereals Deluxe on November 1. When is Cereals Deluxe obligated to pay for the grain?

(B)   On September 15, when the grain was delivered to Great Silos, Commodities Corp. obtained a negotiable warehouse receipt. On October 2, Cereals Deluxe seeks to inspect the grain stored at Great Silos, but the warehouse refuses to allow the inspection. On October 3, Commodities Corp. presents the warehouse receipt and sight draft to Cereals Deluxe and demands payment in exchange for the indorsed warehouse receipt. Does Cereals Deluxe have to pay upon this demand?

Assignment 15: Power to Transfer Title

§ 2-403

As we saw in Assignment 13, section 2-401 tells us when title passes in a contract for sale of goods, but what happens if the title being passed was defective in some way (e.g., the goods were stolen or acquired by fraud or transferred by mistake)? To answer that question, this assignment will look at the derivative title rule in 2-403, the common law concepts of void and voidable title, and the 2-403 rights of good faith purchasers for value and buyers in the ordinary course of business.

The Derivative Title Rule

The first part of the first sentence in 2-403(1) sets out the usual rule for what title is transferred from seller to buyer: "A purchaser of goods acquires all title which his transferor had or had power to transfer . . . ." This rule is called the derivative title rule. If goods are transferred from a first party to a second party, the purchaser usually receives whatever title the transferor had.

Problem 15-1. Transferors and Purchasers. Notice that 2-403 refers to a "purchaser," not a "buyer"; a "transferor," not a "seller"; and a "transfer," not a "sale." Read 1-201(32) and (33). In the diagram below, representing the transactions covered by 2-403, what kinds of transactions are included in the meaning of "transfer"?

A   "Transfer"   B

Transferor   ➡   Purchaser

The final clause of the first sentence of 2-403(1) sets out an exception to the derivative title rule: "except that a purchaser of a limited interest acquires rights only to the extent of the interest purchased." This clause means that the parties may agree that party B receives less than all of party A's title. For instance, if the owner of goods (party A) leases them to another (party B), then party A would retain title to the goods, and party B would receive the agreed leasehold interest:

A	Lease	B
Owner/Lessor	➡	Lessee

A purchaser thus gets all of the transferor's title, unless the agreement specifies that the purchaser is acquiring less than the transferor's full set of rights in the goods.

Voidable Title

The common law says that a transferee receives voidable title if the transferor intended to and did transfer good title at the time of a transaction, but subsequent events or subsequently discovered facts entitle the transferor to rescind the transaction and regain title. Notice that the transaction is void<u>able</u> (able to be voided), not void; the transferor still must perform the action of rescinding the transaction in order to regain title. If he or she does not, the right to rescind the transaction is eventually waived and lost. Examples of defects resulting in voidable title include mutual and unilateral mistake, larcenous[1] fraud in the inducement of a transfer (see, e.g., 2-403(1)(a) and (d)), failure to pay in a "cash sale"[2] (2-403(1)(c)), and receipt of goods by an insolvent buyer (2-702(2)).

If the transferor gave up possession of the goods to the person with voidable title before discovering the facts or events that give the transferor the right to rescind, the transferor is assumed to have given up possession

---

[1] "Larcenous" appears in both 2-403(1)(d) and (3). It is not defined in the UCC, which instead refers to the criminal law definition for that jurisdiction. For instance, the court in *John v. United States*, 79 F.2d 136 (D.C. 1935), defined "larceny" as obtaining possession of property by fraud, trick or device with preconceived design or intent to appropriate, convert or steal.

[2] A "cash sale" is a sale in which payment is agreed to be due upon delivery. Section 2-403(1)(c) rejects the "technical cash sale" approach, used in some pre-UCC cases, under which the seller purports not to transfer title until the buyer has fully paid. *See* William D. Hawkland, *Uniform Commercial Code Series* § 2-403:03 (2001).

voluntarily, even though the transferor may have been deceived into making the transfer.

Problem 15-2. Derivative Title Rule. Let's take that famous cow case from first-year Contracts class, *Sherwood v. Walker*.[3] A cattle breeder arranged to sell the cow, Rose of Aberlone, to a banker, setting the price at $80 because both seller and buyer thought her to be sterile. After they entered into the contract, but before Rose was delivered to the buyer, the breeder discovered that she was pregnant and therefore was worth between $750 and $1000, so he refused to deliver her. The banker sued in replevin to gain possession of Rose. The court ruled that the contract was voidable because of mutual mistake.

Let's extend the facts a bit. The breeder thought Rose was sterile when he delivered her to the banker. Let's say that when the banker discovers that she is already pregnant, he immediately sells Rose to a third party and Rose is delivered into the possession of the third party. Then the breeder sues to recover Rose from the third party, based on his rights arising from the mutual mistake claim between him and the banker at the time of contract formation. Assume the original breeder acts quickly enough so he does not waive any rights.

(A)   As between the breeder and the banker, is there voidable title?

(B)   According to the derivative title rule in the first sentence of 2-403(1), what rights does the third party obtain from the banker?

(C)   Considering only the first sentence of 2-403(1), does the breeder have a superior right to Rose, surpassing the rights of the third party?

(D)   If the breeder can recover Rose from the third party, what Article 2 section provides the best basis for the third party's breach claim against the banker? Think back to previous assignments.

---

[3] 33 N.W. 919 (Mich. 1887). For a renowned poem in praise of Rose, see Brainerd Currie, *Rose of Aberlone*, Student Lawyer, Apr. 1965, at 4.

Void Title

Sometimes the title a purchaser receives from a transferor is not simply voidable; it is void. Title can be passed in only two ways: (1) by the title holder's voluntary and intentional transfer of title to a "purchaser" (remember the broad definition of that word) or (2) by some process of law that transfers title (e.g., a foreclosure). If person B tricks person A into selling a car by misinforming person A about person B's solvency, person B receives voidable title. The transfer was voluntarily and intentionally made, though based on deceit. But if—prior to any sale—person B takes the car for a test drive and never returns it, person B has stolen person A's car. There was no voluntary and intentional transfer of title. Person B has "void title," which more accurately is no title at all. Person A retains title. Instead of title, person B has a right of possession which is superior to everyone else in the world—except person A. When goods are stolen, they do not become fair game for everyone else to steal from the thief. The thief can recover them from any subsequent thief (if he or she has the moxie!). They are recoverable by the original owner, no matter how far down the chain of title they have passed. The tough task for the original owner is finding the goods.

Problem 15-3. The Effect of Void Title. True story. An American soldier was stationed in Germany toward the end of World War II and was one of the first Americans to enter Hitler's residence in Munich, Germany. He picked up some of Hitler's belongings and took them home. Decades later, after he had shown the items to friends and others, his chauffeur stole the items and sold them to a dealer in historical memorabilia.[4]

(A)   What is the nature of the possessory rights of the soldier, the chauffeur, and the dealer, as against each other, Hitler, and the rest of the world?

(B)   If the former soldier sues the dealer to recover the items, who should win?

---

[4] *Lieber v. Mohawk Arms, Inc.*, 314 N.Y.S.2d 510 (Sup. Ct. 1970).

(C)   If Hitler had had an heir who sued to recover the items from whoever held them, who should win?

Acquiring Better Than Derivative Title:
The Good Faith Purchaser for Value

The derivative title rule says that unless a limited interest is specified, a purchaser receives "all title," but not better title than, the transferor had. Section 2-403 adds two exceptions to the derivative title rule to permit certain purchasers to acquire better title than their transferors had. The first of these exceptions concerns the "good faith purchaser for value" and appears in the second sentence of 2-403(1).

Problem 15-4. Parsing 2-403(1).

(A)   Section 2-403(1) identifies the parties to a transaction as "purchaser," "good faith purchaser for value," "person with voidable title," and "transferor." Which of these words are defined in the Code, and where?

(B)   Read the second sentence of 2-403(1). Consider a transfer from A to B and then to C (A => B => C), in which B's title to the goods is flawed in a way that makes it voidable. In the boxes below, label the parties affected by the first and second sentences of 2-403(1), using the words in (A) above. What kind of title is being transferred in each arrow?

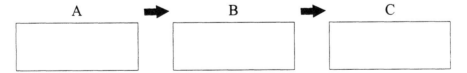

(C)   Read the third sentence of 2-403(1). To what power does "such power" refer? Does "the purchaser" refer to B or to C?

(D)   Read 2-403 comment 1. Consider the language in (a) through (d) of 2-403(1). Which statements below are correct?

           1.   This list is the complete list of facts giving rise to voidable title.
           2.   This list is an incomplete list of facts giving rise to voidable title.
           3.   This list states which fact situations will always result in good title being given to a good faith purchaser for value.
           4.   This list states which fact situations will give a purchaser the power granted by the rule in the second sentence, as long as the goods were delivered to the purchaser before the transfer to a good faith purchaser for value.
           5.   This list states exceptions to the rule in the second sentence.

Problem 15-5. Applying the Exception for the Good Faith Purchaser for Value. Let's return to the facts in Problem 15-2. Recall that a cattle breeder arranges to sell the cow (Rose) to a banker for $80 because both seller and buyer think her to be sterile; assume that the parties' mutual mistake makes that agreement voidable. The breeder delivers Rose to the banker, thinking that she is sterile. The banker then discovers that Rose already is pregnant, so he quickly sells and delivers Rose to a third party without revealing anything about the sale from the breeder to him. The sale price is $800. The breeder then hears that Rose is not sterile and therefore is worth between $750 and $1000, so he sues the third party to recover possession of Rose, based on his rights arising from the mutual mistake defense.

(A)   As between the breeder and the banker, is there voidable title?

(B)   Does the third party qualify as a good faith purchaser for value?

(C)   Does the breeder have a superior right to Rose, surpassing the rights of the third party?

(D) What policies support this result, as compared with the opposite result? Between these two parties (breeder and third party), who needs greater protection in the marketplace?

(E) Does the losing party (the breeder or the third party) have any way to redress its loss, by a claim against the banker?

(F) If the third party, at the time of its agreement with the banker, has knowledge of the breeder's mistake claim, what effect does that have on your answers above?

Acquiring Better Than Derivative Title: Buyer in the Ordinary Course of Business

The second exception to the derivative-title rule concerns the "buyer in the ordinary course of business," as set out in subsections (2) and (3) of 2-403.

Problem 15-6. Parsing 2-403(2) and (3).

(A) Read 2-403(2), and rephrase the rule into "if/then" form.

(B) Section 2-403(2) and (3) labels the parties with the terms "entruster," "merchant who deals in goods of that kind," and "buyer in the ordinary course." Fill in those roles in the boxes below. Label one of the arrows "entrustment."

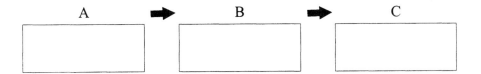

(C)   Look for definitions of the words that you have filled into the above diagram. Which words are defined in the Code, and where?

(D)   Read 2-403(3). What do the two "regardless of" clauses add to the first part of the sentence?

Problem 15-7. Applying the Exception for the Buyer in the Ordinary Course. John takes his great-grandmother's wedding ring to Wanda's Watch Repair and Jewelry Emporium to have the ring cleaned and re-sized so that he can give it to his fiancee for their engagement. After the work is done, an employee, by mistake, places the ring on a shelf marked "Previously Owned Jewelry for Sale." Linda sees the ring there, asks about the "previously owned jewelry" and is told that most of it is from estate sales and families that do not wish to sell the jewelry themselves. She buys the ring, unaware that it is someone else's.

(A)   Can John recover the ring from Linda?

(B)   Does the losing party (John or Linda) have any way to redress its loss, by a claim against Wanda's store?

(C)   What policies support this result, as compared with the opposite result?

Problem 15-8. Comparing 2-403(1) and (2).

(A) Using your answers from Problems 15-4 and 15-6, fill in the following chart comparing the rights of good faith purchasers and buyers in the ordinary course in a transaction from A to B to C.

	Party C is a good faith purchaser for value (2-403(1))	Party C is a buyer in the ordinary course of business (2-403(2))
Nature of right or title obtained and held by party B		
Nature of right or title obtained by party C		
Characteristics required of party B to transfer those rights		
Characteristics required of party C to receive those rights		
Policies supporting this result		

(B) If party C qualifies both as a good-faith-purchaser under 2-403(1) and as a buyer-in-the-ordinary-course under 2-403(2), which subsection transfers more rights to party C?

Problem 15-9. Putting All the Pieces Together. Lest you think that these fact situations cannot get any more complicated . . . .

(A)   Jo buys a 15-speed bike from a bike shop (Yellow Bikes), paying for it with a personal check for $636. However, the night after she buys it, the bike is stolen from her garage, so she stops payment on the check the next morning. The shop brings a small-claims-court action against Jo for the purchase price, to replace the dishonored check. Meanwhile, the police recover the bike in a raid on a bike-theft ring. For reasons not clear to anyone (but true nonetheless), the police place all of the bikes recovered in the raid in a "sheriff's sale" at which abandoned goods, stolen goods, and confiscated goods used in illegal activities are sold. A bicycle dealer who customarily buys bikes at these sheriff's sales buys the bike for $300. He puts it in his shop (Blue Bikes) and sells it to Eileen for $450, who gives it to her son Tim, for a birthday present. Jo is able to track down the bike and sues to recover possession from Tim. Will she prevail? (Hint: a diagram is very helpful.)

(B)   Jo buys a brand new model of 15-speed bike from a bike shop (Yellow Bikes), paying for it with a personal check for $636 that bounces because of insufficient funds in her bank account. The shop brings a small-claims-court action against Jo for the purchase price, to replace the bounced check. Within a week of buying the bike, Jo sells it to Blue Bikes, a shop that buys and sells used bikes; she receives $200 cash for it. Blue Bikes sells it to Eileen for $450. When Yellow Bikes is unable to collect on its small-claims-court judgment against Jo, Yellow Bikes tracks down the bike and sues to recover possession from Eileen. Will it prevail?

Note on Certificate-of-Title Acts

Each of the 50 states has a statute on the issuance of certificates of title, in order to assure orderly, traceable, non-fraudulent transfer of motor vehicles (and often other mobile goods, such as boats, trailers, off-road vehicles, etc.). Many of these certificate-of-title acts (CTAs) contain a rule specifying when title has transferred from seller to buyer; that point in time is often when the state issues the certificate of title. The CTA's rule about when title passes from seller to buyer differs from 2-401, which passes title, generally, upon seller's completion of physical delivery to buyer. This difference has resulted in a muddled set of cases about whether the CTA rule prevails over 2-401 and 2-403, or vice versa.[5] Thus, if the goods involved in the dispute are motor vehicles covered by a certificate of title, be sure to ascertain the result under the applicable certificate-of-title act, as well as the applicable case law about which body of law governs the dispute in the event of a conflict between the UCC and the certificate-of-title act.

2003   Under the 2003 amended version of 2-108(1)(a) and (2), the state's CTA prevails over the UCC in the event of a conflict, except if the rights of a buyer in the ordinary course of business arise before a certificate of title covering the same goods is effective in the name of another buyer.

---

[5] *See* Christina L. Kunz, *Motor Vehicle Ownership Disputes Involving Certificate-of-Title Acts and Article Two of the U.C.C.*, 39 Bus. Law. 1599 (1984).

Assignment 16: Excuse

§§ 2-613 through 2-616

Reading the Code

      The basic obligations of the seller ("to transfer and deliver [the goods] in accordance with the contract") and buyer ("to accept and pay in accordance with the contract") are set forth in 2-301. Failure to fulfill those obligations constitutes a breach, unless performance is excused. The Article 2 provisions on excuse appear in 2-613 through 2-616. Recall that, under 1-103, "the principles of law and equity" supplement the provisions of the UCC "[u]nless displaced by the particular provisions of this Act." Sections 2-613, 2-614, and 2-615 add to but do not pre-empt the common law doctrines of impossibility and frustration of purpose, so common law rulings remain relevant to problems not directly addressed by the provisions of Article 2.

Problem 16-1. Comparing the Article 2 Excuses. Read the UCC sections and comments listed in the left column below. Then fill in the chart below for each type of excuse.

	Elements to be fulfilled to invoke excuse	Effect on seller's obligation to deliver	Effect on buyer's obligation to pay
2-613,[1] comments 1 and 2, 1-201(16)			

---

[1] Ignore the reference to 2-324 and the "no arrival, no sale" term.

	Elements to be fulfilled to invoke excuse	Effect on seller's obligation to deliver	Effect on buyer's obligation to pay
2-614(1), comment 1 ¶ 1			
2-614(2), comment 3			
2-615, comment 1, 2-616			

Problem 16-2. Operation of 2-613 and 2-615. Read 2-615 comments 3, 4, 5, 7, and 8. Answer the following questions, identifying which comment is the source of your answer.

(A)   If a sales agreement specifies that the seller will obtain the goods from Company X and then Company X's inventories are destroyed by a warehouse fire, does 2-613 or 2-615 apply to determine whether the seller is excused from performing?

(B)   If a sales agreement specifies that the farmer-seller will deliver to the buyer a quantity of wheat to be harvested from farmer's fields, and then the wheat crop is destroyed by an insect infestation, does 2-613 or 2-615 apply to determine whether the seller is excused from performing?

(C)   If impracticability affects a minor aspect of performance, will the seller be excused from all, part, or none of the performance due?

(D)   Will a seller be excused from performing if the cost of seller's raw materials doubles?

Applying the Code

For each of the problems below, determine which excuse provision(s) apply and whether each of the required elements of that provision or provisions is likely satisfied for the seller or buyer claiming excuse.

Problem 16-3. Buyer and Seller enter a contract for sale of grain, to be shipped via railroad on April 28 for arrival on May 1. On April 27, Seller is notified of a shortage in rail cars. Seller notifies Buyer that the grain will be shipped instead by truck, and will arrive on May 3.

Problem 16-4. Buyer, a retail jewelry store, and Seller, a manufacturer of watches, enter a contract for sale of two dozen watches, F.O.B. Buyer's store. The shipment of watches is damaged in transit when the truck carrying them is involved in an accident caused by the driver of another vehicle.

Problem 16-5. A milk supplier enters a contract to furnish milk to a school district at a designated price. The market price of milk rises 50% after the contract is entered due to unusually severe crop failures, which raise the price of feed for cows.

Problem 16-6. Force Majeure Clauses. The purchasing agent for your corporate client is negotiating a purchase agreement for electronic parts that your client needs in its manufacturing operation. Seller has proposed its standard clause for force majeure:

> The vendor is excused from breach in the event of war, nuclear holocaust, embargo of essential parts, strike, earthquake, fire, flood, and other sources of substantial delay or destruction beyond vendor's control.

The purchasing agent is seeking advice about whether to accept this clause or bargain for another alternative.

(A)   How does this clause interact with the excuse rules in the UCC? Does it pre-empt, duplicate, or supplement?

(B)   Which particular exemptions are inadvisable for practical, factual, or strategic reasons?

(C)   What aspects of the clause could be drafted with greater clarity? Write better language.

Assignment 17: Buyer's Rights and Duties after Tender, Part I: Inspection, Rejection, and Cure

§§ 2-508, 2-601 through 2-605, 2-612

This assignment picks up where Assignment 13 left off—at the seller's tender and delivery of goods pursuant to the contract. At that point in the transaction, the buyer can judge whether the goods, the means and timing of delivery, and the documents conform to the contract (see 2-106(2)). The buyer can then decide whether to "accept" the goods or to "reject" them, and whether to seek damages for any nonconformity. Even if the buyer accepts the goods, under certain circumstances the buyer may be allowed to "revoke acceptance" of the goods. If the buyer rejects or revokes acceptance of the goods, the seller may have a right to "cure" any nonconformity.

These steps are reflected in the following flowchart. The sections noted in the flowchart are not the only ones applicable to these events, but they are the starting place for analysis.

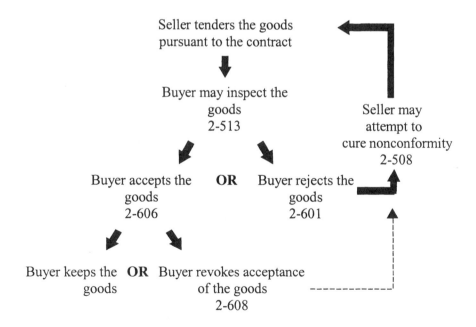

In this assignment, we will address inspection, buyer's rejection, and seller's cure (the right side of the flowchart above). Assignment 18 will complete the picture by addressing buyer's acceptance and revocation of acceptance. Buyer's remedies for breach and their interrelationship with any payments that the buyer has made will be treated in Assignment 20.

Reading the Code: Rejection of Goods by Buyer

Some of the sections that govern rejection, considered below, also refer to revocation of acceptance. For now, consider only the language dealing with rejection. We will return to these sections in Assignment 18 and consider their application to revocation of acceptance.

As you consider the Code sections related to a buyer's rejection of goods, it is important to distinguish between the buyer's *right* to reject and the *process* the buyer must use to reject properly. Article 2 uses the terms *effective* rejection and *ineffective* rejection based on whether the buyer took the required steps to reject. An effective rejection may be *rightful* or *wrongful* depending on whether the buyer is permitted to reject the goods.

Problem 17-1. The Right to Reject. Answer the following questions, using the cited sections.

(A)   Read 2-601. Why do you think the standard for rejection found there is colloquially known as the "perfect tender rule"? Does it mean that the goods must be perfect?

(B)   Based on 2-601, 2-504 (final paragraph), and 1-203,[1] under what circumstances may a buyer rightfully reject goods?

---

[1] Section 1-304 in revised Article 1.

(C)   Read 2-601 comment 1 and 2-105(6).[2] What factors should be considered in deciding whether a buyer is justified in rejecting only part of a shipment of goods?

(D)   Read 2-612(1) and comment 1. Under what circumstances does 2-612 rather than 2-601 govern acceptance and rejection of a shipment? Read 2-612(2) and (3) and comments 4 through 6. What standards govern the buyer's rejection of goods under 2-612? What rationale is suggested for the difference between 2-612 and 2-601?

2003 (E)   Read the 2003 amended version of 2-612(2) and comment 8. What change(s) and clarifications are made in the rejection standard for installment contracts?

Problem 17-2. The Process of Rejection. Answer the following questions, using the cited sections. Note that courts have consistently construed 2-602, 2-603, and 2-604 to apply to both rightful and wrongful rejection, despite the contrary statement in 2-602 comment 3 and the use of "rightful" in all three section titles. The 2003 amended version makes this explicit by deleting "rightful" from the section titles and revising comment 3.

2003 [2] Section 2-105(5) in the 2003 amended version.

(A)   Read 2-602(1) and comment 1. What must the buyer do to effectively reject goods?

(B)   Why is it not an effective rejection if a buyer says to the seller, "I'm not satisfied with the goods you sent. They don't work"?

(C)   Read 2-605 and comments 1 to 3. Under what circumstances must a buyer identify the particular defects leading to rejection?   What are the consequences of failing to convey such information?

2003 (D)   Read the 2003 amended version of 2-605(1) and comment 1. (Ignore the language relating to revocation of acceptance.) How does the answer to (C) change under the 2003 amended version?

Problem 17-3. Handling Goods After Rightful Rejection.

(A)   Read 2-602(2) and comment 2, 2-604 and its comment, and 2-711(3) and comment 2. What *must* a buyer do with rejected goods in buyer's possession? What *may* a buyer do with them, and under what circumstances?

(B)   Read 2-603(1) and comments 1 and 2. What additional responsibilities does a merchant buyer have with respect to rejected goods, and under what circumstances?

2003   (C)   Read 2-608(4)(b) in the 2003 amended version and the second paragraph of new comment 8. What additional obligation is imposed on a buyer who rejects goods? (We will revisit this provision in Assignment 18 to explore it more fully.)

Reading the Code: Cure of Nonconformity by Seller

Problem 17-4. Seller's Right to Cure. Answer the following questions, using 2-508:

(A)   Read 2-508(1) and comment 1.   Under what circumstances after rejection is a seller permitted to cure a nonconformity in tender or goods under this subsection? What must seller do to cure?

(B)   Read 2-508(2) and comments 2 and 3. How does the seller's right to cure after rejection under subsection (2) differ from the seller's right to cure under subsection (1)? What must seller do to cure?

2003 (C) Read the 2003 amended version of 2-508 and comments 3, 4, and 5. How do the amendments change the seller's right to cure after rejection? See 2-508 comment 4.

(D) Is a seller required to cure a nonconforming delivery?

(E) Should a seller cure a nonconforming delivery?

Problem 17-5. Expanding the Definition of Cure. Read *Wilson v. Scampoli*, at page 252. What does this case tell you about how a seller may effectuate a cure? What is the consequence if the buyer refuses to allow the seller to cure after rejection?

Problem 17-6. Cure After Performance Is Due; Money Allowance.

(A) Under 2-508(2), a seller may cure even if the time for performance has expired if the seller "had reasonable grounds to believe [that the nonconforming tender] would be acceptable." Read *Bartus v. Riccardi*, at page 255, and reconsider *Wilson v. Scampoli*. What may constitute "reasonable grounds to believe [the tender] would be acceptable" if the seller knew of the nonconformity at the time of tender, as in *Bartus*? If the seller did not know of the nonconformity, as in *Wilson*?

(B)   If the seller in *Bartus v. Riccardi* had offered the buyer a discount on the hearing aid *at the time it was first delivered,* would the buyer still have been able to reject the hearing aid? Would the seller still have had a right to cure?

(C)   If, *after the buyer in Bartus rejected the hearing aid,* the seller offered buyer a price discount on the rejected goods, would that constitute an attempt to cure? If not, what is it?

Time for Rejection and the Reasonable Opportunity to Inspect

Under 2-602, to be effective a rejection must occur "within a reasonable time after . . . delivery or tender." What constitutes a "reasonable time" depends on the "nature, purpose and circumstances" of the act of rejection (see generally 1-204). Comment 1 to 2-602 adds that "reasonable time" must be understood in connection with Article 2 provisions giving buyer the right to inspect the goods (see 2-513). Consequently, the buyer must be given a reasonable opportunity to inspect and discover defects, but the rejection must occur quickly enough to protect the seller's interests as well. We will explore the concept of reasonable opportunity to inspect further in Assignment 18.

Case law has suggested considering the following additional factors in determining whether the rejecting buyer has acted within a reasonable time:

- whether delay will result in deterioration of the goods;
- whether delay will impair seller's ability to cure;
- the ease or difficulty of communicating notice of rejection;
- whether the value of the goods threatens to decline, so that delay would further injure the seller; and
- whether the contract specifies a reasonable time for rejection.

Applying the Code: Rejection and Cure

Problem 17-7. Brady's Books is planning a reading and book-signing event with an author and orders 100 copies of the author's most recent novel to be delivered "at least two days before author's visit scheduled for April 25." The books arrive on April 23, but all copies have been damaged badly by water during transit. Assuming the seller had the risk of loss during transit and buyer rejects the books, does seller have a right to cure? If so, when must seller effect the cure?

Problem 17-8. Charles buys a new car, which he picks up from the dealer on April 1, the promised delivery date. The next day, Charles discovers that the spare tire compartment in the trunk is empty and the car has a cassette player/radio rather than the CD player/radio that he had ordered. He calls the dealer, describes the problems, and says he does not want to keep the car. The dealer asks Charles to bring the car back, but Charles refuses, telling the dealer the car will be parked in front of his house and can be picked up at any time. Did Charles rightfully and effectively reject? Does seller have a right to cure? Should Charles have brought the car back to the dealer?

Problem 17-9. Nancy purchases a new car. Three days later, the car stalls, and when she starts it again, it makes loud clanging noises. The dealer inspects the car, reports that the engine blew out, and says it will put in a new engine and return the car to her. Can Nancy successfully demand that the dealer give her either a new car or her money back?

Problem 17-10.

(A)   On March 1, Buyer, a liquor store, enters into a contract with Seller, a wine importer and distributor, for purchase of 50 cases of wine (10 cases each of 5 varieties, 24 bottles to each case), F.O.B. Buyer's store, delivery on April 1. When the wine is delivered, six of the cases have one or two broken bottles in them. Buyer receives the goods on Friday, March 30, and phones the seller to reject the whole shipment on Monday, April 2. Did Buyer rightfully and effectively reject? If Buyer did so, would Seller have a right to cure? If so, when must Seller effect the cure?

(B)   Same as (A), but Buyer rejects the six cases with broken bottles and accepts the rest. Did Buyer rightfully reject? Could Buyer reject the nine broken bottles and accept the rest?

Willie Wilson
v.
Nick Scampoli

228 A.2d 848 (D.C. Ct. App. 1967)

Before HOOD, Chief Judge, MYERS, Associate Judge, and QUINN (Associate Judge, retired).

MYERS, Associate Judge.

This is an appeal from an order of the trial court granting rescission of a sales contract for a color television set and directing the return of the purchase price plus interest and costs.

Appellee purchased the set in question on November 4, 1965, paying the total purchase price in cash. The transaction was evidenced by a sales ticket showing the price paid and guaranteeing ninety days' free service and replacement of any defective tube and parts for a period of one year. Two days after purchase the set was delivered and uncrated, the antennae adjusted and the set plugged into an electrical outlet to "cook out."[1] When the set was turned on however, it did not function properly, the picture having a reddish tinge. Appellant's delivery man advised the buyer's daughter, Mrs. Kolley, that it was not his duty to tune in or adjust the color but that a service representative would shortly call at her house for that purpose. After the departure of the delivery men, Mrs. Kolley unplugged the set and did not use it.[2]

On November 8, 1965, a service representative arrived, and after spending an hour in an effort to eliminate the red cast from the picture advised Mrs. Kolley that he would have to remove the chassis from the cabinet and take it to the shop as he could not determine the cause of the difficulty from his examination at the house. He also made a written memorandum of his service call, noting that the television "Needs Shop Work (Red Screen)." Mrs. Kolley refused to allow the chassis to be removed, asserting she did not want a "repaired" set but another "brand new" set. Later she demanded the return of the purchase price, although retaining the set. Appellant refused to refund the purchase price, but renewed his offer to adjust, repair, or, if the set could not be made to function properly, to replace it. Ultimately, appellee instituted this suit against appellant seeking a refund of the purchase price. After a trial, the court ruled that "under the facts and circumstances the complaint is justified. [The court ordered the set returned to the defendant and the purchase price returned to the plaintiff.]

Appellant does not contest the jurisdiction of the trial court to order rescission in a proper case, but contends the trial judge erred in holding that rescission here was appropriate. He argues that he was always willing to comply with the terms of the sale either

---

[1] Such a "cook out," usually over several days, allows the set to magnetize itself and to heat up the circuit in order to indicate faulty wiring.

[2] Appellee, who made his home with Mrs. Kolley, had been hospitalized shortly before delivery of the set. The remaining negotiations were carried on by Mrs. Kolley, acting on behalf of her father.

by correcting the malfunction by minor repairs or, in the event the set could not be made thereby properly operative, by replacement; that as he was denied the opportunity to try to correct the difficulty, he did not breach the contract of sale or any warranty thereunder, expressed or implied.[3]

. . . .

A retail dealer would certainly expect and have reasonable grounds to believe that merchandise like color television sets, new and delivered as crated at the factory, would be acceptable as delivered and that, if defective in some way, he would have the right to substitute a conforming tender. The question then resolves itself to whether the dealer may conform his tender by adjustment or minor repair or whether he must conform by substituting brand new merchandise. The problem seems to be one of first impression in other jurisdictions adopting the Uniform Commercial Code as well as in the District of Columbia.

Although the Official Code Comments do not reach this precise issue,

there are cases and comments under other provisions of the Code which indicate that under certain circumstances repairs and adjustments are contemplated as remedies under implied warranties. In L & L Sales Co. v. Little Brown Jug, Inc., 12 Pa.Dist. & Co.R.2d 469 (Phila.County Ct.1957), where the language of a disclaimer was found insufficient to defeat warranties under §§ 2-314 and 2-315, the court noted that the buyer had notified the seller of defects in the merchandise, and as the seller was unable to remedy them and later refused to accept return of the articles, it was held to be a breach of warranty. In Hall v. Everett Motors, Inc., 340 Mass. 430, 165 N.E.2d 107 (1960), decided shortly before the effective date of the Code in Massachusetts, the court reluctantly found that a disclaimer of warranties was sufficient to insulate the seller. Several references were made in the ruling to the seller's unsuccessful attempts at repairs, the court indicating the result would have been different under the Code.

While these cases provide no mandate to require the buyer to accept patchwork goods or substantially repaired articles in lieu of flawless merchandise, they do indicate that minor repairs or reasonable adjustments are frequently the means by which an imperfect tender may be cured. In discussing the analogous question of defective title, it has been stated that:

> The seller, then, should be able to cure (the defect) under subsection 2-508(2) in those cases in which he can do so without subjecting the buyer to any great inconvenience, risk or loss. Hawkland, Curing an Improper Tender of Title to Chattels: Past, Present and Commercial Code, 46

---

[3] Appellee maintains that the delivery of a color television set with a malfunctioning color control is a breach of both an implied warranty of merchantability (D.C. Code § 28:2-314 (Supp. V, 1966)) and of an implied warranty of fitness for a particular purpose (D.C. Code § 28:2-315 (Supp. V, 1966)) and as such is a basis for the right to rescission of the sale. We find it unnecessary to determine whether a set sold under the circumstances of this case gives rise to an implied warranty of fitness for a particular purpose or whether, as appellant contends, the remedial provisions of the express warranties bind the buyer to accept these same remedial provisions as sole remedies under an implied warranty.

Minn.L.Rev. 697, 724 (1962). See also Willier & Hart, Forms and Procedures under the UCC, 24.07 (4); D.C.Code § 28:2-608(1)(a) (Supp. V, 1966).

Removal of a television chassis for a short period of time in order to determine the cause of color malfunction and ascertain the extent of adjustment or correction needed to effect full operational efficiency presents no great inconvenience to the buyer. In the instant case, appellant's expert witness testified that this was not infrequently necessary with new televisions. Should the set be defective in workmanship or parts, the loss would be upon the manufacturer who warranted it free from mechanical defect. Here the adamant refusal of Mrs. Kolley, acting on behalf of appellee, to allow inspection essential to the determination of the cause of the excessive red tinge to the picture defeated any effort by the seller to provide timely repair or even replacement of the set if the difficulty could not be corrected. The cause of the defect might have been minor and easily adjusted or it may have been substantial and required replacement by another new set—but the seller was never given an adequate opportunity to make a determination.

We do not hold that appellant has no liability to appellee,[4] but as he was denied access and a reasonable opportunity to repair, appellee has not shown a breach of warranty entitling him either to a brand new set or to rescission. We therefore reverse the judgment of the trial court granting rescission and directing the return of the purchase price of the set.

Reversed.

---

[4] Appellant on appeal has renewed his willingness to remedy any defect in the tender, and thus there is no problem of expiration of his warranties. He should be afforded the right to inspect and correct any malfunction. If appellee refuses to allow appellant an opportunity to do so, then no cause of action can lie for breach of warranty, express or implied, and the loss must be borne by appellee.

Frank Bartus
v.
Frank Riccardi

284 N.Y.S.2d 222 (City Ct. 1967)

HAROLD H. HYMES, Judge.

The plaintiff is a franchised representative of Acousticon, a manufacturer of hearing aids. On January 15, 1966, the defendant signed a contract to purchase a Model A-660 Acousticon hearing aid from the plaintiff. The defendant specified Model A-660 because he had been tested at a hearing aid clinic and had been informed that the best hearing aid for his condition was this Acousticon model. An ear mold was fitted to the defendant and the plaintiff ordered Model A-660 from Acousticon.

On February 2, 1966, in response to a call from the plaintiff the defendant went to the plaintiff's office for his hearing aid. At that time he was informed that Model A-660 had been modified and improved, and that it was now called Model A-665. This newer model had been delivered by Acousticon for the defendant's use. The defendant denies that he understood this was a different model number. The hearing aid was fitted to the defendant. The defendant complained about the noise, but was assured by the plaintiff that he would get used to it.

The defendant tried out the new hearing aid for the next few days for a total use of 15 hours. He went back to the hearing clinic, where he was informed that the hearing aid was not the model that he had been advised to buy. On February 8, 1966, he returned to the plaintiff's office complaining that the hearing aid gave him a headache, and that it was not the model he had ordered. He returned the hearing aid to the plaintiff, for which he received a receipt. At that time the plaintiff offered to get Model A-660 for the defendant. The defendant neither consented to nor refused the offer. No mention was made by either party about canceling the contract, and the receipt given by the plaintiff contained no notation or indication that the plaintiff considered the contract canceled or rescinded.

The plaintiff immediately informed Acousticon of the defendant's complaint. By letter dated February 14, 1966, Acousticon writing directly to the defendant, informed him that Model A-665 was an improved version of model A-660, and that they would either replace the model that had been delivered to him or would obtain Model A-660 for him. He was asked to advise the plaintiff immediately of his decision so that they could effect a prompt exchange. After receiving this letter the defendant decided that he did not want any hearing aid from the plaintiff, and he refused to accept the tender of a replacement, whether it be Model A-665 or A-660.

The plaintiff is suing for the balance due on the contract. Although he had made a down payment of $80.00, the defendant made no claim for repayment of his down payment until the case was ready to go to trial. The plaintiff objected to the counterclaim as being untimely. There is nothing in the pleadings to show that such a claim had been previously made by the defendant and, therefore, the court will not consider any counterclaim in this matter.

The question before the court is whether or not the plaintiff, having delivered a model which admittedly is not in exact conformity with the contract, can nevertheless recover in view of his subsequent tender of the model that did meet the terms of the contract.

The defendant contends that since there was an improper delivery of goods, the buyer has the right to reject the same under Sections 2-601 and 2-602(2)(c) of the Uniform Commercial Code. He further contends that even if the defendant had accepted delivery he may, under Section 2-608(1)(b) of the U.C.C., revoke his acceptance of the goods because "his acceptance was reasonably induced . . . by the seller's assurances." He also relies on Section 2-711, claiming that he may recover not only the down payment but also consequential damages.

The defendant, however, has neglected to take into account Section 2-508 of the Uniform Commercial Code which has added a new dimension to the concept of strict performance. This section permits a seller to cure a non-conforming delivery under certain circumstances. Subparagraph (1) of this section enacts into statutory law what had been New York case law. This permits a seller to cure a non-conforming delivery before the expiration of the contract time by notifying the buyer of his intention to so cure and by making a delivery within the contract period. This has long been the accepted rule in New York. (Lowinson v. Newman, 201 App.Div. 266, 194 N.Y.S. 253; Portfolio v. Rubin, 196 App.Div. 316, 187 N.Y.S. 302).

However, the U.C.C. in sub-paragraph (2) of Section 2-508 goes further and extends beyond the contract

time the right of the seller to cure a defective performance.   Under this provision, even where the contract period has expired and the buyer has rejected a non-conforming tender or has revoked an acceptance, the seller may "substitute a conforming tender" if he had "reasonable grounds to believe" that the nonconforming tender would be accepted, and "if he seasonably notifies the buyer" of his intention "to substitute a conforming tender." (51 NY Jur. Sales, p. 41).

This in effect extends the contract period beyond the date set forth in the contract itself unless the buyer requires strict performance by including such a clause in the contract.

"The section (2-508(2) U.C.C.) rejects the time-honored and perhaps time-worn notion that the proper way to assure effective results in commercial transactions is to require strict performance. Under the Code a buyer who insists upon such strict performance must rely on a special term in his agreement or the fact that the seller knows as a commercial matter that strict performance is required." (48 Cornell Law Quarterly 13; 29 Albany Law Review 260).

This section seeks to avoid injustice to the seller by reason of a surprise rejection by the buyer.   (Official Comment, McKinney's Cons.Laws of N.Y., Book 62 1/2, Uniform Commercial Code, Section 2-508).

An additional burden, therefore, is placed upon the buyer by this section. "As a result a buyer may learn that even though he rejected or revoked his acceptance within the terms of Sections 2-601 and 2-711, he still may have to allow the seller additional time to meet the terms of the contract by substituting delivery of conforming goods." (Bender's U.C.C. Service—Sales and Bulk Transfers—Vol. 3, Section 14-02(1)(a)(ii)).

Has the plaintiff in this case complied with the conditions of Section 2-508?

The model delivered to the defendant was a newer and improved version of the model than was actually ordered. Of course, the defendant is entitled to receive the model that he ordered even though it may be an older type. But under the circumstances the plaintiff had reasonable grounds to believe that the newer model would be accepted by the defendant.

The plaintiff acted within a reasonable time to notify the defendant of his tender of a conforming model. (Section 1-204 U.C.C.). The defendant had not purchased another hearing aid elsewhere. His position had not been altered by reason of the original non-conforming tender.

The plaintiff made a proper subsequent conforming tender pursuant to Section 2-508(2) of the Uniform Commercial Code.

Judgment is granted to plaintiff.

Assignment 18: Buyer's Rights and Duties after Tender, Part II: Acceptance and Revocation of Acceptance of Goods, Risk of Loss in Presence of Breach

§§ 2-510, 2-606 through 2-608, 2-717

Recall the flowchart used in Assignment 17 to outline a buyer's handling of the goods after the seller's tender and delivery:

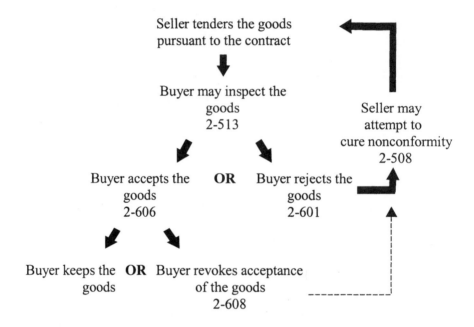

In this assignment, we will address acceptance and revocation of acceptance (the left side of the flowchart). We will also return to the topic of risk of loss, considering what happens when buyer or seller breaches.

Reading the Code: Acceptance of the Goods

Problem 18-1. What Constitutes Acceptance. Read 2-513(1) and 2-606, then fill in the following blanks, based on 2-606(1)(a), (b), and (c):

To prove that the buyer accepted the goods, the seller would have to prove that

(1)   the buyer _____

        and then the buyer _____

        _____

OR

(2)   the buyer _____

        as long as the buyer _____

OR

(3)   the buyer _____

        _____

Problem 18-2. Acts Inconsistent With Seller's Ownership. Recall that 2-606(1)(c) indicates that an "act inconsistent with the seller's ownership" constitutes acceptance.

(A)   What does it mean to say an action is "inconsistent with seller's ownership"? See 2-606 comment 4 (first paragraph). What kinds of action by the buyer with respect to the goods might fit that description?

(B)   Read 2-602(2)(a). When is an act that is inconsistent with seller's ownership *wrongful* as against the seller? What are the consequences if it is wrongful?

(C)   Read 2-606 comment 4 (1st paragraph), and consider 2-603, 2-604, and 2-513. What actions by the buyer with respect to the goods will *not* constitute an acceptance under 2-606(1)(c)?

2003 (D)   Read the 2003 amended version of 2-602(2) and 2-606(1)(c), and new 2-608(4) and comment 8. Under these revised provisions, what actions by the buyer with respect to the goods will *not* constitute an acceptance under 2-606(1)(c)?

Problem 18-3. Consequences of Acceptance. Read 2-607(1) to (4) and the associated comments.

(A)   Can a buyer reject goods after accepting them?

(B)   Does a seller have a right to cure after the buyer has accepted defective goods? Should a seller offer to cure?

(C)   Read 2-717. Does 2-607(1) mean a buyer must pay full price for any accepted goods despite the existence of defects in the goods?

(D)   Who (buyer or seller) has the burden of establishing whether the goods were defective under each of the circumstances given below?

         _____   a buyer rejects goods and then files suit, seeking damages
         _____   a buyer rejects goods and the seller files suit, claiming breach by the buyer
         _____   a buyer accepts goods and then files suit, seeking damages
         _____   a buyer accepts goods and refuses to pay full price, saying the goods were defective; the seller files suit, claiming breach by the buyer

Problem 18-4. Notifying Seller of Breach. In order to permit sellers to correct deficiencies, mitigate damages, prepare for litigation, and negotiate regarding defects in the goods or tender, buyers are required by 2-607(3) to convey information to sellers about the defects. Read 2-607(3)(a) and comments 4 and 5.

(A)   What information must a buyer convey to the seller after discovery of a defect in accepted goods?

(B)   Is notice required only from the immediate buyer to the immediate seller?

(C)   When must 2-607(3)(a) notice be given?

(D)   What happens if the buyer does not give the required notice?

2003 (E)   Read the 2003 amended version of 2-607(3)(a). How does the revision change your answers to (A) through (D) above?

Notice Under 2-607

In an effort to further the purposes of the 2-607 notice requirement, some courts have interpreted 2-607(3) as requiring the buyer to give more detailed information to sellers than seems compelled by the language of the section and its comments. The consequences of failing to give adequate notice are sufficiently severe that buyers are well advised to include more rather than less information when notifying sellers of deficiencies.

Some courts have ruled that a buyer fulfills its duty to notify remote sellers that an injury has occurred by notifying the immediate seller who, it is assumed, will pass the information up the distribution chain. Caution nonetheless suggests that a buyer notify all those against whom the buyer may seek liability.

Buyer's Reasonable Opportunity to Inspect

Recall from Assignment 17 that rejection must occur within a reasonable time after delivery or tender, and a "reasonable time" must include a reasonable opportunity for the buyer to inspect. We now know that a buyer's acceptance of the goods also depends on the existence of a reasonable opportunity to inspect. Just what constitutes a reasonable opportunity to inspect is a question of fact highly dependent upon the circumstances of each case. In deciding whether the buyer has had a reasonable opportunity to inspect, courts consider factors such as the following:

- the contract terms (e.g., does the agreement indicate who will inspect or by when inspection is expected to occur?);
- trade usages (e.g., is it the usual practice for wholesalers to inspect only when a resale contract is created?);
- the way the parties treated previous deliveries under this or other contracts;
- the circumstances of delivery (e.g., were the goods delivered to a remote location?);
- the availability of inspection facilities;
- the nature of the goods (e.g., are the goods likely to change condition rapidly and so should be inspected quickly? are the goods complex, requiring more time and effort to inspect adequately? how long will it take to see if the product will perform as promised?);
- the nature of the defect (e.g., are the goods likely to have hidden defects? can the particular defect at issue be found only after putting the goods to use? should the alleged defects have been detectable quickly?);
- the nature of the buyer (e.g., is the buyer an expert who can detect defects more easily?); and
- whether the seller promised and/or attempted to make repairs to defective goods, which will extend the inspection period.

As one court has noted, a reasonable time to inspect must generally allow the buyer an opportunity to put the product to its intended use or to test the product to verify its capability to perform as intended. The reasonable opportunity to inspect may last as little as a day or as long as a year, depending upon the particular circumstances. For example:

- In *Miron v. Yonkers Raceway, Inc.*, 400 F.2d 112 (2d Cir. 1968), the court found rejection of an auctioned racehorse within 24 hours was untimely because such goods can change condition rapidly so inspection for detectable and easily caused problems (in this instance, a fractured bone in the horse's foreleg) must be conducted immediately after the sale. In *Brodsky v. Nerud,* 414 N.Y.S.2d 38 (App. Div. 1979), on the other hand, the purchased horse was rejected because it was a gelding, not a colt, and rejection the day after delivery was considered to be timely.

- In *Askco Engineering Corp. v. Mobil Chemical Corp.,* 535 S.W.2d 893 (Tex. Civ. App. 1976), the court found no acceptance even though the buyer's representative inspected the purchased scrap plastic before shipment, because the particular defects could not be detected by a visual or manual inspection and the contract provided for inspection upon arrival of the goods.

- In *United Air Lines, Inc. v. Conductron Corp.,* 387 N.E.2d 1272 (Ill. Ct. App. 1979), a reasonable opportunity to inspect had not passed even though the buyer had possession of the purchased flight simulator for 6 weeks. The agreement contemplated that testing would occur on buyer's property after delivery and that acceptance would occur only when the testing was completed and FAA certification received.

- In *Hidden Brook Air, Inc. v. Thabet Aviation,* 241 F. Supp. 2d 246 (S.D.N.Y. 2002), the court found acceptance of the purchased airplane occurred even before the buyer took possession of the aircraft because the buyer had inspected the plane visually twice and had sent the plane to a third party for inspection as provided in the purchase agreement.

- In *Michael M. Berlin & Co. v. Whiting Manufacturing, Inc.,* 5 U.C.C. Rep. Serv. 357 (N.Y. Sup. Ct. 1968), the delivered steel sheets could have been easily measured with a micrometer upon delivery so buyer could not wait six weeks to discover the defect in thickness and an additional seven weeks to notify the seller.

- In *GNP Commodities, Inc. v. Walsh Heffernan Co.,* 420 N.E.2d 659 (Ill. Ct. App. 1981), the buyer's inspection of frozen pork bellies two months after purchase was timely because trade usage contemplated inspection of warehoused goods only when the buyer was ready to deliver the goods under a resale contract. Similarly, in *La Villa Fair v. Lewis Carpet Mills, Inc.*, 548 P.2d 825 (Kan. 1976), rejection of carpet after nine months was considered timely because seller knew the buyer could not install the carpet until a construction strike ended and industry practice was to inspect only when the purchaser was ready to use the carpet.

- In *Oda Nursery, Inc. v. Garcia Tree & Lawn, Inc.*, 708 P.2d 1039 (N.M. 1985), four months was held as a matter of law to exceed the reasonable time to inspect living juniper plants and reject them if defective.
- In *Zabriskie Chevrolet, Inc. v. Smith*, 240 A.2d 195 (N.J. Sup. 1968), a "spin around the block" before purchase was not a reasonable opportunity to inspect a car.
- In *Don's Marine, Inc. v. Haldeman,* 557 S.W.2d 826 (Tex. Civ. App. 1977), thirty days was a reasonable time to inspect a boat to determine if it had a quiet, smooth, and dry ride, especially because the buyer had the opportunity to use the boat only on weekends.

The reasonable opportunity to inspect always involves factual questions and balancing the kinds of factors listed above. Whenever you must determine whether acceptance has occurred (as in Problem 18-5, below), you should consider whether a reasonable opportunity to inspect has passed—and be creative in identifying arguments to extend or narrow the period of time allowed.

Applying the Code: Acceptance of Goods

Problem 18-5. Read comment 3 to 2-606 and review the list of relevant factors in the note above on Buyer's Reasonable Opportunity to Inspect. Each scenario below may or may not result in an acceptance under 2-606. For each scenario, make the best arguments for finding that acceptance has occurred, and the best arguments for finding that acceptance has *not* occurred. If you think one arguments should clearly win, indicate the likely outcome. Be sure to note which subsection of 2-606(1) you rely on in each of your arguments.

(A)   Buyer of a new car arrives at the showroom to pick up the vehicle. She signs all the final paperwork and pays for the car. The car is brought from the service bay to the front of the parking lot, the sales agent hands her the keys, and she drives the vehicle two miles to her home. Did acceptance occur when she signed the paperwork? When she received the keys? By the time she arrived home with the car?

(B)   Same as (A), but one week after Buyer drives the vehicle home, the salesperson calls Buyer to "see how you like the new car." Buyer says, "It's great. Just what I wanted." Has Buyer now accepted the car? Would your answer be affected if Buyer tried to return the car one week later because the car began to vibrate severely at speeds above 60 miles per hour when she first took the car out on the highway?

(C)   Buyer purchases a sweater at a retail store. He puts it in his closet for 3 weeks before noticing a hole in the back of the collar. Is it too late for him to reject the sweater? Would your answer be affected by the existence of a store policy allowing returns with a receipt within 30 days?

(D)   A grocery store receives a shipment of apples it bought from an orchard. The next day, the buyer rejects 20% of the apples because of bruises to the fruit. The remainder of the shipment is set out on the grocery shelves. Has the grocery store accepted the apples not rejected?

(E)   Buyer of a piece of farm equipment notifies Seller upon delivery that the equipment is defective. Seller assures Buyer the problems can be corrected with minor repairs and adjustments. For six months, Buyer continues to use the equipment while Seller attempts unsuccessfully to fix the machinery. At the end of six months, Buyer notifies Seller it wants to return the equipment. Has Buyer already accepted the equipment?

(F)   Buyer is a wholesale distributor of electronic goods. Seller is the manufacturer of DVD players. Seller delivers 1000 DVD players to Buyer, who immediately resells 100 of them to a retail store, still in unopened boxes. The retail store resells the DVD players to its customers (still in unopened boxes), and only then discovers (because of customer complaints) that the DVD players are accompanied by operator manuals written only in Korean. It reports this problem to the distributor. Has the Buyer (the wholesale distributor) accepted the 100 players sold to the retail store? The 900 DVD players remaining in its inventory?

(G)   Buyer takes delivery of defective goods. After notifying seller that the goods are rejected, Buyer resells them to recoup the prepaid contract price. Has Buyer accepted the resold goods?

Problem 18-6. Recall that under 1-102(3),[1] the effect of most provisions of the Code may be varied by agreement. The provisions on acceptance, rejection, and revocation are no exceptions to this general rule. Parties may, for example, agree that the buyer will have no right to inspect before acceptance occurs, leaving the buyer with only alternative remedies to rejection. See 2-513(1). As you answer the questions below, consider both the possibility of variation by agreement and the nature of the usual opportunity to inspect before acceptance.

---

[1] 1-302 in revised Article 1.

(A)   Read 2-513(3)(a) and 2-606 comment 3. Buyer orders a watch C.O.D. Does acceptance occur when the package arrives, and buyer pays the contract price and signs for delivery of the package?

(B)   Buyer of a new car arrives at the showroom to pick up the vehicle. She signs all the final paperwork, including a document entitled "Acknowledgment of Acceptance of Vehicle." She pays for the car, is given the keys, and drives the car off the lot. Did acceptance occur when the buyer signed the "Acknowledgment of Acceptance"?

Reading the Code: Revocation of Acceptance of Goods

Problem 18-7. Justifiable Revocation. Answer the following questions, using the text of 2-608, the indicated comments, and other sections that you already have read.

(A)   Read 2-608 comment 2. Under 2-608(1)(a), what facts must a buyer prove to justify revoking acceptance of goods?

(B)   Read 2-608 comment 3. Under 2-608(1)(b), what facts must a buyer prove to justify revoking acceptance of goods?

(C)   Read 2-608(2) and comments 4, 5, and 6. What must a buyer do to effectively revoke acceptance?

(D)   If a buyer effectively revokes acceptance, what are the buyer's responsibilities and options with respect to the goods?

Problem 18-8. Comparing Rejection and Revocation. It is more difficult for a buyer to establish justification for revoking acceptance (2-608) than for rejecting goods (2-601). What might explain this difference in standards?

Problem 18-9. Cure After Revocation. Because 2-508 refers only to a seller's right to cure after a buyer *rejects* goods, some courts have concluded that a seller has no right to cure after a buyer justifiably revokes acceptance. The trend in court decisions, however, has been to permit cure after revocation, using 2-508 to help determine when cure is appropriate and how long the seller has to effectuate the cure.

2003   The 2003 amended version of 2-508 codifies the court-developed rule giving seller a right to cure after the buyer's justifiable revocation, except in consumer contracts. Why is seller's right to cure limited to revocations under 2-608(1)(b)? If you can't come up with an answer, check the comments.

Applying the Code: Revocation of Acceptance

Problem 18-10. If a buyer seeks to return goods to the seller, the buyer often will argue in the alternative, claiming that it has rightfully and effectively rejected the goods before acceptance but also that, if acceptance already occurred, it has justifiably and effectively revoked acceptance. Full analysis of a problem therefore often requires consideration of both rejection and revocation of acceptance as possibilities and, as with the consideration whether acceptance has occurred, the arguments and conclusions may be highly dependent on the factual circumstances. For each of the following scenarios, make the best arguments for finding that the buyer has rejected and in the alternate has revoked acceptance of the goods. What arguments would you expect from the seller in response? Can you predict a likely outcome?

(A)   Buyer of a copy machine has problems with paper jamming and misfeeds that begin two weeks after the copier is delivered. Seller assures Buyer the problem will "solve itself" within a few days or Seller will perform any necessary repairs. After two months, Seller's repairs have been unsuccessful, and the copier still jams. Buyer notifies Seller it wants a replacement copier.

(B)   Same as (A), but in the two months Buyer has the copier, one of Buyer's employees spills a can of soda pop on the copier, causing a short circuit and sticking keys.

(C)   Charles purchases a new car. One year later, Charles has his car in for servicing and the mechanic notices rust developing on the underside. Charles discovers that the rustproofing and polymer coating listed on the invoice were not applied to the car. Charles tells the dealer he doesn't want to keep the car.

(D)   Buyer of a trailer home tells the salesperson that he needs a three-bedroom home that will fit on an existing foundation that is 70 feet long. The salesperson shows him several models, and he picks one costing $52,000. Several months later, the trailer home drifts off its foundation. Buyer discovers that the home is actually only 67 feet in length. Buyer immediately writes to Seller indicating he wants Seller to take back the trailer home.

2003 (E)   Same as (D), but Seller denies liability and refuses Buyer's demand that Seller take back the trailer and return the purchase price. Buyer continues to live in the trailer home and two months later sues Seller for breach. Consider 2-608(4) and comment 8 in the 2003 amended version, as well as unamended 2-602 and 2-608.

Reading the Code: Effect of Breach on Risk of Loss

In Assignment 13, we explored who has the risk of loss in the absence of breach by either party, as governed by 2-509. Section 2-510 covers risk of loss in the presence of certain breaches by a buyer or a seller.

Problem 18-11. Effect of Seller's Breach on Risk of Loss.

(A)   Read 2-510(1) and comments 1 and 2. What does a buyer have to prove in order to establish that the risk of loss did not shift to the buyer when the goods were delivered?

(B)   If the buyer rightfully rejects goods and the seller sends replacement goods that conform to the contract, who has the risk of loss with respect to the original shipment of goods? With respect to the replacement goods?

(C)   If a seller delivers seriously nonconforming goods but the buyer nevertheless accepts the goods, who then has the risk of loss? Read 2-510(2). Does the risk of loss shift back to the seller if the buyer has a right to revoke acceptance? If the buyer justifiably revokes acceptance?

Problem 18-12. Effect of Buyer's Breach on Risk of Loss. Read 2-510(3) and review 2-509.

(A)   If Buyer repudiates a contract while Seller is still completing manufacture of the goods, who has the risk of loss?

(B)   The parties enter into an F.O.B. destination contract, and Seller delivers conforming goods to the carrier without obtaining insurance for the shipment. Buyer repudiates while the goods are in transit. The goods are damaged while in the hands of the carrier. Who has the risk of loss?

Applying the Code: Effect of Breach on Risk of Loss

Problem 18-13. Agreement between fish merchant in Duluth and a seafood restaurant in New Orleans calling for the sale of "500 lbs. No. 1 Quality Walleye, F.O.B. Duluth, ship to port of New Orleans." The goods are shipped via a refrigerated container and loaded on a boat that travels the Mississippi River. Seller obtains and forwards to the buyer the needed documents. During shipment, the container malfunctions, and the fishspoil. After inspecting the spoiled fish, the buyer's inspection agent claims that 20% of the fish were too small to be "No. 1 Quality."

(A)   If the buyer's agent is right about the size of the fish, who has the risk of loss for the spoilage of the fish, and why?

(B)   If the buyer's agent is wrong, who has the risk of loss for the spoilage of the fish, and why?

(C)   If the contract had been F.O.B. New Orleans, who would have had the risk of loss for the spoilage of the fish? Would it have mattered if the fish had not been "No. 1 Quality"?

Problem 18-14. Stanley makes a contract to buy a new car from a dealer. The parties agree the car will be undercoated and that the car's finish will have a polymer coating. The car is delivered to Stanley on May 19. The next day the dealer calls Stanley and informs him the car was delivered without the coatings and instructs him to return the car so the coatings can be applied. Stanley does so on May 22. Sometime during the night of May 22 the car is stolen and never recovered. Stanley remains liable on his car loan and claims the dealer still owes him a car. Is Stanley right?

Problem 18-15. Return to the facts in Problem 13-14. Assume now that Terra Children does *not* send a postcard to Bianca informing her the goods were shipped. The goods never arrive and Bianca seeks a replacement shipment or a refund from Terra Children. Is she entitled to receive such relief?

Assignment 19: Insecurity, Repudiation, and Retraction

§§ 2-609 through 2-611

Reading the Code

As we have seen, a buyer or seller may breach a contract by failing to perform its obligations when performance is due. Even before the performance date arrives, however, important issues with respect to performance and breach may be raised. A party may become concerned that the other party will not perform as promised, or a party may repudiate a contract before performance is due. This assignment explores the Article 2 provisions dealing with such moments of insecurity before the performance is due.

Problem 19-1. Right to Adequate Assurance of Performance. In 2-609, the UCC provides a mechanism for parties to a contract to respond to serious uncertainties about performance that do not (yet) amount to a material breach.

(A)   Read 2-609 and comment 1. What is the justification for establishing a right to demand adequate assurance of performance?

(B)   Based on 2-609 and comments 1, 3, and 4, what constitutes "reasonable grounds for insecurity"?

(C)   Based on 2-609 and comment 2, if a party has reasonable grounds for insecurity, what actions may that party take?

(D)   Based on 2-609 and comments 3 and 4, what constitutes "adequate assurance of due performance"?

(E)   If adequate assurance of due performance is forthcoming, what should the party who demanded assurance do?

(F)   If adequate assurance of due performance is not forthcoming, what may or should the party who demanded assurance do?

Problem 19-2. Anticipatory Repudiation. Read 2-610 and its comments.

(A)   What action or actions by a party will be considered to constitute a repudiation that triggers the consequences in 2-610(a), (b), and (c)? Note that the 2003 amended version of 2-610(2) and new comment 5 codifies and reinforces standards articulated in unamended 2-610 and its comments.

(B)   Section 2-610 lists the following actions an aggrieved party may take after the other party to the contract repudiates:

•   await performance by the repudiating party, for a commercially reasonable time;
•   resort to any remedy for breach;
•   suspend its own performance;

- if the aggrieved party is the seller and the goods are unfinished, exercise reasonable commercial judgment to choose between ceasing and completing manufacture, and then seek appropriate remedies.

What is the relationship among these options for action? Must the aggrieved party choose only one action to take? If not, what combinations of actions are authorized or contemplated?

(C)   What is the relationship between 2-609 and 2-610? Which comes first, chronologically and analytically? Must a party invoke 2-609 before taking the actions specified in 2-610?

Problem 19-3. Retraction of Repudiation. Read 2-611 and its comments.

(A)   When is retraction no longer an option for the repudiating party?

(B)   How does the breaching party make an effective retraction?

(C)   After an effective retraction, can the repudiating party demand performance by the other party? Who is responsible for the costs or damages caused by any performance delays arising from the repudiation?

(D)   What is the relationship between 2-609 and 2-611?

Applying the Code

Problem 19-4. You are the attorney for a company that has a contract with a vendor, Robotics R Us, that is developing and building complex robotic machines for your client's manufacturing assembly line. Assume that the goods predominate over the services in this contract. Your client is located in Silicon Valley, in California. The contract does not contain any clauses on termination or cancellation. It does require your client to pay progress payments of 10% of the contract price each month of the six-month development and manufacturing process. The remaining 40% of the contract price is spread over the testing and acceptance phases of the contract, after delivery. So far, your client has made four of the six monthly payments. Your client had not seen any indications of trouble in the contractual relationship, until yesterday.

Yesterday, one of the company's purchasing agents attended a training program downtown and overheard two purchasing agents from two other companies talking about Robotics R Us. They each had heard, from other companies, that Robotics R Us was four to six months behind on many deliveries and was experiencing severe shortages of qualified computer engineers and programmers. Neither of these two companies had yet experienced delays on their own contracts with Robotics R Us, but both were trying to figure out how their companies should respond to such delays. Your client's purchasing agent did not participate in the conversation, but listened carefully to every word of the discussion.

She has related the contents of the conversation to you in great detail and would like to know what to do. Robotics R Us is her responsibility, because she negotiated the contract and has been authorizing the progress payments. What do you advise her to do (or not do) on behalf of the company?

Problem 19-5. Same facts as the first two paragraphs of Problem 19-4. However, substitute the following facts in lieu of the third paragraph: Your client's purchasing agent returned from the program and immediately sent Robotics R Us a letter stating that sizable delays by Robotics R Us in its other contracts were grounds for cancellation of your client's contract with Robotics R Us, so this letter served as notice of cancellation, a formal demand for the return of all payments to date, and notice that your client would seek new bids for the manufacture of the machines that were the subject of this contract.

(A)   When Robotics R Us responded that it would be consulting its attorney about the possibility of a lawsuit, the purchasing agent called you for advice. What is your advice?

(B)   If you were instead the attorney for Robotics R Us, what would you advise your client?

Assignment 20: Buyer's Remedies for Seller's Breach

§§ 2-502, 2-711 through 2-717, 2-723

Assignments 17 and 18 covered the first of two groups of buyer's remedies for seller's failure to perform according to the contract: buyer's rights under Part 6 of Article 2 to reject or revoke acceptance of the goods. This assignment covers an aggrieved buyer's additional remedies in Part 7 of Article 2, including damages and specific performance. The availability of many of these remedies depends on whether buyer kept the goods (usually by accepting them) or does not have the goods (because buyer either never received the goods or gave them back to the seller after rejection or revocation). Most of buyer's remedies appear in 2-711 through 2-717.

This assignment is one of four assignments covering the remedy provisions in Part 7 of Article 2. Assignment 20 covers the final set of buyer's remedies, Assignment 21 covers seller's remedies, Assignment 22 covers agreed-upon remedy limitations and exclusions, and Assignment 23 covers the statute of limitations. As you work on these four assignments, keep in mind the policies underlying contract remedies in general and damages in particular:

- preventing double recovery by the aggrieved party,
- abhorring a forfeiture or a windfall,
- requiring reasonable certainty in damage amounts,
- preventing the aggrieved party from recovering damages that it could have avoided (mitigated), and
- preferring the interests of the aggrieved party over those of the breaching party, when both parties' interests can't be accommodated.

These policies underlie and supplement the Code's remedy provisions, by way of 1-103.

As you explore buyer's remedies in this Assignment, keep in mind that the seller may have breached the contract by any of the following means: repudiating (anticipatory or otherwise), failing to give the buyer notice of shipment, not delivering, delivering late, delivering nonconforming goods, not tendering the required documents, tendering defective documents, making a carrier contract inappropriate to the nature of the goods (temperature control, length of trip, packing and cushioning, etc.), or wrongfully requiring the buyer to pay before inspection. Keep this range of possible breaches in mind as you complete the reading problems.

Reading the Code

Problem 20-1. Buyer's Remedies for Unaccepted Goods. Read 2-711.

(A)   Which buyer's remedies does 2-711 list for each type of breach? Place a check in a box if the remedy in the left column is at least sometimes available for the breach specified in the top row.

	Seller fails to deliver	Seller repudiates	Buyer rightfully rejects goods	Buyer justifiably revokes acceptance
2-711 Cancel contract				
2-711 Recover price paid				
2-712 Cover damages				
2-713 Market damages[1]				
2-502 Recovery of identified goods				

---

[1] Although 2-713 is entitled "Buyer's Damages for Non-delivery or Repudiation," the damages in 2-713 are commonly referred to as market damages. Section 2-713 is not limited to non-delivery and repudiation, but is available for the full range of breaches that 2-711 lists. The 2003 amended versions of 2-711 and 2-713 agree with this conclusion and make it explicit.

	Seller fails to deliver	Seller repudiates	Buyer rightfully rejects goods	Buyer justifiably revokes acceptance
2-716 Specific performance or replevin				
2-711(3) Security interest[2] in goods; resale				

(B)   In your answers to (A), does it make sense that the blank squares are blank?

(C)   Why does 2-711 provide for cancellation rather than termination? See 2-106.

[2003]   (D)   Read the 2003 amended version of 2-711. How does its content differ from the unamended version? Which remedies are truly new to Article 2, and which were merely not listed in the previous version of 2-711?

---

[2] A security interest is an interest in goods or other collateral granted to a person who makes a loan or otherwise extends credit to a person with an interest (ownership or less) in the goods. That security interest allows the creditor (now the secured party) to seize the collateral under certain circumstances and resell it to satisfy the debt. Security interests are governed largely by UCC Article 9.

Problem 20-2. Buyer's Recovery of the Goods from the Seller. Consider the plight of the aggrieved buyer who did not receive the goods (because seller repudiated or failed to deliver) but who still would like to get the goods from the seller—perhaps because the goods are scarce in the market or because the seller's skill makes the goods especially desirable. The sections below allow the buyer to recover the goods upon seller's insolvency (2-502), to obtain specific performance (2-716(1), (2)), or to replevy the goods (2-716(3)). These remedies overlap to some extent, but they address somewhat different fact situations.

(A)   Read 2-502 and describe the prerequisites for the buyer to obtain the goods from the seller under this remedy.

(B)   Read 2-716(1) and comment 2. Describe the prerequisites for the buyer to obtain specific performance from the seller under this remedy.

(C)   Read 2-716(3) and the first two sentences of comment 3. Describe the prerequisites for the buyer to obtain replevin of the goods from the seller under this remedy. (Ignore the last sentence of 2-716(3) and the remainder of comment 3, both of which pertain to a security interest issue under Article 9).

2003   (D)   Read the 2003 amended version of 2-716(1). How does its content differ from the unamended version?

Problem 20-3. Comparing Buyer's Cover and Market Damages. Consider the situation of the aggrieved buyer who does not want to obtain the goods from seller, but instead prefers money damages. Read 2-712(2) and 2-713(1).

(A)   Write out the mathematical formula for each type of damages, side by side. Use the following components: incidental damages, consequential damages, market price, cost of cover, expenses saved because of breach, and contract price. Use "+" and "–" as needed. You need not use all of the components. When you are done, consider whether each formula makes sense.

(B)   What is the key difference between the formulas for the two types of damages in (A)?

(C)   Read 2-712(1). What are the requirements for a buyer to effect a valid "cover"? Do the cover goods have to be identical to the contracted-for goods? See 2-712 comment 2.

(D)   Read 2-713(2) and 2-723(1). What do they add to your formulas in (A)?

(E)   Section 2-713(1) says market price should be measured "at the time when the buyer learned of the breach." The courts have split three ways on the question of what "learned of the breach" means when the seller anticipatorily repudiates its performance under the contract,[3] concluding it might mean

- when buyer receives notice of seller's repudiation,
- a commercially reasonable time after buyer receives notice of seller's repudiation, or
- when seller's performance would have been due.

Using 2-610, 2-611, 2-713, and 2-723, describe the arguments in favor of each interpretation above.

2003 (F)   Read the 2003 amended versions of 2-713 and 2-723. When is the market price determined for each kind of mentioned breach? (Note that the 2003 amended version of 2-723 no longer covers anticipatory repudiations.)

Problem 20-4. Expenses Saved Because of Breach. Damage calculations for both cover damages and market damages include "expenses saved in consequence of the seller's breach." In each of the factual settings below, does the buyer save expenses because of the seller's breach?

---

[3] The same issue arises in 2-708(1), the analogous seller's remedy for buyer's repudiation. This remedy is covered in Assignment 21.

_____ A buyer pays freight for the goods, per the contract. The buyer then rightfully rejects the goods and obtains cover in the seller's city, paying freight on the substitute goods.

_____ A buyer pays freight for the goods, per the contract. The buyer then rightfully rejects the goods and decides not to obtain cover, but instead to seek market damages.

_____ A seller repudiates the contract with the buyer, who was supposed to pay freight for the goods. The buyer obtains cover in the buyer's city. The buyer picks up the substitute goods with its own truck.

_____ A seller repudiates the contract with the buyer, who was supposed to pay freight for the goods. The buyer then obtains cover in the seller's city, paying freight on the substitute goods.

_____ A seller repudiates a contract with the buyer, who was supposed to pay freight for the goods under an F.O.B. shipment contract. The market price has risen, and the buyer decides not to obtain cover, but instead to seek market damages.

Problem 20-5. Incidental and Consequential Damages. Damage calculations for both cover damages and market damages include consequential and incidental damages. Under the common law, incidental damages have often been associated with the expenses of "mopping up the breach," that is, the expenses associated with mitigating or avoiding additional losses by the aggrieved party. They do not include lost profits or injuries resulting from the breaching party's defective performance. Those latter two items are instead consequential damages. Read 2-715[4] and comments 2, 3, and 5. Label the following buyer's damages as likely to be considered consequential (C), incidental (I), or neither (N):

_____ Buyer's kitchen is damaged by fire when a defective coffee pot catches fire.

_____ Buyer rejects the defective goods and pays to store them in a third party's warehouse, awaiting seller's retrieval of the goods.

---

[4] Note that 2-715 merely defines consequential and incidental damages; it does not authorize buyer to receive them. The authorization appears in the damage provisions like 2-712(2) and 2-713(1). Section 1-106(1) emphasizes this distinction when it states that "neither consequential or special nor penal damages may be had except as specifically provided in this Act or by other rule of law."

_____   Buyer is liable to its own customer for failure to timely deliver goods that buyer was to manufacture using seller's component goods, had buyer not rejected the goods because they were defective. Seller was aware of that "downstream contract" during the parties' negotiations.

_____   Buyer pulls its administrative staff off its usual duties and assigns them to phone suppliers to find "cover" goods.

_____   Buyer suffers a broken wrist from a defective woodworking tool.

_____   Buyer pays the contract price (which does not include freight) in response to a sight draft attached to the bill of lading, as required by the contract. Buyer then discovers that the goods are defective and decides to reject them. (Skip this problem if you did not complete Assignment 14.)

_____   Buyer pays U.P.S. to ship the rejected goods back to seller, after seller does not offer buyer any reshipping options.

_____   Buyer, a manufacturing company, loses $2555 in profits because it has to shut down a production line for two days to disentangle seller's defective goods from the machinery.

Problem 20-6. Choosing between Cover and Market Damages. Notice that 2-711(1) says that buyer can use 2-712 *or* 2-713. Read 2-712(1), (3), comment 3, and 2-713 comment 5. Answer the questions below, citing the authoritative language in text or comment, as well as the underlying policy that makes that answer sensible.

(A)   May the buyer elect to receive damages under 2-713, even though the buyer has made a proper cover purchase?

(B)   Must buyer effectuate cover, if possible?

(C)   If buyer does not cover, what effect does that have on damages under 2-715?

(D)   Can a buyer ever recover under both 2-712 and 2-713?

Problem 20-7. Buyer's Damages for Accepted Goods. Section 2-711 lists only buyer's remedies for *unaccepted* goods. (Consider writing that point in the margin of 2-711.) If a buyer has accepted (and not revoked acceptance of) the goods, 2-714 specifies buyer's damages, and 2-717 allows a buyer to offset its damages against the price due on the goods.

(A)   Read 2-714. Locate each of the following: a general measure of damages, a specific measure of damages for breach of warranty, and an exception to the latter. Note that subsection (3) applies to each.

(B)   In calculating breach-of-warranty damages, at what place and what time are the values of the goods determined?

(C)   Which of the following are available as 2-714 damages? For those that are, specify the applicable portion of 2-714.

____   cost of repairing the defect
____   market price of conforming goods, minus the resale price of the
         goods delivered
____   rental value of goods during repair
____   the value of the defect, based on an appraiser's testimony
____   contract price of goods minus appraiser's valuation of goods
         delivered

(D)   Read 2-717. Does this section apply to cover damages (2-712)? to market damages (2-713)? to damages to accepted goods (2-714)? If you're stumped, consider when buyer is obligated to pay the contract price.

(E)   If the buyer accepts goods that are defective and has not yet paid any portion of the contract price, what is the formula governing how much buyer has to pay seller?

Problem 20-8. Liquidated Damages. Parties can fashion their own remedies by agreement. A liquidated damage clause sets out an agreed-upon measure of damages in the event of a particular type of breach or a particular type of injury resulting from a breach. It may take the place of direct, consequential, or incidental damages. Such clauses, like other parts of an agreement, are subject to scrutiny for unconscionability. Read 2-718(1). The traditional common law rule is that the reasonableness of the amount of liquidated damages is judged at the time of contract formation. How does the UCC rule differ? What might be the logic for the UCC rule?

Applying the Code

Problem 20-9. Azin, an engineer, orders a scanner for her home computer from a mail-order company. As specified in the catalog, Seller ships it to her F.O.B. Azin's home, buyer to pay seller for shipping. Her credit-card authorization to the mail-order company includes $18.00 shipping (fairly standard price for the industry), in addition to the contract price. When the scanner arrives, the shipping box is pretty beaten up, and the plastic casing of the scanner is cracked, but the scanner works fine. In addition:

- Her mail-order price is $550 on August 28, an especially good deal on the scanner because the scanner is on sale at the beginning of the school year.
- She receives the mail-order scanner on August 30.
- The average mail-order price (without shipping) for the same model of scanner at five similar mail-order businesses is
  $575 on August 28.
  $570 on August 30.
  $600 on September 4.
  $620 on September 6.
- At six stores in Azin's area, the best price for the same model of scanner is
  $589 on August 28.
  $595 on August 30.
  $625 on September 4.
  $640 on September 6.
- Round-trip driving expense to local store, Computer Centre, is $4.70.

Each set of facts below is independent of the other sets of facts. For each question below, first ascertain the formula for the specified remedy, then locate the dollar amount for each element in the formula. You do not need to perform the actual addition and subtraction. You might not use all of the above facts in the questions below.

(A)   On August 30, Azin rightfully and effectively rejects the mail-order scanner by calling the company, describing the damage, saying that she does not want the scanner, and asking for instructions on how to reship it to the company. No instructions are forthcoming. She pays U.P.S. $22.50 to send the damaged scanner back to the mail-order company. Round-trip driving expense to U.P.S. is $9.10. Seller declines to cure.

Azin has a chance to do a quick job over the Labor Day weekend for a client, but she has to decline the job because she doesn't have a scanner at home. The job would have generated $85 in profit. The sale prices in the industry last only until Labor Day, when scanner prices go back up to normal levels. Between August 30 and September 6, Azin spends two hours on the phone getting prices from local and mail-order companies. Her net billing rate in her business is $45 per hour. On September 4, the day after Labor Day, Computer

Centre has the best price in her city on the same model of scanner ($625). Even though the price is $15 more than the average mail-order price as of that date, she decides to buy the replacement scanner locally, to avoid the hassle of possibly receiving another damaged scanner by mail order. She decides to buy the replacement scanner immediately, to avoid any further increase in prices. On September 4, she buys from Computer Centre the same model scanner that she had originally ordered, paying by check. When her credit card bill arrives with the cost of the original scanner and shipping on it, she disputes and therefore does not pay that portion of her payment. Can she get cover damages? If so, how much can she recover?

(B)   On August 30, Azin rightfully and effectively rejects the mail-order scanner by calling the company, describing the damage, saying that she does not want the scanner, and asking for instructions on how to reship the scanner to the company. No instructions are forthcoming. She pays U.P.S. $22.50 to send the damaged scanner back to the mail-order company. Round-trip driving expense to U.P.S. is $9.10. Azin has already paid the mail-order company with a $568 check, and the check cleared before she could stop payment on it. Seller declines to cure. She pays her part-time administrative assistant $24 to phone around town to determine scanner prices at various stores, but then she decides not to buy a replacement, thinking she can get by using a friend's scanner. She uses the friend's scanner to complete a Labor Day job offered by a client. If she had used the same scanner at a nearby photocopy shop, it would have cost her

$123. She pays her friend $40. How much can Azin recover from the seller by way of market and other damages?

(C)   Azin does not contact the mail-order company and does not send the damaged scanner back. She decides to have the scanner checked out by a nearby computer repair shop, to see if she can avoid the hassle of returning it. On August 30, she takes the damaged scanner to a repair shop and asks for an estimate of how much it will cost to replace the outside plastic casing and anything else that is broken. The shop calls her back on September 4 and tells her that the repair cost will be $125. She authorizes the repairs and picks up the repaired scanner on September 6. If Azin gives the mail-order company notice under 2-607(3)(a), how much does she owe the mail-order company, using 2-714 and 2-717? How much does she owe if she does not give 2-607(3)(a) notice? Assume that the credit card bill has not yet arrived and that she has not paid yet.

(D)   On August 30, Azin rightfully and effectively rejects the mail-order scanner by calling the company, describing the damage, saying that she does not want the scanner, and asking for instructions on how to reship the scanner to the company. The company asks her to ship it back via U.P.S., and says that the company will reimburse her. She does so. Her round-trip driving expense to U.P.S. is $9.10. The mail-order company replaces the cracked case and sends the scanner back to her, along with reimbursement for her shipping and driving expenses. Delighted, Azin pays the credit card bill for the scanner and uses it for a month before part of the motor overheats because a self-lubricating bearing in the scanner was damaged in the shipping accident but took a month to fail. The scanner motor is destroyed by the overheating, but the motor can be replaced. Otherwise, the scanner is fine. What are Azin's options, in terms of remedies? What is her best course of action?

Problem 20-10. Sometimes the damages formula in a Code remedy must be adjusted in order to provide full compensation but not a windfall. Consider the following examples.

(A)   What happens to your answer to Problem 20-9(A) if the buyer obtains cover with a slightly better and more expensive model of scanner (perhaps because the model she is replacing is unavailable or because buyer's needs have changed)? How might you adjust the Code formula to fit the actual solution?

(B)   What happens to your answer to Problem 20-9(C) if the buyer is not able to get the scanner fully repaired but is able to make it functional, save one or two features that still do not work? How might you adjust the Code formula to fit the actual solution? Assume that the buyer gave 2-607(3)(a) notice.

(C)   Assume that when Azin purchases her scanner, the seller also agrees to install it into her existing computer network. If goods predominate over services in the purchase, what remedies are available to Azin if the seller fails to install the scanner or installs it defectively?

Problem 20-11. For the following liquidated damage clause, what additional facts do you need to evaluate the clause's validity under 2-718(1)?

> "If Seller does not deliver each weekly installment of goods by 8 p.m. Sunday to Buyer's manufacturing plant, Seller must pay Buyer the current FedEx price of shipping substitute goods overnight from Buyer's designated alternate supplier, as well as $600."

Assignment 21: Seller's Remedies for Buyer's Breach

§§ 2-702 through 2-710, 2-718

In Assignment 20, we explored the buyer's remedies for seller's breaches. In this assignment, we turn to a consideration of buyer's breach and the remedies seller has for those breaches. Because buyer's obligation is simply to accept the goods and to pay for them (2-301), the buyer can breach in fewer ways than the seller might: repudiation (anticipatory or otherwise), wrongful rejection of the goods, unjustified revocation of acceptance, and failure to pay. Seller's remedies for buyer's breach appear in 2-702 through 2-710.

Reading the Code

Problem 21-1. Overview of Seller's Remedies. Read 2-703. This section provides an overview of the remedies available to the aggrieved seller when the buyer breaches.

(A)   Unlike 2-711, which lists the buyer's remedies according to the type of seller's breach, 2-703 lists *all* of seller's remedies for *any* kind of buyer's breach. Consider the language of 2-703 and use your own common sense to determine which of the remedies are available to the seller for each type of buyer's breach. In the chart on the next page, place a check in each applicable box if the remedy in the left column is at least sometimes available for the breach specified in the top row. (This chart omits the action for the price under 2-709 because that remedy applies only to a narrow set of facts that we will examine in Problem 21-8.)

	Buyer repudiates	Buyer fails to make payment due on or before delivery	Buyer wrongfully rejects goods	Buyer wrongfully revokes acceptance of goods
2-703 Withhold delivery				
2-705 Stop delivery				
2-704 Identify goods, resale/ completion option				
2-706 Resale and damages				
2-708 Market damages[1]				
2-703 Cancel contract				

(B)   Read comment 1 to 2-703, and note the lack of connecting conjunctions among the parts of 2-703. Recall 1-106(1)[2] and the policies underlying contract remedies (see page 279). Why is a seller not able to recover all provable remedies listed in 2-703 for any given breach by the buyer?

---

[1] Although 2-708 is entitled "Seller's Damages for Non-acceptance or Repudiation," the damages in 2-708(1) are commonly referred to as market damages. "Non-acceptance" can be wrongful rejection or unjustified revocation of acceptance of the goods."

[2] Section 1-305(a) in revised Article 1.

2003 (C)   Read the 2003 amended version of 2-703. How does its content differ from the unamended version? Which of those changes actually change the law?

Problem 21-2. Comparing Seller's Resale and Market Damages. Read 2-706(1) and 2-708(1), which provide two measures of seller's damages when the buyer has not accepted the goods.

(A)   Write out the mathematical formula for each type of damages, side by side. Use the following components: incidental damages, market price, resale price, expenses saved because of breach, and contract price. (Ignore the word "unpaid" used to describe "contract price" in 2-708(1); it probably was included in error and is omitted in the 2003 amended version.) Use "+" and "–" as needed. You need not use all of the components. When you are done, consider whether each formula makes sense.

(B)   What is the key difference between the formulas for the two types of damages in (A)?

(C)   Look back to your answer for part (A) of Problem 20-3. Compare the formulas for buyer's and seller's market damages. Then compare the formulas for buyer's cover damages and seller's resale damages. Aside from the recoverability of consequential damages, the other key difference between the two buyer's formulas and the two seller's formulas is that the order of the two main components is reversed. That is, the contract price is the item *subtracted* in one formula, but the item *subtracted from* in the other formula. Why does that difference make sense?

(D)   What do 2-708(1) and 2-723(1) say about determining the time and place at which the market price is measured?

2003   (E)   Read the 2003 amended version of 2-708(1), and note that 2-723(1) is deleted in the 2003 version. When and where is the market price determined for each kind of mentioned breach? What changes are made in the measurement of market price?

(F)   Read 2-704 and comments 1 and 2. What alternative courses of action may an aggrieved seller take under this section? How should the seller decide among these alternatives? Of what relevance are the market and resale measures of damage?

Problem 21-3. Expenses Saved Because of Breach. Damage calculations for both resale damages and market damages include "expenses saved in consequence of the buyer's breach." In each of the factual settings below, did the seller save expenses because of the buyer's breach?

_____   A buyer repudiates the contract before shipment by the seller, who was contractually obligated to pay freight for the goods. The seller resells the goods in its own city to a buyer who picks up the goods with its own truck.

_____ A seller pays freight for the goods, per the contract. The buyer then wrongfully rejects the goods, which the seller resells in the buyer's city with only a small additional shipment expense.

_____ A seller is obligated by contract to pay for cold storage of the goods in a warehouse until the buyer picks them up some time during the specified three-month period. The buyer repudiates at the end of the first week of the three-month period, so seller resells the goods to another buyer a week later.

Problem 21-4. Incidental and Consequential Damages.

(A)   Recovery for both resale and market damages include incidental damages.   Read 2-710.   Notice that there is no definition of seller's consequential damages, nor does any remedy section provide seller with consequential damages.[3]   The choice by the Code drafters not to include consequential damages for seller is inconsistent with the Restatement (Second) of Contracts § 351 but consistent with the common law rule, which originated in *Hadley v. Baxendale*.

Label the following seller's damages as likely to be considered consequential (C), incidental (I), or neither (N), keeping in mind that consequential damages are not recoverable by a seller in a contract for sale of goods:

_____ Buyer repudiates, and the seller pays for freight, inspection, and certification in the course of reselling the goods.

_____ Buyer wrongfully rejects the goods, which are perishable, and the seller pays for cold storage while looking for another buyer.

_____ Buyer wrongfully revokes acceptance, and the seller pays commission to a broker, in order to find a new buyer.

_____ Buyer repudiates, and the seller, who has not yet ordered the goods it intends to send to the buyer, loses its volume discount with its supplier. Seller then has to pay more for goods it is ordering for other buyers and so loses some profit on those sales.

---

[3] Recall from footnote 4 in Assignment 20 that 1-106(1) states that consequential damages are recoverable only as "specifically provided by this Act or by other rule of law."

_____ Seller has to take out a loan in order to cover the buyer's late payment and has to pay interest on that loan until the buyer finally pays the contract price.

_____ In the facts immediately above, the seller then pays off the principal due under the loan.

2003 (B)   The 2003 amended version of Article 2 makes a dramatic change by allowing consequential damages for the seller/payee.[4] Read the 2003 amended version of 2-710(2) and (3) and compare them to 2-715(2), which was not amended. How do the two differ? Read comment 2 to amended 2-710. In what circumstance is seller likely to have consequential damages?

Problem 21-5. Requirements for Resale. Read 2-706.

(A)   Under 2-706(1) and (2), what are the requirements for a valid resale?

(B)   What function do 2-706(3) and (4) serve, relative to (1) and (2)?

Problem 21-6. Choosing between Resale and Market Damages.

(A)   Read 2-703 comment 1 and 2-706 comment 2. Also review your answers to Problem 20-6 on buyer's ability to choose between cover and market damages. Both resale and market damages are available to a seller, which poses

---

2003 [4] The effects of this change ripple through amended 2-706(1), 2-708(1) and (2), and 2-709(1), all of which include consequential damages in the list of damages that seller can recover.

a similar problem: 2-703 seems to give the seller a choice between 2-706 resale damages and 2-708(1) market damages. But may the seller freely choose between these two measures of damages? The case law on this issue is split.

To see the problem clearly, consider the following hypothetical: Suppose that the contract price is $1000. Buyer wrongfully repudiates. The market price at the time and place of the would-be tender is $800. Seller resells for $900, complying in all respects with 2-706. Seller could, therefore, sue Buyer for damages under 2-706, recovering $100. However, Seller could get a larger recovery ($200) under 2-708(1), because the resale brought a price higher than the market price at the time and place of tender.[5]

Must Seller attempt a resale, if it seems commercially feasible? If Seller does not attempt to resell when it is commercially feasible, does that choice bar some of Seller's damages? May Seller elect to recover under 2-708(1), even though a proper resale has occurred? Be prepared to argue, as appropriate, from the statute and its comments, from your answers to Problem 20-6, and from public policy, including whether the buyer or the seller should reap the advantage of the market's fluctuations.

---

[5] How could this be possible? Seller might have found a buyer willing to pay above market price for fast delivery or may simply have driven a hard bargain and done better than market value. Or perhaps the market price rose after the time of tender (which is the time at which 2-708 damages are measured), allowing the seller to resell at the then market price, which is higher than the amount used for 2-708(1).

2003   (B)   Read the 2003 amended version of 2-706(7) and comment 11, and 2-710(2). How does this change your answer to some or all of the questions above?

Problem 21-7. Recovery of Prepayment by Breaching Buyer. Recall that 2-711(3) allows an *aggrieved* buyer to recover any price already paid (unless buyer has accepted the goods). What rights does a *breaching* buyer have to recover part or all of the price already paid, and how does that affect seller's right to collect damages?

(A)   Read 2-718(2). What part of the buyer's prepayment is an aggrieved seller allowed to keep under this provision?

(B)   Read 2-718(3). What part of the buyer's prepayment is an aggrieved seller allowed to keep under this provision?

(C)   Buyer and Seller enter a contract for $1000. Buyer pays a deposit of $500. Buyer breaches, and Seller justifiably withholds delivery. Seller establishes damages under 2-706 in the amount of $150. What portion of the prepayment may Seller keep under 2-718(2)? under 2-718(3)? What arguments can you make for and against the seller being able to keep both amounts? (The case law on this latter question is split.)

2003 (D)   Read the 2003 amended version of 2-718(2) and (3) and comments 5 and 6. How do these changes affect the rules in these subsections?

Problem 21-8. Action for the Price.

(A)   A seller's first preference is to be able to recover the full contract price, rather than the usually smaller amount available under 2-706 or 2-708(1). However, 2-703(e) says that an aggrieved seller may recover the price only "in a proper case." Read 2-709. In what three instances can a seller recover the contract price?

      (1)

      (2)

      (3)

(B)   What restriction does the opening clause of 2-709(1) place on the applicability of this section? Consider that phrase in light of 2-507(1).

(C)   Why is seller's right to recover the price so limited? Why doesn't a seller always get the price instead of damages? Think back to the policies underlying common law contract remedies, which are listed at the beginning of Assignment 20.

Problem 21-9. Seller's Alternative to Market and Resale Damages. Recall that 2-708(1) (market damages) is "subject to subsection (2)." Read 2-708(2) and reread comment 2.

This subsection contains an alternative measure of damages when the damages in 2-708(1) are inadequate to fulfill a seller's expectation interest.[6] In addition, case law and commentators agree that 2-708(2) damages are available only if 2-706 also is inadequate to fulfill the seller's expectation interest. *Commonwealth Edison Co. v. Decker Coal Co.*, 653 F. Supp. 841 (N.D. Ill. 1987). (The 2003 amended version of 2-708(2) and comment 1(d) agree with and adopt this line of cases and commentary.) Furthermore, a seller who is able to recover the price and accompanying damages under 2-709 will be made whole under that section and will not instead choose to seek the lesser damages under 2-708(2).

(A)   Write out the mathematical formula for the damages in 2-708(2), using "+" and "−" as needed.

(B)   Consider the situation of a manufacturer who is specially manufacturing components that are suited *solely* to the needs of its buyer, where the buyer repudiates before the goods have been completed. Under 2-704(2) and comments 1 and 2 (see Problem 21-2(F)), the seller must exercise reasonable commercial judgment and therefore will decide not to complete the manufacture

---

[6] See 1-106(1), which emphasizes the Code's preference for expectation damages.

of the goods. If the seller can sell the unfinished goods for scrap or salvage value, 2-704 allows the seller to be made whole with resale damages under 2-706. But if the partially completed goods cannot be resold for scrap or salvage value, then seller cannot be fully compensated by 2-706. Nor will there be a market price for these goods, so 2-708(1) will not apply. Buyer's repudiation will prevent seller from being able to recover the price under 2-709 because the requirements of that rule will not have been met.

Write the formula for 2-708(2) damages as it would apply to these facts. Will those damages meet the requirement of 1-106 by putting the components manufacturer in as good a position as performance would have? Leaving aside the issue of overhead, for the moment, what facts would you need to calculate seller's profit?

(C)   Accountants have spent many hours on the witness stand analyzing what constitutes "overhead" under 2-708(2). White and Summers sum up the debate with the following advice:

> Presumably the Code gives the seller net profit after taxes plus that part of his fixed costs which he would have satisfied out of the proceeds from this contract. Courts should not be hesitant to award more than the plaintiff's net profit; a contract with a theoretical net profit of zero may nevertheless carry a substantial economic benefit to the contracting party. . . . [I]t is logical and also consistent with the policy of 1-106 to award the seller not only its net profit but also that pro rata share of its fixed costs which the broken contract would have satisfied.[7]

---

[7] James J. White & Robert S. Summers, *Uniform Commercial Code* § 7-13, at 290 (5th ed. 2000).

What facts would you need to calculate the recoverable overhead of the components manufacturer, based on the facts in (B)?

(D)   Damages under 2-708(2) also are used to compensate a "lost-volume seller"—a seller who is left with the goods and must "use up" a future customer in order to resell those goods, thereby losing the extra profit on the additional sale that is no longer possible. The case law has furnished additional criteria for judging whether a seller is a lost-volume seller and therefore entitled to 2-708(2) damages. Some of those criteria are now compiled in the second paragraph of comment 5 to the 2003 amended version of 2-708. Read that comment and list the criteria.

Case law has furnished two additional criteria. Read the following case summaries and identify these criteria.

Buyer entered into contract to buy gasoline from seller, then repudiated. Seller was able to resell the gasoline to another buyer. Court held that a seller had lost volume and could recover under 2-708(2) because the resale buyer would have been solicited by seller had there been no breach, that solicitation would have been successful, and seller could have performed the additional contract. *Tri-State Petroleum Corp. v. Saber Energy, Inc.*, 845 F.2d 575 (5th Cir. 1988).

When a buyer repudiated his contractual obligation to buy a mobile home, the buyer's father offered to buy that mobile home from the seller. After the seller instead sold that mobile home to another buyer, the court denied recovery of 2-708(2) damages to seller, reasoning that the seller could have mitigated its damages by selling to the father, in which case the seller would not have lost the profit associated with "using up" the resale buyer. The father would not have been available as a second buyer if his son had not repudiated the first contract. *Schiavi Mobile Homes, Inc. v. Gironda*, 463 A.2d 722 (Me. 1983).

(E)   Courts and commentators have found it necessary to "tweak" the 2-708(2) formula when applying it to different types of fact situations, so as to fashion a remedy that fully meets seller's expectation interest, while preventing seller's double recovery and barring damages for avoidable losses. For example, courts sometimes have ignored the phrases giving "due allowance for costs reasonably incurred" and "due credit for payments or proceeds of resale." The 2003 amended version of 2-708(2) no longer contains these phrases. Read comment 1(e), which explains this deletion. Explain, in your own words, in which fact situations these two aspects of damages should *not* apply.

Problem 21-10. Seller's Right to Stop Delivery.

(A)   Read 2-705(1).[8] In what four situations may an aggrieved seller stop delivery of the goods?

2003 [8] The 2003 amended version of 2-705(1) does not include the phrase "and may stop delivery of carload, truckload, planeload or larger shipments of express or freight." Although the comments do not explain this deletion, Professor Kunz learned firsthand during the drafting meetings that the shipping industry is now able to stop containers smaller than car-, truck-, or plane-loads, so the size minimum is no longer necessary to prevent undue burden on carriers, the rationale offered in comment 1 to the unamended version of 2-105.

(B)   Read 2-705(2) and the second paragraph of comment 2. What is the common idea behind (a) through (d)?

(C)   Read 2-705(3). For whose primary benefit are these subsections?

Problem 21-11. Seller's Right to Keep or Reclaim the Goods.

(A)   Read 2-702(1) and (2). What remedies do those subsections give seller, in brief?

(B)   Under 2-702(2), what two factual elements must be present in order for the seller to be able to reclaim the goods from the buyer?

2003   (C)   Read the 2003 amended version of 2-507(2).[9] What factual elements must be present for the seller to have a right of reclamation?

---

[9] The 2003 amended version of 2-507(2) and comment 3 unify the rules and explanations in amended 2-507(2), comment 3, and PEB Commentary No. 1 (available in an appendix of the UCC).

2003 (D)   Read amended 2-702, as well as comment 3 to amended 2-507. What insight does the comment provide about the 2003 amendments to 2-507(2) and 2-702(2)?

Problem 21-12. Comparing Buyer's and Seller's Remedies. Many of buyer's and seller's remedies resemble each other or are the mirror image of each other. Fill in the chart below showing those relationships.

Buyer's remedy	Commonality	Seller's remedy
2-711	overview list	2-703
	market damages	
	substitute performance and damages	
	B keeps goods	
	specific performance	
2-711(3) (buyer's security interest)	resale of goods in possession to mitigate damages	2-704(2) (unfinished goods)
	cancellation	
	incidental damages	
	consequential damages	(what is seller's closest equivalent?)
	insolvency of other party	

Applying the Code

Problem 21-13. On February 23, the parties contract to have electrical motors shipped (F.O.B. seller's place of business) on March 6, to arrive at the buyer's factory on March 8, where the buyer is planning to install them immediately in its production line, as components in electric drills. The quantity is 1230 motors, and the buyer contracts to buy at $38 per motor. In addition:

- When bought in quantities similar to buyer's order, the price of this type of motor in buyer's city is
  - $37 on February 23.
  - $34 on March 3.
  - $33 on March 6.
  - $32 on March 8.
- When bought in quantities similar to buyer's order, the price of this type of motor in seller's city is
  - $39 on February 23.
  - $36 on March 3.
  - $35 on March 6.
  - $33 on March 8.
- When bought in quantities similar to buyer's order, seller's price for this type of motor is
  - $38 on February 23.
  - $35 on March 3.
  - $34 on March 6.
  - $32 on March 8.
- The contract calls for seller to pay freight. The freight cost is (or would be) $388.
- Seller's costs for materials and labor on each motor are $25.
- Seller's overhead expenses (taxes, building costs, administrative costs, etc.) included in the price of each motor are $2.

Each set of facts below is independent of the other sets of facts. Merely list the numbers to be added, subtracted, or multiplied; do not do the math.

(A)   On March 3, the buyer repudiates the contract before the seller ships the electric motors to buyer. Between March 3 and 8, the seller does not find any buyers who need quantities similar to buyer's order, so the seller does not resell the motors until March 8, when seller's broker finds another buyer for the seller's price on that day (seller to pay $124 freight). The seller pays the broker

$450. Assume that the seller gives the original buyer proper notice under 2-706(3) for a private sale. What are the seller's resale damages?

(B)   On March 3, the buyer repudiates the contract before the seller ships the electric motors to buyer. What are the seller's market damages?

(C)   Why can't the seller recover the price in (A) or (B)?

(D)   On March 3, the buyer repudiates the contract before the seller ships the electric motors to buyer. The motors were specially manufactured for buyer, have no reliable market price, and are not easily resalable, except to just a few of seller's customers. Seller contacts those customers and finally, on March 8, finds a customer who was planning to buy motors in May but is willing to buy these 1230 motors now for $38 apiece (seller to pay $124 freight). Assume that the seller gave the original buyer proper notice under 2-706(3) for a private sale and that the resale is in good faith and is conducted in a commercially reasonable manner. What are the seller's damages under 2-708(2)?

Assignment 22: Modification or Limitation of Remedies

§§ 2-302, 2-719

As permitted by 1-102(3), the buyer and seller are free to vary by agreement the default remedies in Parts 6 and 7 of Article 2 "except as otherwise provided in this Act." Section 2-719 expressly permits the parties to supplement, replace, or limit the default remedies, while also specifying constraints on contractual modification or limitation of remedies, as explored more fully below.

2003   As seen in Assignment 9, the 2003 version of Article 2 incorporates additional provisions on agreed remedies, specifying that a seller is obligated to perform in accordance with "remedial promises" made in a sales transaction (2-313(4)), in a record packaged with or accompanying the goods (2-313A(3)), or in an advertisement or similar communication to the public (2-313B(3)). A remedial promise is "a promise by the seller to repair or replace goods or to refund all or part of the price of goods upon the happening of a specified event," 2-103(1)(m). The specified event is usually the discovery of a defect or the failure of the goods to perform. See 2-103 comment 9. "Remedial promises" are thus a subset of the remedies that the parties may agree to under 2-719 and 1-102(3). "Remedial promises" are treated like all other agreed remedies except as they are affected by the statute of limitations. See Assignment 23.

Limitation of remedies, governed by 2-719, must be distinguished from disclaimer of warranties, governed by 2-316. A warranty disclaimer limits or excludes the extent of seller's responsibility with respect to the nature and quality of the goods. A remedy limitation modifies the nature and extent of relief otherwise available for a party's breach of warranty or other contract obligation (e.g., damages, right to reject or revoke acceptance, specific performance).

A note of explanation on vocabulary: This assignment refers to any agreed-to changes in the parties' remedies as "remedy limitations." A remedy after it has been altered by the remedy limitation is a "limited remedy."

Reading the Code

Problem 22-1. Remedy Limitations in General. Read 2-719(1) and (3).

(A)   How do these subsections restrict the seller's ability to limit or exclude buyer's consequential damages?

(B)   What other restrictions do these subsections place on the buyer's or seller's ability to limit or exclude the other party's remedies?

Problem 22-2. Making Limited Remedies Exclusive. Read 2-719 comment 2. Do any of the following clauses prevent buyer from collecting damages?

(A)   "Seller may repair or replace any defective goods."

(B)   "Buyer's remedy for any defect in manufacture is refund or replacement, at seller's option."

(C)   "Buyer's sole and exclusive remedy shall be repair or replacement of defective parts, at seller's option."

Problem 22-3. Minimum Adequate Remedy. Read 2-719 comments 1 and 3. Comment 1 says that there must be "minimum adequate remedies" or "a fair quantum of remedy" available to compensate the aggrieved party for breach of the obligations or duties created by the agreement. Comment 1 does not dictate what contractual obligation a party must assume, but rather

> aims at preventing a surprise result from occurring in which the aggrieved party, usually the buyer, is led to believe that certain obligations have been assumed by the other party to the contract, only

to find that these obligations are meaningless because other provisions of the contract unduly qualify any redress for their breach.

William D. Hawkland, *Uniform Commercial Code Series* § 2-719:2, at 2-611 (2001). Similarly, 2-313 comment 4 notes that parties are free to "make their own bargain as they wish," but "the probability is small that a real price is intended to be exchanged for a pseudo-obligation."

Section 2-719(3) and comments 1 and 3 explicitly note that unconscionable restrictions on remedies are impermissible. Section 2-302 more generally bars contract clauses that a court finds to have been unconscionable when made, and 2-302 comment 1 illustrates the "underlying basis" for that section with cases refusing to enforce certain remedy restrictions. But courts applying the common law doctrine often will not find unconscionability unless the claimant is disadvantaged by a gross disproportionality of bargaining power and has an absence of meaningful choice. Such elements are rarely present in contracts between merchants so the requirement that a party (merchant or non-merchant) must have a minimum adequate remedy expands the law's protections against surprising terms.

We have seen that, although a seller need make only the most limited representations about the goods and may disclaim all implied warranties, whatever warranties are made must be enforceable with at least minimum remedies designed to compensate in some fashion for the breach of whatever obligations remain. With that in mind, consider each of the following clauses. Is buyer deprived of a minimum adequate remedy or a fair quantum of remedy for breach in each instance?

(A)   "Seller shall not in any circumstance be liable to buyer for consequential or incidental damages."

(B)   "Return for any reason within 30 days. Store credit only."

(C)   "Seller disclaims all implied warranties, including the warranty of merchantability and the warranty of fitness for a particular purpose."

(D)   "Seller's liability for any breach of warranty shall not in any event exceed the purchase price paid to date by the buyer." (Assume the buyer has paid only 10% of the purchase price by the time buyer rightfully rejects the goods for breach of warranty.)

(E)　"Upon breach, buyer may not recover any amount in excess of $500." (Assume the contract price was $759.)

(F)　"All claims of breach must be made in writing, within 24 hours of delivery."

Remedy Provisions of the Magnuson-Moss Warranty Act

As discussed in Assignment 10, the Magnuson-Moss Warranty Act applies if (either at the time of sale or within ninety days thereafter) a supplier gives a "written warranty" or enters into a "service contract" as to a "consumer product." Recall the following definitions, focusing on the italicized portions, which pertain to remedies:

- A "written warranty" is
    (1) a written affirmation of fact or promise (by a direct or indirect supplier to the buyer) that affirms or promises that the material or workmanship of the goods is defect-free or will meet a specified level of performance over a specified period of time, or
    (2) a supplier's written *undertaking to refund, repair, replace, or take other remedial action* as to the goods upon the failure of the goods to meet contract specifications,
  if the affirmation, promise, or *undertaking* becomes part of the basis of the bargain between the supplier and the buyer for purposes other than resale of the goods.
- A "service contract" is a written *contract to perform maintenance or repair services* over a fixed period of time.

Note that neither a written representation nor a supplier's written undertaking to refund, repair, replace, or take other remedial action is a "written warranty" under Magnuson-Moss unless it is part of the basis of the bargain.[1]

---

[1] Recall that under Article 2, express warranties are effective only if they are part of the basis of the bargain, but Article 2 does not impose the same requirement on other terms of a sales contract, including promises to repair or replace.

As also discussed in Assignment 10, Magnuson-Moss establishes a mandatory two-tier system of warranty labeling for "written warranties": Full Warranty or Limited Warranty. Recall that a warrantor[2] giving a Full Warranty cannot disclaim or limit any of the implied warranties. In addition, the warrantor giving a Full Warranty must abide by the following rules on remedies and remedy limitations:

- The warrantor cannot require the consumer product owner to do more than notify the warrantor of the defect, in order to be entitled to a remedy, unless the warrantor can prove that the additional duty is reasonable.
- The warrantor must give the minimum adequate remedy of curing any breach of a written warranty within a reasonable time and without charge.
- After the warrantor has made a reasonable number of attempts to remedy defect(s), the warrantor must allow the consumer product owner to elect between refund and replacement (without charge).
- The warrantor cannot limit or exclude consequential damages for breach of a written or implied warranty, unless the limitation or exclusion is conspicuous and on the face of the warranty.

A warrantor giving a Limited Warranty has no additional restrictions, aside from those discussed in Assignment 10.

The Magnuson-Moss Warranty Act encourages consumers and warrantors to resolve their disputes without litigation by use of "informal dispute settlement mechanisms" that operate under rules set up by the Federal Trade Commission. These informal dispute settlement mechanisms often involve mediation or arbitration in private forums set up by manufacturers, trade associations, or large vendors. If a warrantor sets up a dispute settlement mechanism that complies with the Magnuson-Moss regulations, the warrantor can contractually require the consumer product owner to resort to that mechanism before pursuing judicial remedies.

---

[2] Magnuson-Moss defines a "supplier" as a person in the business of making a consumer product directly or indirectly available to consumers. A "warrantor" is a supplier or any other person who makes (or offers to make) a "written warranty" or who is (or may be) obligated under an implied warranty.

In addition, the consumer product owner must allow the warrantor a reasonable opportunity to cure before bringing suit. Federal jurisdiction is available if the total amount in controversy is at least $50,000 and, if the dispute is a class action, if it consists of at least 100 plaintiffs, each with an individual claim of at least $25. Otherwise, the suit can be brought in state court. If the consumer product owner prevails, the owner also can recover costs and attorneys' fees (based on actual time).

Problem 22-4. Magnuson-Moss Provisions.

(A)   What effect do the above provisions of Magnuson-Moss have on the following agreement term, assuming that the goods are a "consumer product"?

Full Warranty for the Life of the Product
Paragon warrants this product, for its life, to be free from defects in materials and workmanship. If a defect is found, our entire liability and your exclusive remedy shall be, at our option, free repair or replacement or a full refund, provided that you return the goods to us, postage prepaid. Paragon has no liability for any incidental or consequential damages, such as data loss. Some states do not allow the exclusion or the limitation of incidental or consequential damages, so the above limitation or exclusion may not apply to you.

(B)   How does your answer to (A) change if the heading on the above warranty is instead labeled "Warranty of Quality"?

Problem 22-5. Failure of Essential Purpose. As you have seen earlier in this assignment, the parties' remedy limitations are policed by the doctrine of unconscionability, by a requirement that exclusiveness of remedy be explicit, by the policy requiring a minimum adequate remedy, and by the provisions of Magnuson-Moss. In addition to these protections, which apply to the agreement upon formation, another doctrine—failure of essential purpose—applies to the agreement during its performance and enforcement phase. Read 2-719(2) and the last sentence of comment 1.

In order to determine whether a remedy limitation failed of its essential purpose, one must first ascertain the purpose(s) of the remedy limitation. By far, the most common limited remedy is seller's promise to repair or replace the defective goods. A common back-up limited remedy is seller's refund of the price paid to date. Other remedy limitations include a time limit on reporting defects, notice requirements for reporting defects, and buyer's obligation to transport the goods to a particular repair facility. These remedy limitations serve a variety of purposes for the parties, depending on the parties' intent, the nature of the remedy limitation, and the circumstances of the contract. For instance:

- An exclusive remedy of repair or replacement makes the buyer whole by providing the buyer with the promised goods in a reasonably timely fashion, thereby fulfilling buyer's expectation. Repair or replacement also prevents or reduces buyer's consequential damages and keeps down the cost of the goods (because seller doesn't incur litigation costs, isn't liable for consequential damages, and can furnish the repair or replacement cheaply).
- An exclusive remedy of a refund prevents seller's unjust enrichment by providing restitution to the buyer, gives back to the buyer the financial resources to obtain substitute goods, and keeps down the cost of the goods (because seller doesn't incur litigation costs and isn't liable for consequential damages).
- Time limits on buyer's reporting of defects allow the seller to have "repose," i.e., know when no further claims on the goods can be made, while encouraging buyer to act promptly to find and report defects.
- Notice requirements for buyer's reporting of defects (e.g., specifications about addressee, format, and content) allow the seller to receive the notice with certainty, reduce administrative processing costs, and promptly receive the information necessary for seller to give buyer the needed relief.

When circumstances cause "an apparently fair and reasonable" remedy limitation to fail of its essential purpose or "to deprive either party of the substantial value of the bargain," the party whose remedies were limited (usually the buyer) then can avail itself of the full range of remedies, including all of the remedies in Parts 6 and 7 of UCC Article 2. Below is a sampling of cases in which courts have found that the exclusive remedy failed of its essential purpose:

- *Bishop Logging Co. v. John Deere Industrial Equipment Co.*, 455 S.E.2d 183 (S.C. Ct. App. 1995) (exclusive remedy of repair or replacement failed of its essential purpose when seller was not able to repair several pieces of equipment for mechanized swamp logging operation, after many breakdowns and attempts to repair).
- *Murray v. Holiday Rambler, Inc.*, 265 N.W.2d 513 (Wis. 1978) (exclusive remedy of repair or replacement of defective parts in motor home contract failed of its essential purpose when many parts of motor home malfunctioned over a seven-month period and buyer took motor home to seller for repairs nine or ten times).
- *International Financial Services, Inc. v. Franz*, 515 N.W.2d 379 (Minn. App. 1994) (exclusive remedy of repair or replacement failed of its essential purpose when purchased photoplotting system was inoperable between 16% and 25% of time in the 9 months following purchase; system was serviced 19 times), *rev'd on other grounds*, 534 N.W.2d 561 (Minn. 1995).
- *Coastal Modular Corp. v. Laminators, Inc.*, 635 F.2d 1102 (4th Cir. 1980) (remedy of repair or replacement of panels Coastal had installed in air traffic control towers failed of its essential purpose because remedy contemplated replacement before panels were incorporated in construction, and buyer's cost to remove defective panels and install replacements was more than six times the cost of the panels).
- *Phillips Petroleum Co. v. Bucyrus-Erie Co.*, 388 N.W.2d 584 (Wis. 1986) (crane manufacturer sold cranes and adapters to oil company for installation on 13 of buyer's North Sea oil drilling platforms; after one crane broke loose from platform and fell into sea because seller had used nonconforming steel in adapters, Norway forbade use of all cranes until adapters were replaced on the platforms; seller's exclusive remedy of replacing defective parts in seller's plant failed of its essential purpose because buyer could be made whole only by having adapters replaced and cranes certified safe on site).

(A)   Read *Evans Industries, Inc. v. International Business Machines Co.*, at page 321. Which limited remedies were found to have failed of their essential purposes? What factual circumstances caused each failure?

(B)   Upon the failure of the limited remedy's purpose, did the law of the governing jurisdiction allow the buyer to recover consequential damages?

Note that some jurisdictions have a blanket rule permitting buyers to recover consequential damages after failure of the limited remedy, while others employ a case-by-case approach. As noted in *Ritchie Enterprises v. Honeywell Bull, Inc.*, 730 F. Supp. 1041, 1050 (D. Kan. 1990), cited by the *Evans* court, "[t]he case-by-case approach requires an evaluation of the relative bargaining strength of the parties and the allocation of risks reflected by the specific terms of the agreement," including whether the agreement contained an independent clause excluding consequential damages, to determine whether consequential damages should be excluded after failure of the limited remedy.

Problem 22-6. The Relationship between 2-718 and 2-719. As discussed in Problem 20-8, a liquidated damages term establishes an agreed-to amount that a party is to recover upon the occurrence of a particular kind of breach. The validity of liquidated damages terms is determined under the criteria in 2-718(1).

(A)   Can a liquidated damages term also be affected by the rules in 2-719? Must it be exclusive to be effective? Can it fail of its essential purpose? As you answer, consider the introductory clause in 2-719(1).

`2003`   (B)   Read the 2003 amended version of 2-718(1) and comments 1 and 4. Are your answers to (A) still valid for the 2003 amended versions of 2-718 and 2-719?

Applying the Code

Problem 22-7. Buyer runs a game arcade in a shopping mall. He purchases a flight-simulator game in which the customer sits in a chair and pilots a simulated plane using hand and foot controls while watching the simulated screen of the scene outside of the plane. The contract states that "buyer's sole and exclusive remedy for defects in the simulator is to return the defective parts to the seller, at buyer's expense, for repair or replacement, seller's choice. Seller is not, in any event, responsible for any consequential damages." The simulator catches fire and is completely destroyed. The fire also damages four other games in Buyer's arcade. The fire was caused by a wiring defect in the simulator. Buyer has nothing but a few melted plastic pieces and some charred wires to return to Seller. Seller maintains that its sole responsibility under the contract is to replace the defective wiring, which it has offered to do. Is Seller correct?

Problem 22-8. Seller is a manufacturer of nuts, bolts, and washers that hold together large items like planes, ships, trains, and buildings. Buyer is a manufacturer of construction cranes. Seller sells Buyer 150 bolts (27 inches long!), which Buyer uses in its manufacture of construction cranes. The parties' written agreement contains the following clause:

> If the bolts do not conform to Buyer's specifications, Buyer's sole and exclusive remedy is to return the nonconforming bolts to Seller for repair or replacement, Seller's choice.

Buyer sells its cranes to various customers (downstream buyers); each of those agreements contains the following clause: "Crane manufacturer promises to indemnify customer for all losses directly resulting from defects in parts or workmanship." One of its customers suffers a $456,000 loss when two of the bolts sheer off, causing the crane to topple and resulting in damage to the crane and other property, but no personal injuries. No one disputes that the accident was caused by the two bolts, both of which were defective and did not meet the Buyer's specifications in the agreement with Seller.

Buyer pays its customer for the $456,000 loss under the indemnity clause and now maintains that Seller owes the same to Buyer, as consequential damages. Seller, of course, argues that the repair-or-replacement clause is valid and has offered to replace the two defective bolts, but refuses to pay any damages. What arguments would you expect from each party?

Evans Industries, Inc.
v.
International Business Machines Co.

No. Civ.A. 01-0051, 2004 WL 241701
(E.D. La. Feb. 6, 2004)

ORDER AND REASONS

DUVAL, J.

. . . .

This case arises out of Evans Industries, Inc. ("Evans") purchase of software from J.D. Edwards[1] ("JDE") and the alleged failure thereof. . . .

. . . .

---

[1] JDEdwards has apparently been merged into PeopleSoft, Inc. Nonetheless, they will be referred to as JDE herein.

JDE develops, markets and supports Enterprise Resource Planning ("ERP") software that operates on multiple computing platforms. These software application suites support manufacturing, finance, distribution, logistic and human resources operations. There are two versions of its software application suites—World and One World.

Evans manufactures, reconditions and packages 55-gallon steel containers. It packages more than 500,000 containers a year with over 300 different products. It has plants in Harvey, Louisiana, Houston, Texas, and Cushing, Oklahoma. It is a family owned and closely-held corporation owned by Robert Evans, Janice Evans, Ronald Evans, Jan Hamilton and various grandchildren of Janice and Robert Evans.

In 1998, Evans decided it required new computer software to integrate its business onto one central system.

Responding to Evans' request, JDE on August 17, 1998, proposed its OneWorld Enterprise Software Package ("OneWorld") to meet all of Evans' needs. Evans contends that it evaluated the OneWorld package proposal, which evaluation included presentations and demonstrations by JDE and IBM. (Amended Complaint ¶¶ 8 & 9). Evans contends that there were a series of meetings with Evans, IBM, IBM Credit Corporation ("IBMCC") and JDE which culminated in a joint venture of the four entities "for the acquisition, licensing, installation, configuration and implementation of the One World package on Evans' existing computer system. (*Id.*)

Pursuant to Evans' agreement with the joint venture, Evans would be a customer of "Big Tiger" which was allegedly a joint venture between JDE and the IBM companies for the successful installation, configuration and implementation of the OneWorld package. (Amended Complaint, ¶ 10). Evans maintains that it entered into three separate agreements, the subject Agreement, another . . . on February 10, 1999 which was an Agreement for Services with IBM for the installation, configuration and implementation of the OneWorld package, and a third with IBMCC, a Term Lease Master Agreement, which purports to lease to Evans the OneWorld package and the services needed to install, configure and implement the package on Evans' computer system. (Amended Complaint ¶¶ 13-24.

JDE vehemently denies the formation of a joint venture. It contends that it suggested for purposes of completing the implementation of the OneWorld software, the Summit Group, its business partner that had successfully implemented OneWorld software at other companies, for Evans' implementation consultant. The Summit Group quoted a $693,310 estimate; JDE avers that Evans rejected the bid because it was not a fixed amount.

Furthermore, JDE argues that IBM directly contacted Evans and proposed that it would implement the OneWorld software on Evans' DEC-Alpha platform. It alleges that IBM's first proposal consisted of IBM's using "two proven methodologies- IBM's Joint Application Development Methodology (JAD) and J.D. Edward's Rapid, Economic and Predictable Implementation Methodology (REP)". That proposal allegedly envisioned:

- 8,084 [hours] of IBM's consulting time
- 9,640 in Evans core team hours
- 8 full time equivalents for Evans to complete
- 10 months completion time
- $1,800,000 cost.

Evans rejected that bid.

In February of 1999, JDE contends that IBM made a second proposal to Evans to do the implementation using "IBM's Solution Factory Implementation Methodology." JDE maintains that it is not a party to this proposal and had no obligations thereunder. JDE urges that the IBM methodology proposed was "under development" and as allegedly stated in the contract, was to be developed by IBM "in partnership with Evans and other pilot customers." That proposal provided:

- 3603 hours at $222 per hour
- fixed bid of $800,000

- four Evans employees to comprise the core team and 3800 hours of work for it
- six months to complete.

A CSMS module was not part of this proposal but was part of the first bid. Without the CSMS module ascertaining the functionality of the OneWorld software was delayed.

Thus, JDE maintains that with the February 9, 1999, contract, Evans accepted the second proposal and contracted directly with IBM for implementation services. JDE maintains that Evans knew of the risk [. . .] of going with a pilot program.

Evans alleges that to date, the OneWorld package has never been successfully installed, configured, and/or implemented and Evans has not utilized such system in its business operation. (Amended Complaint ¶ 26). Furthermore, Evans maintains that the OneWorld package provided by defendants was deficient and defective and failed to operate and function as promised. Thus, the program did not run properly and could not be remedied. Apparently, IBM did not complete its task and abandoned the job.

The instant suit was filed against IBM; that suit was removed to this Court. On May 25, 2001, JDE and IBM Credit Corporation were then joined in this suit. Evans alleged in the Amended Complaint fraud, error regarding the cause and object of its agreements with the defendant, breach of contract, detrimental reliance, unfair trade practices, and negligence.

. . . [T]he Court granted JDE's Motion to Compel Arbitration, denied Evans' Motion to Compel Arbitration as to IBM and denied IBM Credit Corporation's Motion to Dismiss. Thus, in August of 2003, after an extensive motion practice before that panel, the instant matter proceeded to Arbitration.

At the core of the dispute was J.D. Edwards' Software License, Services and Maintenance Agreement ("the Agreement") and the limits to liability that the Agreement provided. Arkansas law applied thereto. The relevant contract language is as follows:

ARTICLE V

4. WARRANTIES (A) Licensed Products: J.D. Edwards warrants that for a period of 12 months following the date of delivery of the Licensed Products to Customer's first designated site, the Licensed Products will perform in all material respects in accordance with the J.D. Edwards Source Published Product Specifications in effect at the date of this Agreement. J.D. Edwards further warrants that the J.D. Edwards Source Published Product Specifications are accurate in all material respect . . . . J.D. Edwards shall have no responsibility for problems in the Licensed Products caused by alterations or modifications made by [Evans] or a third party, or arising out of the malfunction of [Evans'] equipment or other software products not supplied by J.D. Edwards.

6. EXCLUSIVE REMEDIES For any breach of warranties contained in Section 4 of this Article, [Evan's] exclusive remedy shall be as follows:

(A) Licensed Products: Customer shall have twelve (12) months following delivery of the Licensed Products to Customer's first designated site to verify that the Licensed Products conform in all material respects with J.D. Edwards Source Published Product Specifications. [Evans] shall provide written notice of any material nonconformance to J.D. Edwards within this twelve (12)[2] month period. Such notice shall be in sufficient detail to allow J.D. Edwards to duplicate the nonconformance. J.D. Edwards shall at no additional charge, correct such nonconformance or provide a mutually acceptable plan for correction by sixty (60) days following the receipt of Customers notice by J.D. Edwards. Should J.D. Edwards fail to provide such correction or mutually acceptable plan by such date, Customer's sole and exclusive remedy shall be to terminate this Agreement as a default incapable of cure by written notice . . . . Notwithstanding the payment provisions hereof, [Evans] shall be entitled to receive a refund of the license fees paid.

(C) Maintenance: J.D. Edward agrees to correct any material nonconformance of the unmodified portion of the Licensed Product(s) to J.D. Edwards Source Published Products Specifications at no additional charge subject to the following conditions . . . . Customer shall provide notice to J.D. Edwards in sufficient detail to allow J .D. Edwards to duplicate the nonconformance. Should J.D. Edwards fail to provide such correction, Customer's sole and exclusive remedy shall [be to] receive a refund of maintenance fees paid for the nonconforming Licensed Products for the Period of Coverage during which the nonconformance occurred.

8. LIMITED LIABILITY EXCEPT FOR A) FAILURE TO COMPLY WITH THE PROPRIETARY RIGHTS OR B) THE INFRINGEMENT INDEMNITY PROVISIONS CONTAINED HEREIN:

(A) IN NO EVENT SHALL EITHER PARTY BE LIABLE TO THE OTHER PARTY FOR A MONETARY AMOUNT GREATER THAN THE AMOUNTS PAID OR DUE PURSUANT TO THIS AGREEMENT.

(B) IN NO EVENT SHALL EITHER PARTY BE LIABLE TO THE OTHER PARTY FOR ANY LOSS OR INJURIES TO EARNINGS, PROFITS OR GOODWILL, OR FOR ANY INCIDENTAL, SPECIAL, PUNITIVE OR CONSEQUENTIAL DAMAGES OF ANY PERSON OR ENTITY WHETHER ARISING IN CONTRACT, TORT OR OTHERWISE, EVEN IF EITHER PARTY HAS BEEN ADVISED OF

---

[2] While the contract called for a 6 month period, certain amendments . . . apparently included an increase to 12 month period with respect to ARTICLE V, Section 6, Exclusive Remedies, Paragraph A.

THE POSSIBILITY OF SUCH DAMAGES.

(C) THE LIMITATIONS SET FORTH IN THIS SECTION SHALL APPLY EVEN IF ANY OTHER REMEDIES FAIL OF THEIR ESSENTIAL PURPOSE.

On December 16, 2003, the Arbitration Award issued. The Panel found, *inter alia:*

1) One World Software failed to perform and was never corrected despite Evans' installation of at least three releases of the Software as well as numerous updates and corrections. The Software had not been fully developed when . . . it was sold to Evans. Apparently there is no proof that the 7.3.3.2 release had ever run on the DEC-Alpha hardware other than in a "debug" mode;

2) As such, the express warranty set forth in Paragraph 4(A) of Section V of the Software License was not performed in a professional and workmanlike manner;

3) timely notice of the failures was given;

4) "Exclusive Remedies" provision (presumably Paragraph 6) failed of its essential purpose allowing for damages in [excess] of return of the moneys paid;

5) The clause seeking to void the application of the "failure of essential purpose" theory is against public policy and unenforceable. (presumably Paragraph 8);

The Panel awarded Evans the direct cost of the IBM implementation either as a direct cost by reason of the JDE-IBM Joint Venture, or as an incidental cost because the exclusive remedies failed of their essential purposes. It further found that Evans was not entitled to further incidental or consequential damages such as lost cost savings and employee expense.

. . . .

. . . [T]he key issue before the Court on the Motion to Vacate is whether the arbitrators exceeded their powers by "ignoring" the contractual limitations, 9 U.S.C. § 10(a), or if such an award demonstrates that the arbitrator acted with "manifest disregard for the law." *Williams v. Cigna Fin. Advisors, Inc.,* 197 F.3d 752, 761 (5th Cir.1999).

. . . .

THE MOTION TO VACATE

JDE primarily contends in its Motion to Vacate that the Arbitration Panel's failure to uphold the contractual damages limitation manifestly disregards the law. It maintains that the Agreement is a fully integrated contract. Furthermore, because no fraud was found, the Panel was bound to uphold the terms of the Agreement as written, and it thus committed manifest error by awarding damages arising out of the "alleged" joint venture or as incidental damages.

Relying on Paragraph 6(a) of Section V, JDE maintains that the exclusive remedy for any breach of warranties was to terminate the Agreement as "a default incapable of cure by written notice in accordance with the termination provisions hereof." Thus, JDE contends that Evans' exclusive remedy was a refund of the License Fees it paid to JDE. Similarly as Evans purchased maintenance services from JDE under the Agreement separate from its License, Paragraph 6(c) ostensibly provided an exclusive remedy for the failure to repair which was to "receive a refund of the Maintenance fees paid for the nonconforming Licensed Product(s) for the Period of Coverage during which the nonconformance occurred" which amounts to $35,828. Moreover, Paragraph 8 of Section V as previously noted stated in essence that under no circumstances would either party be liable to the other for monetary amounts greater than the amounts paid or due under the agreement and that there could be no incidental, special, punitive or consequential damages. The paragraph then provided, "The limitations set forth in this section shall apply even if any other remedies fail of their essential purpose."

Based on these provisions, JDE contends that Evans was limited to these remedies. JDE emphasizes that JDE and Evans had even bargaining power and that Evans knew that these limitations on damages were potentially dangerous for Evans. JDE maintains that Evans was able to buy its products at a reduced price because of these limitations on liability. Because the Panel used the doctrine of "failure of purpose" as provided by Arkansas law to eliminate the limitations, JDE maintains that the Panel manifestly disregarded the law.

. . . .

A. Arkansas Law—Failure of Purpose

The leading Arkansas case discussing "failure of purpose" is *Kohlenberger, Inc.*

v. Tyson's Food, Inc., 256 Ark. 584, 510 S.W.2d 555 (1979). There, the Arkansas Supreme Court explained that under Ark.Stat.Ann.. § 85-2-719:

it was permissible for a contract to provide for remedies in substitution for those provided in the UCC or to limit or alter the measure of damages recoverable by limiting the buyer's remedies to return of the goods and repayment of the price or to repair and replacement of non-conforming goods or parts and to make the remedy agreed upon the sole remedy, unless circumstances cause the exclusive or limited remedy to fail of its essential purpose. It was also permissible, under the same section, to limit or exclude consequential damages, unless the limitation or exclusion is unconscionable.

Kohlenberger at 597-98, 510 S.W.2d 555. . . . [I]n *Great Dane v. Malvern Pulpwood, Inc.*, 301 Ark. 436, 785 S.W.2d 13 (Ark.1990), the Arkansas Supreme Court reiterated that Arkansas case law indicates consequential damages are recoverable upon the failure of a limited remedy's essential purpose. *Id.* at 444, 785 S.W.2d 13; *see CIBA-Geigy Corp. v. Alter*, 809 Ark. 426 (1992).

JDE argues that because there is alternative remedy—that is first the repair of the product, then the return of the purchase price, that this Agreement is not subject to the concept of "failure of purpose." *See Marr Enterprises, Inc. v. Lewis Refrigeration Co.*, 556 F.2d 951, 955 (9th Cir.1977); *Ritchie Enterprises v. Honeywell Bull, Inc.*, 730 F.Supp. 1041, 1048 (D.Kan.1990). From the Court's research it appears that these cases have never been cited in the Eighth Circuit nor in Arkansas. The idea is that the "back-up" remedy of repayment prevents a limited remedy of repair from failing of its essential purpose. Moreover, even the *Ritchie* case notes that:

> Of course the backup remedy may also fail of its essential purpose. For example, the seller may refuse to refund the purchase price after failure of the front-line repair-or-replacement remedy. Or the seller might conceal facts regarding the breach of warranty until such time that [rescission] by the buyer could not be [pursued] as a backup remedy because it would cause [severe] financial strain."

Ritchie at 1049.

Thus, it is clear that Arkansas law contemplates instances where based on the totality of the circumstances, contract provisions which seek to limit . . . damages to (1) repair, (2) repayment of purchase price and/or (3) the exclusion of consequential damages are ineffective. It is equally apparent that such determinations are imbedded in findings of fact—the circumstances surrounding the transaction and its consequences.

B. Manifest Disregard of the Law Analysis

Obviously, the next inquiry is the reasons stated for the Panel's decision. The Panel stated in its Order:

> JDE's efforts to limit its liability to repair or return of the license fee or even to all sums paid to JDE [violate 2-719] under the circumstances of this case where Evans was required to incur substantial and significant

additional costs just to install and implement the Software. Moreover, the limitation in the "Exclusive Remedy" provision to nonconformities that are discerned within six months after delivery of the software is not reasonable under the circumstances of this case. Neither the implementation of the software nor the CNC configuration were completed [within] that period so the extent of the non-conformities could not be determined [within] that time frame. The remedies of correction of deficiencies or termination and return of the license fee were inadequate and failed of their essential purposes for other reasons too. JDE never offered to refund any payment to Evans. JDE's main efforts were directed to getting Evans to pay more, not less. In fact, J.D. Edwards stopped supporting the Software on the DEC-Alpha hardware and offered only to continue to perform services for Evans at the rate of $300 per hour—hardly an approach that could be deemed a warranty remedy. J.D. Edwards was unable to provide the promised functionality after three releases of software and countless SARS, which Evans had to pay to install despite the fact that Evans had paid JDE substantial sums for "maintenance". Nor did JDE offer to return the license fees or other payments it received from Evans. It did "write off" some of the charges but then offered to complete various tasks at $300 per hour!

(Award of Arbitrators, p. 3). The panel then stated in a footnote that "The clause which attempts to void the application of the "failure of essential purpose" theory is against public policy and unenforceable.

Thus, taking into consideration the analysis of this area of the law, there is a basis for Panel to make ineffective those clauses upon which JDE relies to limit the damage award to Evans including the clause seeking to void the application of the "failure of essential purpose" theory. The facts recited above clearly indicate and provide a sufficient basis to find that the warranty remedies provided failed of their essential purpose as defined by Arkansas law . . . . Based on the standard of review mandated by Fifth Circuit precedent, this Court finds that there has been no manifest error of law made by the Panel. Accordingly, the Motion to Vacate must be denied.

. . . .

Assignment 23: Statute of Limitations

§ 2-725

Even if liability and a remedy would otherwise exist under Article 2, a party must file suit before the statute of limitations has expired in order to get relief. The limitations period for contracts for sales of goods is found in 2-725. The problems in this assignment will help you to identify

- when the statute of limitations begins running,
- the length of the limitations period, and
- under what circumstances the limitations period will be extended beyond the length of time specified in the section.

Reading the Code

Problem 23-1. Triggering the Statute of Limitations. Read 2-725(1).

(A)   What triggers the running of the statute of limitations?

(B)   Once the running of the statute of limitations is triggered, how long does the aggrieved party have to file suit?

Problem 23-2. Accrual of the Cause of Action. Read 2-725(2).

(A)   Complete the chart on the following page, based on the three rules for when a cause of action accrues:

Nature of claim	When cause of action accrues
	When the breach is or should have been discovered
	When tender of delivery occurs
	When the breach occurs

(B)   How would a warranty "explicitly extend" to future performance of the goods?

(C)   For violation of the implied warranties under 2-312, 2-314, or 2-315, does the cause of action ever accrue when the breach is or should have been discovered, rather than when tender of delivery occurs?

Problem 23-3. Application to Mixed Transactions. Recall from Assignment 2 that a contract including a sale of goods *and* a sale of services falls within the scope of Article 2 if the predominant purpose test is satisfied. For example, a sales contract between a buyer and a seller might contain both a sale of goods and a promise of services associated with installation of the goods. If the seller breaches its contract by failing to perform its installation services effectively, when does the statute of limitations begin to run for a claim regarding the installation?

Problem 23-4.   Extension of the Limitations Period.   Read 2-725(3). Rephrase the rule in 2-725(3) using an if/then statement.

Applying the Code

Applying the language of 2-725 raises several critical issues of interpretation, some of which cannot be settled solely by reference to the statutory language. These issues are treated in the textual material and problems that follow.

Problem 23-5. Suit Against a Remote Seller. Under 2-725(2), the cause of action for a breach of warranty accrues "when tender of delivery [of the goods] is made." But what does this mean if the goods have been sold (from manufacturer to retailer, for example) and then resold (from retailer to consumer)? Does the cause of action accrue for the consumer's suit against the manufacturer when the goods are tendered from the manufacturer to the retailer or when they are tendered from the retailer to the consumer?

(A)   Read *Patterson v. Her Majesty Industries, Inc.*, at page 339. What answer does the case give to the question posed above? What policy considerations and statutory arguments support that result?

(B)   What policy considerations and statutory arguments would support the alternative result?

Problem 23-6. Suit for Indemnification. A seller who buys and resells goods and is then found liable for a breach of warranty on the resale (the "intermediate seller") may seek to recover what it owes to its own buyer by filing a claim against the person from whom it bought the goods (the "original seller"). The claim by the intermediate seller against the original seller is an indemnity claim, although it is based on a warranty breach.

(A)   Read *City of Wood River v. Geer-Melkus Construction Co.*, at page 344. What conclusion did this court reach about the applicability of 2-725 to a claim of this sort? What policy considerations and statutory arguments support the result reached?

(B)   What policy considerations and statutory arguments would support the alternative result? With respect to statutory arguments, pay particular attention to the second sentence of 2-725(1) and the first sentence of 2-725(2).

Problem 23-7. Warranting Future Performance. Section 2-725(2) specifies that a cause of action for breach of warranty accrues not upon delivery (the general rule given in 2-725(1)) but rather when the breach is or should have been discovered "where a warranty explicitly extends to future performance of the goods." The critical task is the identification of warranty language that fits this requirement. The courts have reached inconsistent results, but most construe the standard narrowly, often requiring an express statement referring to performance at a specific time in the future ("guaranteed to last for 10 years") rather than a general promise of performance that implicitly or generally includes the future ("promised to be durable"). With that standard in mind, consider the following phrases that might appear in a contract. Which of them appear to articulate a warranty that "explicitly extends to future performance of the goods"? Which do not? Be prepared to defend your conclusions or articulate arguments supporting one or the other result (or both). Also keep in mind the difference between a warranty and a remedy.

(A)   Goods are warranted to be free from defects in material and workmanship.

(B)   This boat is unsinkable.

(C)   Muffler guaranteed as long as you own your car.

(D)   Goods when purchased new are warranted to be free from substantial defects of material and workmanship under normal use and service for a period of 12 months from the date of delivery to the first retail purchaser.

(E)   The sales clerk tells the buyer that "these hiking boots will survive even the toughest trail."

(F)   Goods are warranted to be free from defects in material and workmanship. Seller will at its option repair or replace defective part or parts within the scope of this warranty, provided that notice of the defect is received from the purchaser within one year from the date of delivery.

Problem 23-8. Statute of Limitations and Remedial Promises. Seller expressly promises to repair the purchased goods if a defect appears during the warranty period, but then Seller fails to repair as promised. Construct arguments for the following alternative conclusions.

(A)   Buyer's cause of action accrued when tender of delivery occurred.

(B)   Buyer's cause of action accrued when Seller failed to repair the goods.

Note on the Tolling of the Statute of Limitations

Because 2-725 "does not alter the law on tolling of the statute of limitations" (2-725(4)), the usual common law principles and otherwise applicable state law provisions apply. Thus the statute of limitations is generally tolled if the seller prevents the buyer from discovering a defect,[1] if the seller engages in fraud or concealment of a defect,[2] while the party seeking relief is a

---

[1] *See, e.g.,* Balog v. Center Art Gallery-Hawaii, Inc., 745 F. Supp. 1556 (D. Haw. 1990).

[2] *See, e.g.,* Freiberg v. Atlas-Turner, Inc., 37 UCC Rep. Serv. 1592 (D. Minn. 1984).

minor,[3] or during the pendency of a prior suit between the parties on the same claim that was dismissed without prejudice.[4]

The courts have disagreed, however, regarding whether the statute of limitations is tolled when the seller attempts unsuccessfully to make repairs. Some courts have applied estoppel to toll the statute when evidence reveals that the seller attempted to repair the goods and made representations that the repairs would cure the defect, and the plaintiff relied upon the representations.[5] Other courts have rejected this so-called "repair doctrine."[6] For goods that are replaced rather than repaired, however, the statute of limitations begins to run anew when the replacement goods are delivered.[7]

2003 **Problem 23-9. The 2003 Amended Version.** We have seen that 2-725

> (1) states three rules for when accrual of a cause of action for sale of goods occurs, and then
> (2) declares the default statute of limitations to be four years from that date, except when a claim is brought and terminated under the circumstances described in 2-725(3).

The 2003 amended version changes both of these aspects of the statute of limitations.

(A)   Read the 2003 amended version of 2-725(1). What changes do the amendments make in the time permitted to file suit after accrual of a cause of action?

---

[3] *See, e.g.,* Evans v. General Motors Corp. 732 N.E.2d 79 (Ill. Ct. App. 2000).

[4] *See, e.g.,* Zahler v. Star Steel Supply Co., 213 N.W.2d 269 (Mich. Ct. App. 1973).

[5] *See, e.g.,* Keller v. Volkswagen of America, Inc., 733 A.2d 642 (Pa. Super. 1999); Aced v. Hobbs-Sesack Plumbing Co., 55 Cal. 2d 573 (1961).

[6] *See, e.g.,* Zahler v. Star Steel Supply Co., 213 N.W.2d 269 (Mich. Ct. App. 1973); Binkley Co. v. Teledyne Mid-America Corp., 333 F. Supp. 1183 (E.D. Mo. 1971).

[7] *See* Coakley & Williams, Inc. v. Shatterproof Glass Corp., 706 F.2d 456 (4th Cir. 1983).

(B)   What change does the 2003 amended version of 2-725(1) make to the parties' ability to modify the default statute of limitations?

(C)   In 2-725(2) and (3), the 2003 amended version provides a complex series of provisions detailing when a cause of action for sale of goods accrues for a variety of different kinds of claims. The chart below lists the obligations that may give rise to a cause of action and asks you to fill in the 2-725 rule regarding when that kind of cause of action accrues, as well as which subsection is the source of the rule.

Read 2-725(2) and (3) and fill in the chart below. Because the section repeatedly states rules "except as otherwise provided in" some subsequent section or sections, we suggest that you read the sections in the following order to help you understand how the various parts fit together:

    2-725(3)(d)
    2-725(3)(c)
    2-725(3)(a)
    2-725(3)(b)
    2-725(2)(b)
    2-725(2)(c)
    2-725(2)(d)
    2-725(2)(a)

Kind of claim	Source of claim in amended Article 2	2-725 sub-section that applies	When cause of action accrues
Breach of warranty of title	2-312		
Breach of warranty against infringement	2-312		

Kind of claim	Source of claim in amended Article 2	2-725 sub-section that applies	When cause of action accrues
Breach of express warranty (but not remedial promise) to immediate buyer, warranty does not extend to future performance	2-313(2)		
Breach of express warranty (but not remedial promise) to immediate buyer, warranty extends to future performance	2-313(2)		
Breach of implied warranty of merchantability	2-314		
Breach of implied warranty of fitness for a particular purpose	2-315		
Breach of remedial promise to immediate buyer	2-313(4), 2-103(1)(n) & comment 9		
Breach of remedial promise made in a record accompanying the goods	2-313A (3)(b)		
Breach of obligation (not re-medial promise) created by record accompanying goods, obligation does not extend to future performance	2-313A		

Kind of claim	Source of claim in amended Article 2	2-725 sub-section that applies	When cause of action accrues
Breach of obligation (not remedial promise) created by record accompanying goods, obligation extends to future performance	2-313A		
Breach of remedial promise made in communication to the public	2-313B (3)(b)		
Breach of obligation (not remedial promise) created by communication to the public, obligation does not extend to future performance	2-313B		
Breach of obligation (not remedial promise) created by communication to the public, obligation extends to future performance	2-313B		
Breach by repudiation	2-610		
Indemnity claim by intermediate buyer	---		
Other	---		

Kathleen Patterson
v.
Her Majesty Industries, Inc.

450 F. Supp. 425 (E.D. Pa. 1978)

DITTER, District Judge.

This is a diversity suit for personal injuries sustained by minor plaintiff when a pair of pajamas she was wearing caught fire. Presently before the court is the motion of the garment's manufacturer for summary judgment on the ground that the statute of limitations for plaintiffs' breach of warranty claim expired before the action was brought. For the reasons hereafter advanced, I find that the statute of limitations began to run on the date of the retail sale to plaintiffs, the suit was timely brought, and the motion must be denied.

1.   Factual and Procedural History

On September 24, 1971, plaintiff, Carole Patterson, purchased a pair of pajamas from Lit Brothers, a retail store, for her daughter Kathleen, then age 12. Her Majesty Industries, Inc., (Her Majesty), had manufactured the pajamas and sold them to Lit Brothers for resale to the public. On the evening of October 11, 1971, Kathleen wore these pajamas to bed for the first time. The next morning, while preparing breakfast in her home, Kathleen reached over a gas stove to get a teabag. As she did, a spark from the stove contacted the lower portion of the pajama top. Almost instantaneously, the top was consumed by flames and Kathleen was badly burned.

On June 6, 1975, plaintiffs started suit against Her Majesty on theories of breach of warranty, negligence, and strict

liability because the pajamas were not resistant to flame and Her Majesty had failed to provide appropriate warning. Thereafter, on December 9, 1975, leave was granted to join Lit Brothers as a third party defendant.[1] By order dated July 15, 1976, I entered judgment on the pleadings in favor of Her Majesty on those counts of the complaint based on negligence and strict liability since they were barred by the applicable two-year statute of limitations.

Her Majesty has now moved for summary judgment with respect to the breach of warranty claim, contending that 1) Pennsylvania would apply a two-year statute of limitations,[2] and 2) if a four-year statute of limitations does apply, as provided in Section 2-725 of the Uniform Commercial Code, 12 P.S. § 2-725, it began to run as of the date of the sale by Her Majesty to Lit Brothers, which was more than four years prior to the start of suit.[3] Plaintiffs urge the motion be denied

---

[1] The other defendants were joined as follows. On March 1, 1976, Her Majesty joined Burlington Industries, which made the nylon tricot used to make spaghetti bow decorations on the pajama top, Avondale Mills, which sold the fabric to Burlington Industries, and Fab Industries, which allegedly manufactured the lace decorating the pajama top. Avondale Mills filed a third party complaint against Wade Manufacturing which actually manufactured the fabric used by Burlington on June 15, 1976.

[2] See n. 6, infra.

[3] Defendant contends that it must have shipped the pajamas in question to Lit Brothers prior to June 6, 1971. For support, Her Majesty points to its records and those of Lit Brothers which indicate that there were no

and maintain that a four-year statute of limitations does apply and that it runs from the date of the retail sale and, alternatively, that Her Majesty's warranty explicitly extended to future performance so the statute started to run as of the date of the accident. After an analysis of Pennsylvania cases and those of other state and federal tribunals, I have concluded that the statute of limitations begins to run from the retail sale date and is of four years duration.

Oddly, this appears to be a case of first impression. Neither my continuous and exhaustive research nor that of counsel has disclosed any case that addresses this particular issue. Inasmuch as no Pennsylvania cases are on point, my decision must be governed by a prediction of what a Pennsylvania court would rule if this matter came before it. . . .

---

shipments of pajamas in 1971 prior to October 12, 1971, the date of the accident and, thus, the pajamas were delivered to Lit Brothers sometime in 1970.

Plaintiffs, on the other hand, have argued that the pajamas were shipped sometime between June and September, 1971. This contention is based on plaintiffs' identification of the pajama style as Style 47177, a type manufactured during the time frame from April to June, 1971, and shipped to retailers in the summer of 1971.

Based upon this dispute, I expressed my hesitation in considering a summary judgment motion because of what appeared to be a material issue of fact. Defendant then moved under F.R.Civ.P. 42(b) to sever the factual issue from the statute of limitations question. Plaintiffs, however, withdrew the affidavit which had created the factual dispute and agreed that the motion for summary judgment should be decided purely on the legal question.

2. Section 2-725: The Statute of Limitations

The parties agree that Section 2-725 of the Uniform Commercial Code (Code), 12 A.P.S. § 2-725, is the relevant limitation provision to be applied here. It states . . . that an action for breach of any contract for sale must be commenced within four years after the cause of action has accrued. It is Her Majesty's position that under the clear language of Section 2-725(2), the limitation period as to any seller commences when he tenders delivery of the goods to his immediate purchaser, the retailer, and the four-year period would have expired prior to June, 1975. Plaintiffs' position is there could be no tender of delivery as to them until they had purchased the merchandise, and, under their computations, the four-year period would have expired in September, 1975.

Although the Code is silent on the issue, defendant asserts that one purpose of the limitation is to enable firms to destroy their records four years after a commercial sale "without fear of being unable to defend against liabilities subsequently asserted." Engelman v. Eastern Light Co., Inc., 30 Pa.D. & C.2d 38, 45 (1962). To some extent, this is supported by the comments of the National Conference of Commissioners on Uniform State Laws and The American Law Institute:

> This Article takes sales contracts out of the general laws limiting the time for commencing contractual actions and selects a four year period as the most appropriate to modern business practice. This is within the normal commercial record keeping period.

If the limitation period was held to begin only upon sale by the retailer to the ultimate consumer, defendant argues it would not run for 25 years if the retailer were not able to sell the product for 21 years. Similarly, with respect to a machine which might be sold and resold a number of times over a great number of years, the manufacturer's warranty liability would be extended for even longer periods of time. Conversely, if defendant's reasoning were adopted, a calculation of the statute of limitations from the date of delivery to the retailer could bar an injured consumer before his cause of action even existed. For example, a sale and an injury could take place four years and one day after delivery of the product to the retailer. While the customer could maintain an action against the retail establishment, he would be foreclosed from bringing a breach of warranty claim against the manufacturer.[4]

The initial step in my inquiry as to the probable reaction of Pennsylvania

---

[4] Judge Frank, in his dissenting opinion in Dincher v. Marlin Firearms Co., 198 F.2d 821, 823 (2d Cir. 1952), cited with approval in Vescio v. Chrysler Corp., 125 P.L.J. 353 (1977), described the "Alice in Wonderland" effect of this result as follows:

Except in topsy-turvy land, you can't die before you are conceived, or be divorced before ever you marry, or harvest a crop never planted, or burn down a house never built, or miss a train running on a non-existent railroad. For substantially similar reasons, it has always heretofore been accepted, as a sort of legal "axiom," that a statute of limitations does not begin to run against a cause of action before that cause of action exists, i. e., before a judicial remedy is available to the plaintiff.

courts to this issue must be an examination of the development of warranty law in this state and the courts' recognition of the economic reality in cases involving manufacturers and users of allegedly defective products. Thereafter, I shall address those cases from other jurisdictions which have impliedly considered this issue.

3. The Pennsylvania law

[The court first concludes that section 2-725 rather than Pennsylvania's two-year trespass statute of limitations applies to the plaintiff's claim.]

The only state court case that has even remotely considered whether the retail or wholesale date controls is Rufo v. Bastian-Blessing Co., supra, where the court intimated that it is the retail sale which provides the significant date. Rufo had bought a refilled, portable cylinder of liquefied gas from Martin in March, 1956. Defendant, Bastian-Blessing, had manufactured a valve which was connected to the cylinder. On December 8, 1957, plaintiff was injured in an explosion, caused by gas which escaped from the valve and caught fire. Alleging that defendant had violated an implied warranty of fitness, Rufo brought suit on July 12, 1960. In ruling that the action was barred by the statute of limitations, the court held:

Applying the statute, the latest time that the alleged breaches of implied warranties could have occurred and, therefore, the latest time that the cause could have accrued was when Rufo took delivery of the allegedly defective cylinder in March of 1956. Because the complaint was filed more than four years later, in August of 1960, it was too late (emphasis added). 417 Pa. at 113, 207 A.2d at 826.

There was no mention of the date defendant sold the valve to Martin nor was there any indication that Martin was a retailer. However, it certainly can be strongly argued that if the date of sale from defendant to Martin was crucial, the court would have revealed it and measured the statute of limitations from that date. Admittedly, however, Rufo is less than conclusive.

The federal district court cases from Pennsylvania that have bordered on this issue are not very helpful. In Peeke v. Penn Central Transportation Co., 403 F.Supp. 70 (E.D.Pa.1975), Judge Becker faced a different question, i. e., whether the accrual date was the date of injury. But, in discussing Rufo, he concluded:

> The court held plaintiff's claim barred because the accrual date of § 2-725's four year limit was the date of the breach; that is, of tender of delivery; and certainly no later than the date of resale by the retailer (emphasis added). Id. at 72.

. . . .

Today's business world is no longer one of direct contact. It is, instead, based on advertising. Manufacturers make extensive use of newspapers, periodicals, radio, and television to call attention to the qualities of their products. This advertising is directed at the ultimate consumer. In addition, many products are shipped in sealed packages and the retailer is, in reality, merely a conduit through which the manufacturer distributes his goods. Klages v. General Ordnance Equipment Corp., 240 Pa.Super. 356, 364-65, 367 A.2d 304,

308-09 (1976). . . .

While the policy espoused in these cases must be tempered by the realization that the courts were dealing with decidedly different questions of law from the one at issue here, I believe that if confronted with it a Pennsylvania court would adopt a rule of law that would best spread the risk of loss and protect the consumer. [footnote omitted] Having adopted a four-year statute of limitations, eliminated the requirements of vertical and horizontal privity in breach of warranty actions, and described the manufacturer as a guarantor of his product's safety, Salvador v. Atlantic Steel Boiler Co., supra, 457 Pa. at 32, 319 A.2d at 907, Pennsylvania, in my judgment, would more likely adopt plaintiffs' theory and hold the statute of limitations runs from the retail sale date.

4. Other Jurisdictions

A survey of other jurisdictions has revealed no case which has directly addressed and answered this question, although some courts impliedly lean in plaintiff's direction. For instance, in Raymond v. Eli Lilly & Co., 412 F.Supp. 1392 (D.N.H.1976), aff'd 556 F.2d 628 (1st Cir. 1977), plaintiff brought an action for personal injuries against the manufacturer of an oral contraceptive for breach of implied warranty. Suit was filed February 28, 1975. In barring plaintiff's claim on this ground the court concluded:

> NH RSA 382-A:2-725(1) establishes a four year statute of limitations for any action based upon a contract for sale. The statute begins to run from the time a cause of action accrues, which is when the breach occurs.

The breach of warranty occurs when the tender of delivery is made regardless of the aggrieved party's knowledge of the breach. NH RSA 382-A:2-725(2). Plaintiff's last purchase of C-Quens (the contraceptive) was on or about May 20, 1968, more than four years prior to the commencement of her action. She is, therefore, barred from pursuing her breach of warranty claim against defendant by NH RSA 382-A:2-725(1) (emphasis added). Id. at 1403.

Presumably plaintiff would have filled prescriptions for the drug at a pharmacy and not directly from the manufacturer. Thus, the court focused on the retail sale date as the date which would trigger the statute of limitations.

Along the same lines is Berry v. G. D. Searle & Co., 56 Ill.2d 548, 309 N.E.2d 550 (1974). There, a woman and her husband brought suit against the manufacturer of an oral contraceptive for a stroke and paralysis she sustained. The record showed that contraceptives had been sold to wife plaintiff on May 29, 1965, by the Planned Parenthood Association of Chicago.[5] Suit was started on May 29, 1969, and defendant moved

to dismiss the action on the ground that the statute of limitations had run. In rejecting defendant's argument that suit should have been started on or before May 28, 1969, the court found that "if the evidence would indicate that the drug causing the injury was delivered to the plaintiff on May 29, 1965, an action based on liability under the Code commenced four years thereafter was timely filed." Id. at 557, 309 N.E.2d at 555. Unfortunately, for the purposes of this discussion, Searle did not argue that the statute should begin to run from the date of its delivery to Planned Parenthood, since there is a strong likelihood that the wholesale sale took place more than four years prior to the start of the suit. However, it is clear that the court concentrated on the date of retail sale.

One other decision merits attention. In Waldron v. Armstrong Rubber Co., 64 Mich.App. 626, 236 N.W. 722 (1975), plaintiff had brought an action for personal injuries based on alleged defects in a tire he purchased from Sears, Roebuck & Company on August 27, 1968. Suit was started against the retailer, Sears, and the manufacturer, Armstrong Rubber, on July 6, 1972. The Michigan Court of Appeals found that the action was timely brought under Section 2-725(2) and concluded that August 27, 1968, was the date of the breach of warranty and, therefore, that plaintiff's cause of action accrued as of that time. Once again, it is obvious that the delivery of the tire to Sears from Armstrong Rubber would have taken place sometime prior to August 27, 1968, but the court looked exclusively to the retail date. [footnote omitted]

---

[5] Planned Parenthood argued that it was primarily a service organization, i. e., to give birth control advice, and that its dispensation of birth control devices was merely an adjunct to performing that service. It asserted, therefore, that it was not engaged in selling these items. The court disagreed and found that the association was a seller. Thus, the case involved two sales, one from Searle to Planned Parenthood and one from Planned Parenthood to plaintiffs, similar to the situation posed here.

5. Conclusion

It must be recognized that the Code gives no clear answer to the question posed here, for it does not specify to whom tender of delivery must be made in order to commence the four-year statute of limitations. In addition, Pennsylvania has not decided nor been faced with the issue. Therefore it has been necessary to examine Pennsylvania as well as other state and federal court decisions in order to determine how a Pennsylvania court might resolve the matter. Since only one case, Rufo v. Bastian-Blessing Co., supra, has come remotely close to considering the question, the policy formulated by Pennsylvania courts has been most instructive. In abolishing the doctrines of vertical and horizontal privity, the Supreme Court placed a great deal of reliance on today's business world and the economic realities of marketing goods in our society.   It does not seem conceivable that the court which looked to the consumer, and not the middleman, as the party to be protected, Kassab v. Central Soya, supra, and which termed the manufacturer the guarantor of his product's safety, Salvador v. Atlantic Steel Boiler Co., supra, would adopt an interpretation which might allow a statute of limitations to run before a consumer ever received the goods.

Moreover, it is important to remember the purpose for which warranties are primarily made, the protection of the ultimate user or consumer. The benefit of such warranties to the retail merchant are tangential they provide a means to recoup losses suffered from the sale of a defective product. Therefore, the warranty should begin to run when the ultimate purchaser receives the goods, not when a merchant obtains the goods for resale.

For these reasons, I find that the statute of limitations began to run when plaintiffs purchased the pajamas. Since the suit was commenced within four years from the date of the retail sale, the action is not barred by Section 2-725(1) of the Code.[6] Accordingly, defendant's motion for summary judgment must be denied.

City of Wood River
v.
Geer-Melkus Construction Co.

444 N.W.2d 305 (Neb. 1989)

WITTHOFF, District Judge.

This is an appeal from an order of the Hall County District Court finding the third-party action of Geer-Melkus Construction Company, Inc., and United States Fidelity & Guarantee Company (Geer-Melkus) against Geo. A. Hormel & Company (Hormel) was barred by the statute of limitations.

FACTS

Appellant Geer-Melkus contracted with the City of Wood River to construct a waste water treatment facility. Appellee Hormel manufactured and supplied the rotating media aeration system for the facility. The media system was delivered on or about September 14,

---

[6] Because I have found in plaintiffs' favor, I need not decide whether defendant's warranty extended to future performance and, thus, whether the statute of limitations began to run as of the date of the accident. See Section 2-275(2).

1976, and the plant became operational in the summer of 1977. In the following years, many repairs were made to the media system, and in December 1982 the system broke down completely and could not be repaired.

Wood River filed an action for breach of contract against Geer-Melkus on July 6, 1981. With the court's consent, on December 22, 1981, Geer-Melkus filed a third-party complaint against Hormel, alleging that if it was found liable to Wood River, Hormel was liable to it for breach of warranty.

Specifically, Geer-Melkus complained (1) Hormel warranted the rotating media aeration system would, without further modification, provide a minimum of 22,000 square feet of biological support media in each of the first two stages and 33,000 square feet in the final two stages, for a total of 110,000 square feet of biological support media; (2) Geer-Melkus installed the waste water treatment facility in exact accordance with the plans and specifications; (3) the waste water treatment facility was made operational on or about July 27, 1977; (4) the media rotary disk unit deteriorated and shifted on its shaft; (5) the deterioration and shifting subsequently caused damage to the bearings of the shaft and the shaft itself; (6) the shifting and deterioration required Wood River to replace portions of the waste water treatment system; and (7) the deterioration and shifting were contrary to the specifications for the fixed media rotating disk unit. Geer-Melkus attached, and incorporated by reference, a copy of Wood River's petition as an exhibit to their third-party complaint, and alleged that

if the allegations of the Plaintiff's Petition are found to be true and if the Plaintiff recovers a judgment against the Defendants and Third Party Plaintiffs, the Third Party Defendant would be liable to the Defendants and Third Party Plaintiffs for the entire amount of the Plaintiffs [sic] claim against them for the reason that said allegations constitute a breach of the Third Party Defendant's express warranty set forth in paragraph 8 hereof.

On February 12, 1982, Hormel filed a demurrer, based primarily upon the statute of limitations defense, which the court overruled. Hormel filed an answer to the third-party complaint on March 5, 1982, admitting it manufactured and supplied the rotating system and stating the system was delivered on February 12, 1978. Hormel raised as affirmative defenses that (1) the action was barred by the statute of limitations; (2) the amount of the claim exceeded the coverage of the warranty; (3) Wood River failed to properly operate and maintain the system; (4) Hormel was not notified of the alleged breach of warranty; and (5) the warranty expired on February 12, 1978. Geer-Melkus filed a reply, alleging the statute of limitations had not run because they were asking for indemnity.

Hormel then moved for summary judgment, once again asserting the statute of limitations. The motion for summary judgment was overruled.

On November 12, 1985, a separate trial was held on the issue of the statute of limitations. At trial, Hormel demurred ore tenus, which demurrer the court also overruled. At the conclusion of this trial, the judge ruled the statute of limitations was tolled because of repairs and replacements made by Hormel.

Trial on the merits was held on October 28, 1986. The court found for Wood River and against Geer-Melkus in the amount of $57,379.54 on the original petition. On the third-party petition, the court found for Hormel and against Geer-Melkus, holding that the third-party action was barred by the statute of limitations. Pursuant to statute, the court allowed attorney fees of $19,000 to Wood River against Geer-Melkus. Geer-Melkus appeals the court's ruling on their third-party complaint, and Hormel cross-appeals the earlier failures to dismiss the action.

. . . .

ISSUE OF INDEMNITY RAISED BY THE PLEADINGS

Before we can determine whether the statute of limitations bars Geer-Melkus' third-party claim, we must determine whether Geer-Melkus seeks damages on a breach of warranty or seeks indemnification. Geer-Melkus does not specifically ask for "indemnity," but, instead, asks for damages for breach of warranty. The third-party complaint specifically set forth the problems with the "rotating media aeration system" manufactured by Hormel. It incorporated Wood River's petition and all its allegations. Finally, the third-party complaint alleged that if Wood River recovered a judgment against Geer-Melkus, Hormel would be liable to Geer-Melkus for the entire amount of Wood River's claim because of the expressed warranty.

While the term "indemnity" is not specifically used,

[t]he essential character of a cause of action or the remedy or relief it seeks, as shown by the allegations of the complaint, determines whether a particular action is one at law or in equity, unaffected by conclusions of the pleader or what the pleader calls it, or the prayer for relief.

Waite v. Samson Dev. Co., 217 Neb. 403, 408, 348 N.W.2d 883, 887 (1984); Brchan v. The Crete Mills, 155 Neb. 505, 52 N.W.2d 333 (1952).

Even if the pleading mistakenly identifies a cause of action, the right to recover under the facts alleged is not affected.

In order to decide the form of the redress, whether contract or tort, it is necessary to know the source or origin of the duty or the nature of the grievance. Attention must be given to the cause of the complaint; in other words, the character of the action must be determined from what is asserted concerning it in the petition in the cause. It is not important what the plaintiff calls his action. If he does attempt to identify it and is mistaken, that is immaterial. This is the rationale of the code provision that a petition is a statement of facts constituting a cause of action in ordinary and concise language.

Fuchs v. Parsons Constr. Co., 166 Neb. 188, 192, 88 N.W.2d 648, 651 (1958).

It is evident from the pleadings Geer-Melkus claims that (1) appellant Geer-Melkus purchased the rotary system from Hormel; (2) Hormel manufactured the same to meet certain specifications; (3) the system did not meet those specifications; and (4) if Geer-Melkus suffered damages because of the failure of Hormel to fulfill its contractual obligation, they would look to Hormel for payment of their loss. The third-party complaint sets out specifically what Hormel's aeration system did wrong. A duty to indemnify will always arise out of another more basic obligation whether it arises on contract or tort. Although Utah chose to bring sales indemnification actions within § 2-725 of the Uniform Commercial Code, the Utah Supreme Court identified an allegation of a breach of warranty as raising the issue of indemnification.

> Perry argues that [§ 2-725] does not apply because his action is in reality one for indemnity, not one for breach of warranty. We consider this argument in the context of the undeniable fact that the subject matter of this entire lawsuit is the sale of goods, which will be governed where applicable by the Utah version of the Uniform Commercial Code. . . . *The underlying action was for breach of contract, and the amended third-party complaint alleges only a cause of action for breach of warranty. It nowhere mentions indemnity. Nonetheless, we look to the substance of Perry's claim, regardless of what he chose to call it.*

(Emphasis supplied.) Perry v. Pioneer Wholesale Supply Co., 681 P.2d 214, 217 (Utah 1984).

Hormel cannot claim that it did not understand the theory upon which the third-party complaint was predicated or that it had no warning in time to defend itself. The motion for leave to file a third-party complaint against Hormel specifically stated that "a rotating media aeration system manufactured by George A. Hormel & Co. was defective and was not merchantable and if such allegations are true these Defendants would be entitled to indemnification from George A. Hormel & Co."

In addition thereto, the reply filed by Geer-Melkus specifically addressed § 2-725 and alleged that it did not apply

> for the reason that under the substantive law of the State of Nebraska the periods of limitation set forth in the foregoing statutes, if applicable in the instant case, do not start to run upon a claim for indemnity until such time as the indemnitee's liability has been fixed and discharged.

Therefore, the third-party complaint raised an indemnification cause of action.

APPLICABILITY OF § 2-725 TO INDEMNIFICATION CAUSES OF ACTION

All parties agree the sale which is the subject matter of the third-party complaint is a sale of goods within the meaning of the Uniform Commercial Code. As such, the original contract and warranty were covered by the statute of limitations of contracts for sale.

In examining the statute and the proposed scope of the statute, it should be noted that any action for breach of contract must be commenced within 4 years after the cause of action has accrued. The statute further specifically defines accrual of a cause of action by saying that the breach occurs when a tender of delivery is made, except where a warranty specifically extends to future performance of the goods, and discovery of the breach must await time of such performance. In this case the warranty did not specifically extend to future performance.

We have not previously addressed the question of whether the limitation set out in § 2-725 applies to an indemnity claim. Other jurisdictions have split on the issue.

Georgia, Utah, Illinois, and Idaho have held indemnity claims are controlled and limited by § 2-725. PPG Industries v. Genson, 135 Ga.App. 248, 217 S.E.2d 479 (1975); Perry v. Pioneer Wholesale Supply Co., supra; Anixter Bros., Inc. v. Cen. Steel & Wire, 123 Ill.App.3d 947, 79 Ill.Dec. 359, 463 N.E.2d 913 (1984); Farmers Nat. Bank v. Wickham Pipeline, 114 Idaho 565, 759 P.2d 71 (1988). These jurisdictions view the strict application of § 2-725 as necessary to avoid the problem of unending litigation.

> The four-year statute applicable to the indemnity theory does not apply in this case because a sale of goods occurred in 1974 with observable defects (if any), and any cause of action against Third-Party Defendants arose at that time. Otherwise, anyone buying defective goods could resell them before or after the statute had run, and upon being sued for the original defects, file a third-party complaint for indemnity and thus defeat the policy of repose underlying the statute of limitation.

Perry v. Pioneer Wholesale Supply Co., 681 P.2d 214, 217 n. 1 (Utah 1984).

Maryland, New Hampshire, Missouri, Maine, North Carolina, and New York have ruled indemnity claims do not come under the time limitation found in § 2-725. McDermott v. City of N.Y., 50 N.Y.2d 211, 428 N.Y.S.2d 643, 406 N.E.2d 460 (1980); Walker Mfg. Co. v. Dickerson, Inc., 619 F.2d 305 (4th Cir.1980) (applying North Carolina law); Cyr v. Michaud, 454 A.2d 1376 (Me.1983); City of Clayton v. Grumman Emer. Prod., 576 F.Supp. 1122 (E.D.Mo.1983) (applying Missouri law); Jaswell Drill Corp. v. General Motors Corp., 129 N.H. 341, 529 A.2d 875 (1987); Hanscome v. Perry, 75 Md.App. 605, 542 A.2d 421 (1988). These jurisdictions follow the reasoning advanced by the New York Court of Appeals in McDermott v. City of N.Y., supra 50 N.Y.2d at 216-17, 406 N.E.2d at 462, 428 N.Y.S.2d at 646:

> Conceptually, implied indemnity finds its roots in the principles of equity. It is nothing short of simple fairness to recognize that "[a] person who, in whole or in part, has discharged a duty which is owed by him but which as between himself and another should have been discharged by the other, is entitled to indemnity" (Restatement, Restitution, § 76). To prevent unjust enrichment, courts have assumed the duty of placing the obligation where in equity it belongs (see, e.g., Dunn v. Uvalde Asphalt Paving Co., 175 NY 214, 217-218 [67 N.E. 439]; Oceanic S.N. Co. v. Compania Transatlantica Espanola, 134 NY 461, 465-468 [31 N.E. 987] . . .).

In deciding the statute of limitations question was governed by the indemnity rule rather than the contract or warranty rule, the Maryland Court of Special

Appeals stated:

> In approaching this issue, both sides have focused their attention on when limitations begins to run in an action for indemnification and have given but scant consideration to the nature of the indemnity claim actually made by appellant. As to the limitations question, we think that appellant is correct in her view that an action for indemnification accrues and the limitations period commences not at the time of the underlying transaction but when the would-be indemnitee pays the judgment arising from the underlying transaction. That seems to be the majority view, and it is certainly in keeping with the nature of an indemnity action.

(Citations omitted.) Hanscome v. Perry, supra 75 Md.App. at 614, 542 A.2d at 425.

In applying the Missouri rule, the U.S. District Court used the same rationale. In City of Clayton v. Grumman Emer. Prod., supra, the issue was which party was financially responsible for cracks in a firetruck frame. The firetruck was purchased by the city from Howe Fire Apparatus Co., Inc., which was subsequently merged into Grumman Emergency Products, Inc. The frame was manufactured by The Warner and Swayse Company. Clayton sued Grumman as the successor in interest to Howe, which brought in Warner and Swayse as third-party defendants. Warner and Swayse responded by pleading the statute of limitations.

> Although Grumman raises the issue of the future performance exception to § 2-725, the Court need not address that question. Counts I and III of Grumman's third-party complaint state causes of action for indemnity based on breaches of express and implied warranties. The statute of limitations for indemnity does not start to run until the indemnitee is found liable to a third party. *See* Simon v. Kansas City Rug Co., 460 S.W.2d 596, 600 (Mo.1970). Therefore, Grumman's claims for indemnity from Warner are not time barred. This result does not imprudently enlarge the statute of limitations for breach of warranty. A party who buys and then resells a product is not in a position to discover the latent defect within the warranty's limitation period because the product is in the hands of the consumer during that time. Only when the consumer sues the retailer does the retailer gain notice of the latent defect. *See* Walker Manufacturing Co. v. Dickerson, Inc., 619 F.2d 305, 310 (4th Cir.1980) (North Carolina U.C.C. law).

City of Clayton, supra at 1127.

Nebraska has long held a claim for indemnity accrues at the time the indemnity claimant suffers loss or damage. City of Lincoln v. First Nat. Bank of Lincoln, 67 Neb. 401, 93 N.W. 698 (1903).

In Waldinger Co. v. P & Z Co., Inc., 414 F.Supp. 59 (D.Neb.1976), the trial court held the underlying statute of limitations dealing with political subdivision tort claims did not apply to actions seeking contribution or indemnification. Waldinger Co. instituted an action on January 16, 1976, against P & Z, Metropolitan Utilities District of Omaha, and the City of Omaha, alleging negligence proximately resulting in the collapse of a slurry trench wall which surrounded the Omaha-Douglas Civic Center. On May 3, 1976, the City of Omaha filed a third-party complaint against Hawkins Construction Company, Leo A. Daly Company, and Omaha-Douglas Public Commission for indemnification or contribution. Thereafter, the commission moved to dismiss the third-party complaint for failure to file a tort claim pursuant to the Political Subdivisions Tort Claims Act, Neb.Rev.Stat. § 23-2401 et seq. (Reissue 1974). The commission argued that any claims not filed within 1 year of the injury were extinguished.

In interpreting Nebraska law on contribution and indemnity, the trial court held:

These decisions are based on sound equitable principles. Contribution and indemnification are inchoate rights which do not arise until one tort feasor has paid more than his share of the damages or judgment. A plaintiff may sue one tort feasor or he may join all tort feasors in one suit. He may also wait more than a year to file his suit. To accept the Commission's argument that the claim for contribution or indemnification arises when the injury is incurred would allow plaintiff to choose which defendant would bear the burden by simply filing his lawsuit after the one year statute of limitations has run. The defendant joint tort feasor, having no

prior knowledge of a claim, would be unable to file a claim prior to being joined in the lawsuit.

Waldinger Co. v. P & Z Co., Inc., supra at 60.

The reasoning in McDermott, Hanscome, and City of Clayton is consistent with Nebraska law. If we were to adopt the opposite position, a party who might have a claim for indemnification would have to bring his action before the underlying claim was brought to avoid the running of the statute of limitations. Therefore, we hold § 2-725 does not apply where a party is seeking indemnification.

The present case is a classic example of the inequity which would result from adopting the theory advanced by Hormel. Geer-Melkus could not have brought their cause of action for indemnity until the original suit was brought by Wood River on July 6, 1981. The statute of limitations on the indemnity action would have expired on December 14, 1980. Geer-Melkus would be left with no recourse under these circumstances.

It is generally recognized that the party seeking indemnification must have been free of any wrongdoing, and its liability is vicariously imposed. Therefore, it should recover from another. See, Danny's Const. Co., Inc. v. Havens Steel Co., 437 F.Supp. 91 (D.Neb.1977); Barber-Greene Company v. Bruning Company, 357 F.2d 31 (8th Cir.1966); Farmers Elevator Mut. Ins. Co. v. American Mut. Lia. Ins. Co., 185 Neb. 4, 173 N.W.2d 378 (1969). In this case, the product was manufactured and sold by Hormel. The evidence in the record indicates any problems with the product were directly attributable to Hormel, not to Geer-Melkus. . . .

For the foregoing reasons, we find the statute of limitations does not bar the third-party complaint brought by Geer-Melkus.

CONCLUSION

The trial court's findings that the pleadings and evidence establish that Geer-Melkus Construction Company, Inc., and United States Fidelity & Guarantee Company's claim was for a breach of warranty and not for a claim of indemnification and that the claim was barred by the statute of limitations, § 2-725, are reversed. As noted above, the uncontroverted evidence establishes that the loss was directly attributable to Hormel. The action is therefore remanded with instruction to enter judgment against Hormel.

REVERSED AND REMANDED WITH DIRECTION.

Assignment 24: Overlapping Tort and Contract Claims and Development of the Economic Loss Doctrine

Litigants often have alternative bases for claiming relief, but the juxtaposition of Article 2 and tort claims presents special difficulties. Buyers or others who suffer losses caused by defects in purchased goods may seek to hold the seller liable for those losses not only by claiming breach of obligation under Article 2, but also by alleging that the seller was negligent or is strictly liable for distributing a defective and unsafe product. If a contract contains effective disclaimers of warranty liability or exclusions of consequential damages, should the buyer be permitted to bypass the contractual restrictions by seeking damages in tort? If Article 2 relief is barred because the statute of limitations has run under 2-725, should a buyer be able to seek tort recovery, which may not be barred because the statute of limitations for tort claims began to run when the injury occurred rather than when the goods were tendered?

Article 2 itself says nothing about how such alternative claims for relief should be handled, so the courts address the problem as a matter of a common law. As we will see below, the rule that has been adopted by the courts—commonly called the "economic loss doctrine"—establishes restrictions on the damages that will be recoverable in tort for defects in goods when Article 2 also applies to the sale culminating in the claimed injury.

Problem 24-1. Origins of the Economic Loss Doctrine. Read *East River Steamship Corp. v. Transamerica Delaval, Inc.*, at page 358, and answer the following questions:

(A)   Defects in purchased goods may cause several different kinds of injury to the buyer, all of which are compensable in a resulting breach of contract action under Article 2 (though recovery for some or all may be barred in an individual case by warranty disclaimers, remedy limitations, or other defenses). Complete the following chart, noting what *East River Steamship* says or suggests about whether these kinds of injury should *also* be compensable in a *tort* claim:

Nature of damage claim	Cognizable in tort?
Loss in value of the goods purchased	
Lost profits from failure of performance of the goods	
Personal injury	
Injury to property other than the goods purchased	

(B)   Why did the court conclude that tort liability should be restricted in the manner outlined in (A)?

Variations of the Economic Loss Doctrine

In the years since *East River*, the overwhelming majority of jurisdictions have been in accord with *East River,* adopting what is commonly called the "economic loss doctrine": if injury results from defects in goods bought and sold, negligence or strict liability claims are available only for personal injury and for injury to other property, real or personal. Other forms of injury (e.g., damage to the purchased goods, lost profits, expenses incurred as a result of the breach) are considered to be "economic loss"[1] and are governed only by Article 2.[2]

---

[1] The terminology is a bit confusing, because damage to the person and to other property also represents a form of economic loss, but it is not within the definition of "economic loss" as used in the cases.

[2] A few states have disagreed. *See, e.g., Thompson v. Nebraska Mobile Homes Corp.*, 647 P.2d 334 (Mont. 1982), in which the court voiced skepticism that warranty law is adequate to protect consumers and ruled that sellers might be strictly liable for damages to the goods

The general rule is only a starting place, however. Courts applying the economic loss rule have developed a variety of exceptions and variations permitting tort recovery under additional circumstances:

Serious risk of personal injury: As noted above, the economic loss doctrine does not bar recovery for personal injury. A few jurisdictions permit recovery in tort even for classic economic loss (e.g., damage to the goods) if the product defect creates an unreasonable risk of death or serious personal injury, concluding that such liability is needed to deter manufacturers from engaging in unsafe practices. *See, e.g., Morris v. Osmose Wood Preserving*, 667 A.2d 624 (Md. 1995); *Alloway v. General Marine Industries, L.P.*, 695 A.2d 264 (N.J. 1997).

Sudden and calamitous failure: Some courts have permitted tort recovery for economic loss if the defect causes the purchased goods to fail in a "sudden and calamitous" manner. "For courts adopting this distinction, the line drawn for purposes of recovering for damage to the defective product itself typically falls between damage resulting merely from deterioration, internal breakage, depreciation, or failure to live up to expectations and damage that is 'sudden and calamitous,' resulting from a violent or hazardous accident." *S.J. Groves & Sons Co. v. Aerospatiale Helicopter Corp.*, 374 N.W.2d 431, 434 (Minn. 1985) (declining to adopt an exception for sudden and calamitous injury, at least where claimant was buyer with substantial bargaining power). Examples of "sudden and calamitous" events include the failure of brakes on a truck, explosion of a grain storage tank, and a roof collapse. *See* R. Fox & Patrick J. Loftus, *Riding the Choppy Waters of East River: Economic Loss Doctrine Ten Years Later,* 64 Def. Coun. J. 260, 262 (1997). But some courts have rejected any exception for sudden and calamitous events, arguing that most calamitous failures result from gradual deterioration that simply manifests at a time and in a manner that will cause great harm, so no principled distinction can be drawn. *See, e.g., S.J. Groves,* 374 N.W.2d at 435. Where the distinction *is* recognized, determining whether a failure is "sudden and calamitous" or a normal failure is problematic. Is the collapse of a roof in a windstorm

---

themselves. And not every jurisdiction recognizes an exception for damage to other property. *See, e.g., Citizens Ins. Co. v. Osmose Wood Preserving, Inc.*, 585 N.W.2d 314, 316 (Mich. App. 1998) ("[T]he economic loss rule applies in Michigan even when the plaintiff is seeking to recover for property other than the product itself.")

a sudden and calamitous failure? In *Chicago Heights Venture v. Dynamit Nobel of America, Inc.,* 782 F.2d 723, 729 (7th Cir. 1986), the court found it was not, noting that the nature of the product meant the defect would manifest itself "most acutely in times of adverse weather. . . . The gravamen of the complaint—simply stated—is that the roof did not work."

Consumer buyers: Many jurisdictions apply the economic loss doctrine to both commercial and consumer buyers. The purpose of barring recovery for economic loss under tort law is to permit sellers to determine by contract their liability for breach of warranty, these courts conclude, and the same rationale supports the rule no matter who the buyer is. However, some courts do distinguish between commercial and consumer buyers, barring tort suits brought by buyers seeking commercial recovery for property damage but concluding that non-commercial buyers generally have less bargaining power to ensure that the sales contract reflects a reasonable allocation of risks so they should be permitted to recover in tort the damages that might not be available to them in contract. *Compare, e.g., Hapka v. Paquin Farms,* 458 N.W.2d 683, 688 (Minn. 1990) *with Lloyd F. Smith Co. v. Den-tal-Ez, Inc.,* 491 N.W.2d 11, 15 (Minn. 1992). *See also, e.g., Mainline Tractor & Equip. Co. v. Nutrite Corp.,* 937 F. Supp. 1095 (D. Vt. 1996); *Rousseau v. K.N. Constr., Inc.,* 727 A.2d 190 (R.I. 1999).

Misrepresentation and fraud: The economic loss doctrine arose to prevent litigants from bringing claims sounding in strict liability or negligence for injury caused by defective goods subject to Article 2. The courts are divided on whether the economic loss rule also bars recovery for none, some, or all claims of fraud or misrepresentation related to the sale of goods. *See* R. Joseph Barton, *Drowning in a Sea of Contract: Application of the Economic Loss Rule to Fraud and Negligent Misrepresentation Claims,* 41 Wm. & Mary L. Rev. 1789 (2000).

Even the "usual" rule—which states that buyers may not obtain tort damages for injury to the goods themselves but may recover for injury to "other property"—creates enormous questions of interpretation. When goods are purchased and are attached to other personal property or are incorporated as components into a larger device, what happens if the purchased goods cause damage to the attached property or to the larger device? Does that constitute damage to the goods themselves or damage to other property? For example, if the turbines in *East River* had caused injury to the ships in which they were installed, should the buyer have been able to collect damages under tort law? What if the problem with the turbines was caused by a defective switch that had been manufactured by and purchased from another company and then installed by Delaval into its turbines? Could Delaval claim tort damages for injury to "other property" against the manufacturer of the switch? Could the purchaser of the ships?[3]

Courts have generally concluded that loss to property that was foreseeable by the contracting parties does not constitute loss to "other property" that would allow tort recovery, because the parties should have determined (or did determine) in the contract the allocation of risks for such injury. The distinction between "the goods themselves" and "other property" thus does not depend solely on whether the purchased goods and the property injured were physically separate but rather on whether injury to the particular property at issue should have been contemplated based on the nature of the goods sold and the use to which they were to be put. Courts have also concluded that a small amount of damage to something legitimately labeled "other property" will not trigger tort liability for the usually much greater economic loss arising from damage to the goods themselves.

Some examples of what the courts have found does *not* constitute damage to "other property" (and therefore is not recoverable in tort):

1.   Damage to walls into which defective brick was incorporated (although the court implied that structural damage to the building might have constituted damage to other property), *Minneapolis Society of Fine Arts v. Parker-Klein Associates Architects, Inc.*, 354 N.W.2d 816 (Minn. 1984).

2.   Damage to property underneath a defective roof, *Hartford Fire Ins. Co. v. Huls America, Inc.*, 893 F. Supp. 465 (E.D. Pa. 1995).

3.   Damage to a building caused by a defective roof, *Pulte Home Corp. v. Ply Gem Indus., Inc.*, 804 F. Supp. 1471 (M.D. Fla. 1992).

4.   Damage to potatoes ruined by a sprout suppressant, *King v. Hilton-Davis*, 855 F.2d 1047 (3d Cir. 1988).

---

[3] In *Saratoga Fishing Co. v. J.M. Martinac & Co.*, 117 S.Ct. 1783 (1997), the Supreme Court answered some of these questions as a matter of admiralty law. Whether other jurisdictions will choose to follow the particular holdings in *Saratoga Fishing Co.* is unclear. *See* Chadwidk Mollere, *Saratoga Fishing Co. v. J.M. Martinac & Co.: Charting the Course of "Other Property" in Products Liability Law*, 58 La. L. Rev. 1281 (1998).

5. Damage to machinery and other property caused by explosion of a defective power plant pipe, *Detroit Edison Co. v. NABCO, Inc.*, 35 F.3d 236 (6th Cir. 1994).
6. Damage to property owned by someone other than the buyer, even if the buyer is held responsible for the damage, *Myrtle Beach Pipeline Corp. v. Emerson Electric Co.*, 843 F. Supp. 1027 (D.S.C. 1993).

On the other hand, the following have been found to constitute damage to "other property" so that the buyer could recover damages under tort theories:

7. Damage to brick panels and steel infrastructure of bank building caused by defective mortar additive, *Philadelphia Nat'l Bank v. Dow Chem. Co.*, 605 F. Supp. 60 (E.D. Pa. 1985).
8. Damage to building in fire caused by defective dental chair, *Lloyd F. Smith Co. v. Den-tal-Ez, Inc.*, 491 N.W.2d 11 (Minn. 1992).
9. Damaged food resulting from defective refrigerator's repeated failure, *In re Merritt Logan, Inc.*, 901 F.2d 349 (3d Cir. 1990).

Problem 24-2. Manufacturer sells a grain dryer to Buyer. After Buyer installs the grain dryer, an electrical malfunction in the unit causes a fire in the dryer. As a result, the grain dryer itself is damaged severely, the grain in the dryer at the time of the fire is destroyed, and the fire causes damage to nearby equipment and injures a visitor to Buyer's facility. Buyer sues Manufacturer in tort for the injury to the grain dryer and the visitor, for the loss of the grain destroyed in the fire, for damage to other equipment, and for profits lost as a result of the fire. Manufacturer moves for summary judgment, claiming that all of these claims must be litigated as a matter of contract, not tort.

Analyze Buyer's claim and Manufacturer's summary judgment motion under the principles established in *East River Steamship Corp.* and the other cases discussed in this Assignment. Which of these claims will certainly survive Manufacturer's motion for summary judgment? Which claims will certainly be dismissed? Which claims are difficult to resolve, and what more will you need to know to resolve them?

East River Steamship Corp.

v.

Transamerica Delaval, Inc.

106 S. Ct. 2295 (1986)

Justice BLACKMUN delivered the opinion of the Court.

In this admiralty case, we must decide whether a cause of action in tort is stated when a defective product purchased in a commercial transaction malfunctions, injuring only the product itself and causing purely economic loss. The case requires us to consider preliminarily whether admiralty law, which already recognizes a general theory of liability for negligence, also incorporates principles of products liability, including strict liability. Then, charting a course between products liability and contract law, we must

determine whether injury to a product itself is the kind of harm that should be protected by products liability or left entirely to the law of contracts.

I

In 1969, Seatrain Shipbuilding Corp. (Shipbuilding), a wholly owned subsidiary of Seatrain Lines, Inc. (Seatrain), announced it would build the four oil-transporting supertankers in issue—the T.T. Stuyvesant, T.T. Williamsburgh, T.T. Brooklyn, and T.T. Bay Ridge. Each tanker was constructed pursuant to a contract in which a separate wholly owned subsidiary of Seatrain engaged Shipbuilding. Shipbuilding in turn contracted with respondent, now known as Transamerica Delaval Inc. (Delaval), to design, manufacture, and supervise the installation of turbines (costing $1.4 million each, see App. 163) that would be the main propulsion units for the 225,000-ton, $125 million, ibid., supertankers. When each ship was completed, its title was transferred from the contracting subsidiary to a trust company (as trustee for an owner), which in turn chartered the ship to one of the petitioners, also subsidiaries of Seatrain. Queensway Tankers, Inc., chartered the Stuyvesant; Kingsway Tankers, Inc., chartered the Williamsburgh; East River Steamship Corp. chartered the Brooklyn; and Richmond Tankers, Inc., chartered the Bay Ridge. Each petitioner operated under a bareboat charter, by which it took full control of the ship for 20 or 22 years as though it owned it, with the obligation afterwards to return the ship to the real owner. See G. Gilmore & C. Black, Admiralty §§ 4-1, 4-22 (2d ed. 1975). Each charterer assumed responsibility for the cost of any repairs to the ships. Tr. of Oral Arg. 11, 16-17, 35.

The Stuyvesant sailed on its maiden voyage in late July 1977. On December 11 of that year, as the ship was about to enter the Port of Valdez, Alaska, steam began to escape from the casing of the high-pressure turbine. That problem was temporarily resolved by repairs, but before long, while the ship was encountering a severe storm in the Gulf of Alaska, the high-pressure turbine malfunctioned. The ship, though lacking its normal power, was able to continue on its journey to Panama and then San Francisco. In January 1978, an examination of the high-pressure turbine revealed that the first-stage steam reversing ring virtually had disintegrated and had caused additional damage to other parts of the turbine. The damaged part was replaced with a part from the Bay Ridge, which was then under construction. In April 1978, the

ship again was repaired, this time with a part from the Brooklyn. Finally, in August, the ship was permanently and satisfactorily repaired with a ring newly designed and manufactured by Delaval.

The Brooklyn and the Williamsburgh were put into service in late 1973 and late 1974, respectively. In 1978, as a result of the Stuyvesant's problems, they were inspected while in port. Those inspections revealed similar turbine damage. Temporary repairs were made, and newly designed parts were installed as permanent repairs that summer.

When the Bay Ridge was completed in early 1979, it contained the newly designed parts and thus never experienced the high-pressure turbine problems that plagued the other three ships. Nonetheless, the complaint appears to claim damages as a result of deterioration of the Bay Ridge's ring that was installed in the Stuyvesant while the Bay Ridge was under construction. In addition, the Bay Ridge experienced a unique problem. In 1980, when the ship was on its maiden voyage, the engine began to vibrate with a frequency that increased even after speed was reduced. It turned out that the astern guardian valve, located between the high-pressure and low-pressure turbines, had been installed backwards. Because of that error, steam entered the low-pressure turbine and damaged it. After repairs, the Bay Ridge resumed its travels.

II

The charterers' second amended complaint, filed in the United States District Court for the District of New Jersey, invokes admiralty jurisdiction. It contains five counts alleging tortious conduct on the part of respondent Delaval and seeks an aggregate of more than $8 million in damages for the cost of repairing the ships and for income lost while the ships were out of service. The first four counts, read liberally, allege that Delaval is strictly liable for the design defects in the high-pressure turbines of the Stuyvesburgh, the Williamsburgh, the Brooklyn, and the Bay Ridge, respectively. The fifth count alleges that Delaval, as part of the manufacturing process, negligently supervised the installation of the astern guardian valve on the Bay Ridge. The initial complaint also had listed Seatrain and Shipbuilding as plaintiffs and had alleged breach of contract and warranty as well as tort claims. But after Delaval interposed a statute of limitations defense, the complaint was amended and the charterers alone brought the suit in tort. The nonrenewed claims were dismissed with prejudice by the District Court. Delaval then moved for summary judgment, contending that the charterers' actions were not cognizable in tort.

The District Court granted summary judgment for Delaval, and the Court of Appeals for the Third Circuit, sitting en banc, affirmed. East River S.S. Corp. v. Delaval Turbine, Inc., 752 F.2d 903 (1985). The Court of Appeals held that damage solely to a defective product is actionable in tort if the defect creates an unreasonable risk of harm to persons or property other than the product itself, and harm materializes. Disappointments over the product's quality, on the other hand, are protected by warranty law. Id., at 908, 909-910. The charterers were dissatisfied with product quality: the defects involved gradual and unnoticed deterioration of the turbines' component parts, and the only risk created was that

the turbines would operate at a lower capacity. Id., at 909. See Pennsylvania Glass Sand Corp. v. Caterpillar Tractor Co., 652 F.2d 1165, 1169-1170 (CA3 1981). Therefore, neither the negligence claim nor the strict-liability claim was cognizable.

Judge Garth concurred on "grounds somewhat different," 752 F.2d, at 910, and Judge Becker, joined by Judge Higginbotham, concurred in part and dissented in part. Id., at 913. Although Judge Garth agreed with the majority's analysis on the merits, he found no strict-liability claim presented because the charterers had failed to allege unreasonable danger or demonstrable injury.

Judge Becker largely agreed with the majority's approach, but would permit recovery for a "near miss," where the risk existed but no calamity occurred. He felt that the first count, concerning the Stuyvesant, stated a cause of action in tort. The exposure of the ship to a severe storm when the ship was unable to operate at full power due to the defective part created an unreasonable risk of harm.

We granted certiorari to resolve a conflict among the Courts of Appeals sitting in admiralty.

[Citations omitted]

III

[A and B omitted]

C

With admiralty jurisdiction comes the application of substantive admiralty law. See Executive Jet Aviation, 409 U.S., at 255, 93 S.Ct., at 498. Absent a relevant statute, the general maritime law, as developed by the judiciary, applies. . . .

The Courts of Appeals sitting in admiralty overwhelmingly have adopted concepts of products liability, based both on negligence . . . and on strict liability, Pan- Alaska Fisheries, Inc. v. Marine Constr. & Design Co., 565 F.2d 1129, 1135 (CA9 1977) (adopting Restatement (Second) of Torts § 402A (1965)). Indeed, the Court of Appeals for the Third Circuit previously had stated that the question whether principles of strict products liability are part of maritime law "is no longer seriously contested." . . .

We join the Courts of Appeals in recognizing products liability, including strict liability, as part of the general maritime law. This Court's precedents relating to injuries of maritime workers long have pointed in that direction. . . . The Court's rationale in those cases—that strict liability should be imposed on the party best able to protect persons from hazardous equipment—is equally applicable when the claims are based on products liability. . . . And to the extent that products actions are based on negligence, they are grounded in principles already incorporated into the general maritime law. . . . Our incorporation of products liability into maritime law, however, is only the threshold determination to the main issue in this case.

IV

Products liability grew out of a public policy judgment that people need more protection from dangerous products than is afforded by the law of warranty. See Seely v. White Motor Co., 63 Cal.2d 9, 15, 45 Cal.Rptr. 17, 21, 403 P.2d 145, 149 (1965). It is clear, however, that if this development were allowed to progress too far, contract law would

drown in a sea of tort. See G. Gilmore, The Death of Contract 87-94 (1974). We must determine whether a commercial product injuring itself is the kind of harm against which public policy requires manufacturers to protect, independent of any contractual obligation.

A

The paradigmatic products-liability action is one where a product "reasonably certain to place life and limb in peril," distributed without reinspection, causes bodily injury. See, e.g., MacPherson v. Buick Motor Co., 217 N.Y. 382, 389, 111 N.E. 1050, 1051, 1053 (1916). The manufacturer is liable whether or not it is negligent because "public policy demands that responsibility be fixed wherever it will most effectively reduce the hazards to life and health inherent in defective products that reach the market." Escola v. Coca Cola Bottling Co. of Fresno, 24 Cal.2d, at 462, 150 P.2d, at 441 (opinion concurring in judgment).

For similar reasons of safety, the manufacturer's duty of care was broadened to include protection against property damage. See Marsh Wood Products Co. v. Babcock & Wilcox Co., 207 Wis. 209, 226, 240 N.W. 392, 399 (1932); Genesee County Patrons Fire Relief Assn. v. L. Sonneborn Sons, Inc., 263 N.Y. 463, 469-473, 189 N.E. 551, 553-555 (1934). Such damage is considered so akin to personal injury that the two are treated alike. See Seely v. White Motor Co., 63 Cal.2d, at 19, 45 Cal.Rptr., at 24, 403 P.2d, at 152.

In the traditional "property damage" cases, the defective product damages other property. In this case, there was no damage to "other" property. Rather, the first, second, and third counts allege that each supertanker's defectively designed turbine components damaged only the turbine itself. Since each turbine was supplied by Delaval as an integrated package, see App. 162-163, each is properly regarded as a single unit. "Since all but the very simplest of machines have component parts, [a contrary] holding would require a finding of 'property damage' in virtually every case where a product damages itself. Such a holding would eliminate the distinction between warranty and strict products liability." Northern Power & Engineering Corp. v. Caterpillar Tractor Co., 623 P.2d 324, 330 (Alaska 1981). The fifth count also alleges injury to the product itself. Before the high-pressure and low-pressure turbines could become an operational propulsion system, they were connected to piping and valves under the supervision of Delaval personnel. See App. 78, 162-163, 181. Delaval's supervisory obligations were part of its manufacturing agreement. The fifth count thus can best be read to allege that Delaval's negligent manufacture of the propulsion system—by allowing the installation in reverse of the astern guardian valve—damaged the propulsion system. Cf. Lewis v. Timco, Inc., 736 F.2d 163, 165-166 (CA5 1984). Obviously, damage to a product itself has certain attributes of a products-liability claim. But the injury suffered—the failure of the product to function properly—is the essence of a warranty action, through which a contracting party can seek to recoup the benefit of its bargain.

B

The intriguing question whether injury to a product itself may be brought in tort has spawned a variety of answers.[4] At one end of the spectrum, the case that created the majority land-based approach, Seely v. White Motor Co., 63 Cal.2d 9, 45 Cal.Rptr. 17, 403 P.2d 145 (1965) (defective truck), held that preserving a proper role for the law of warranty precludes imposing tort liability if a defective product causes purely monetary harm. See also Jones & Laughlin Steel Corp. v. Johns-Manville Sales Corp., 626 F.2d 280, 287, and n. 13 (CA3 1980) (citing cases).

At the other end of the spectrum is the minority land-based approach, whose progenitor, Santor v. A & M

---

[4] The question is not answered by the Restatement (Second) of Torts §§ 395 and 402A (1965), or by the Uniform Commercial Code, see Wade, Is Section 402A of the Second Restatement of Torts Preempted by the UCC and Therefore Unconstitutional?, 42 Tenn.L.Rev. 123 (1974).

Congress, which has considered adopting national products-liability legislation, also has been wrestling with the question whether economic loss should be recoverable under a products-liability theory. See 1 L. Frumer & M. Friedman, Products Liability § 4C (1986). When S. 100, 99th Cong., 1st Sess. (1985) (the Product Liability Act) was introduced, it excluded, § 2(6), recovery for commercial loss. Suggestions have been made for revising this provision. See Amendment 16, 131 Cong.Rec. 5461 (1985); Amendment 100, id., at 11850, 11851. Other bills also have addressed the issue. See S. 1999, id., at 38772 (1985); Amendment 1951, 132 Cong.Rec. 10304 (1986). See also H.R. 2568, 99th Cong., 1st Sess. (1985); H.R. 4425, 99th Cong., 2d Sess. (1986). The issue also is of concern in the area of conflict of laws. See R. Weintraub, Commentary on the Conflict of Laws § 6.29 (2nd ed. 1980).

Karagheusian, Inc., 44 N.J. 52, 66-67, 207 A.2d 305, 312-313 (1965) (marred carpeting), held that a manufacturer's duty to make nondefective products encompassed injury to the product itself, whether or not the defect created an unreasonable risk of harm.[5] See also LaCrosse v. Schubert, Schroeder & Associates, Inc., 72 Wis.2d 38, 44-45, 240 N.W.2d 124, 127-128 (1976). The courts adopting this approach, including the majority of the Courts of Appeals sitting in admiralty that have considered the issue,[6] e.g., Emerson G.M. Diesel, Inc. v. Alaskan Enterprise, 732 F.2d 1468 (CA9 1984), find that the safety and insurance rationales behind strict liability apply equally where the losses are purely economic. These courts reject the Seely

approach because they find it arbitrary that economic losses are recoverable if a plaintiff suffers bodily injury or property damage, but not if a product injures itself. They also find no inherent difference between economic loss and personal injury or property damage, because all are proximately caused by the defendant's conduct. Further, they believe recovery for economic loss would not lead to unlimited liability because they think a manufacturer can predict and insure against product failure. See Emerson G.M. Diesel, Inc. v. Alaskan Enterprise, 732 F.2d, at 1474.

Between the two poles fall a number of cases that would permit a products-liability action under certain circumstances when a product injures only itself. These cases attempt to differentiate between "the disappointed users . . . and the endangered ones," Russell v. Ford Motor Co., 281 Or. 587, 595, 575 P.2d 1383, 1387 (1978), and permit only the latter to sue in tort. The determination has been said to turn on the nature of the defect, the type of risk, and the manner in which the injury arose. See Pennsylvania Glass Sand Corp. v. Caterpillar Tractor Co., 652 F.2d, at 1173 (relied on by the Court of Appeals in this case). The Alaska Supreme Court allows a tort action if the defective product creates a situation potentially dangerous to persons or other property, and loss occurs as a proximate result of that danger and under dangerous circumstances. Northern Power & Engineering Corp. v. Caterpillar Tractor Co., 623 P.2d 324, 329 (1981).

We find the intermediate and minority land-based positions unsatisfactory. The intermediate positions, which essentially turn on the

---

[5] Interestingly, the New Jersey and California Supreme Courts have each taken what appears to be a step in the direction of the other since Santor and Seely. In Spring Motors Distributors, Inc. v. Ford Motor Co., 98 N.J., at 579, 489 A.2d, at 672, the New Jersey court rejected Santor in the commercial context. And in J'Aire Corp. v. Gregory, 24 Cal.3d 799, 157 Cal.Rptr. 407, 598 P.2d 60 (1979), the California court recognized a cause of action for negligent interference with prospective economic advantage.

[6] Most of the admiralty cases concerned fishing vessels. See Emerson G.M. Diesel, Inc. v. Alaskan Enterprise, 732 F.2d 1468, 1472 (CA9 1984) (relying on solicitude for fishermen as a reason for a more protective approach). Delaval concedes that the courts, see Carbone v. Ursich, 209 F.2d 178, 182 (CA9 1953), and Congress, see 46 U.S.C.App. § 533 (1982 ed., Supp. II), at times have provided special protection for fishermen. This case involves no fishermen.

degree of risk, are too indeterminate to enable manufacturers easily to structure their business behavior. Nor do we find persuasive a distinction that rests on the manner in which the product is injured. We realize that the damage may be qualitative, occurring through gradual deterioration or internal breakage. Or it may be calamitous. Compare Morrow v. New Moon Homes, Inc., 548 P.2d 279 (Alaska 1976), with Cloud v. Kit Mfg. Co., 563 P.2d 248, 251 (Alaska 1977). But either way, since by definition no person or other property is damaged, the resulting loss is purely economic. Even when the harm to the product itself occurs through an abrupt, accident-like event, the resulting loss due to repair costs, decreased value, and lost profits is essentially the failure of the purchaser to receive the benefit of its bargain—traditionally the core concern of contract law. See E. Farnsworth, Contracts § 12.8, pp. 839-840 (1982).

We also decline to adopt the minority land-based view espoused by Santor and Emerson. Such cases raise legitimate questions about the theories behind restricting products liability, but we believe that the countervailing arguments are more powerful. The minority view fails to account for the need to keep products liability and contract law in separate spheres and to maintain a realistic limitation on damages.

C

Exercising traditional discretion in admiralty, see Pope & Talbot, Inc. v. Hawn, 346 U.S. 406, 409, 74 S.Ct. 202, 204, 98 L.Ed. 143 (1953), we adopt an approach similar to Seely and hold that a manufacturer in a commercial relationship has no duty under either a

negligence or strict products-liability theory to prevent a product from injuring itself.[7]

"The distinction that the law has drawn between tort recovery for physical injuries and warranty recovery for economic loss is not arbitrary and does not rest on the 'luck' of one plaintiff in having an accident causing physical injury. The distinction rests, rather, on an understanding of the nature of the responsibility a manufacturer must undertake in distributing his products." Seely v. White Motor Co., 63 Cal.2d, at 18, 45 Cal.Rptr., at 23, 403 P.2d, at 151. When a product injures only itself the reasons for imposing a tort duty are weak and those for leaving the party to its contractual remedies are strong.

The tort concern with safety is reduced when an injury is only to the product itself. When a person is injured, the "cost of an injury and the loss of time or health may be an overwhelming misfortune," and one the person is not prepared to meet. Escola v. Coca Cola Bottling Co., 24 Cal.2d, at 462, 150 P.2d, at 441 (opinion concurring in judgment). In contrast, when a product injures itself, the commercial user stands to lose the value of the product, risks the displeasure of its customers who find that the product does not meet their needs, or, as in this case, experiences increased costs in performing a service. Losses like these

---

[7] We do not reach the issue whether a tort cause of action can ever be stated in admiralty when the only damages sought are economic. Cf. Ultramares Corp. v. Touche, 255 N.Y. 170, 174 N.E. 441 (1931). But see Robins Dry Dock & Repair Co. v. Flint, 275 U.S. 303, 48 S.Ct. 134, 72 L.Ed. 290 (1927).

can be insured. See 10A G. Couch, Cyclopedia of Insurance Law §§ 42:385-42:401, 42:414-417 (2d ed. 1982); 7 E. Benedict, Admiralty, Form No. 1.16-7, p. 1-239 (7th ed. 1985); 5A J. Appleman & J. Appleman, Insurance Law and Practice § 3252 (1970). Society need not presume that a customer needs special protection. The increased cost to the public that would result from holding a manufacturer liable in tort for injury to the product itself is not justified. Cf. United States v. Carroll Towing Co., 159 F.2d 169, 173 (CA2 1947).

Damage to a product itself is most naturally understood as a warranty claim. Such damage means simply that the product has not met the customer's expectations, or, in other words, that the customer has received "insufficient product value." See J. White and R. Summers, Uniform Commercial Code 406 (2d ed. 1980). The maintenance of product value and quality is precisely the purpose of express and implied warranties.[8] See UCC § 2-313 (express warranty), § 2-314 (implied warranty of merchantability), and § 2-315 (warranty of fitness for a particular purpose). Therefore, a claim of a nonworking product can be brought as a breach-of-warranty action. Or, if the customer prefers, it can reject the product or revoke its acceptance and sue for breach of contract. See UCC §§ 2-601, 2-608, 2-612.

Contract law, and the law of warranty in particular, is well suited to commercial controversies of the sort involved in this case because the parties may set the terms of their own agreements.[9] The manufacturer can restrict its liability, within limits, by disclaiming warranties or limiting remedies. See UCC §§ 2-316, 2-719. In exchange, the purchaser pays less for the product. Since a commercial situation generally does not involve large disparities in bargaining power, cf. Henningsen v. Bloomfield Motors, Inc., 32 N.J. 358, 161 A.2d 69 (1960), we see no reason to intrude into the parties' allocation of the risk.

---

[8] If the charterers' claims were brought as breach-of-warranty actions, they would not be within the admiralty jurisdiction. Since contracts relating to the construction of or supply of materials to a ship are not within the admiralty jurisdiction, see Thames Towboat Co. v. The Schooner "Francis McDonald", 254 U.S. 242, 243, 41 S.Ct. 65, 66, 65 L.Ed. 245 (1920); Kossick v. United Fruit Co., 365 U.S., at 735, 81 S.Ct., at 889, neither are warranty claims grounded in such contracts. See 1 E. Benedict, Admiralty § 188, p. 11-36 (7th ed. 1985). State law would govern the actions. See North Pacific S.S. Co. v. Hall Brothers Marine Railway & Shipbuilding Co., 249 U.S. 119, 127, 39 S.Ct. 221, 223, 63 L.Ed. 510 (1919). In particular the Uniform Commercial Code, which has been adopted by 49 States, would apply.

[9] We recognize, of course, that warranty and products liability are not static bodies of law and may overlap. In certain situations, for example, the privity requirement of warranty has been discarded. E.g., Henningsen v. Bloomfield Motors, Inc., 32 N.J. 358, 380-384, 161 A.2d 69, 81-84 (1960). In other circumstances, a manufacturer may be able to disclaim strict tort liability. See, e.g., Keystone Aeronautics Corp. v. R.J. Enstrom Corp., 499 F.2d 146, 149 (CA3 1974). Nonetheless, the main currents of tort law run in different directions from those of contract and warranty, and the latter seem to us far more appropriate for commercial disputes of the kind involved here.

While giving recognition to the manufacturer's bargain, warranty law sufficiently protects the purchaser by allowing it to obtain the benefit of its bargain. See White & Summers, supra, ch. 10. The expectation damages available in warranty for purely economic loss give a plaintiff the full benefit of its bargain by compensating for forgone business opportunities. See Fuller & Perdue, The Reliance Interest in Contract Damages: 1, 46 Yale L.J. 52, 60-63 (1936); R. Posner, Economic Analysis of Law § 4.8 (3d ed. 1986). Recovery on a warranty theory would give the charterers their repair costs and lost profits, and would place them in the position they would have been in had the turbines functioned properly.[10] See Hawkins v. McGee, 84 N.H. 114, 146 A. 641 (1929). Thus, both the nature of the injury and the resulting damages indicate it is more natural to think of injury to a product itself in terms of warranty.

A warranty action also has a built-in limitation on liability, whereas a tort action could subject the manufacturer to damages of an indefinite amount. The

limitation in a contract action comes from the agreement of the parties and the requirement that consequential damages, such as lost profits, be a foreseeable result of the breach. See Hadley v. Baxendale, 9 Ex. 341, 156 Eng.Rep. 145 (1854). In a warranty action where the loss is purely economic, the limitation derives from the requirements of foreseeability and of privity, which is still generally enforced for such claims in a commercial setting. See UCC § 2-715; White & Summers, supra, at 389, 396, 406-410.

In products-liability law, where there is a duty to the public generally, foreseeability is an inadequate brake. Cf. Kinsman Transit Co. v. City of Buffalo, 388 F.2d 821 (CA2 1968). See also Perlman, Interference with Contract and Other Economic Expectancies: A Clash of Tort and Contract Doctrine, 49 U.Chi.L.Rev. 61, 71-72 (1982). Permitting recovery for all foreseeable claims for purely economic loss could make a manufacturer liable for vast sums. It would be difficult for a manufacturer to take into account the expectations of persons downstream who may encounter its product. In this case, for example, if the charterers—already one step removed from the transaction—were permitted to recover their economic losses, then the companies that subchartered the ships might claim their economic losses from the delays, and the charterers' customers also might claim their economic losses, and so on. "The law does not spread its protection so far." Robins Dry Dock & Repair Co. v. Flint, 275 U.S. 303, 309, 48 S.Ct. 134, 135, 72 L.Ed. 290 (1927).

And to the extent that courts try to limit purely economic damages in tort,

---

[10] In contrast, tort damages generally compensate the plaintiff for loss and return him to the position he occupied before the injury. Cf. Sullivan v. O'Connor, 363 Mass. 579, 584-586, 588, n. 6, 296 N.E.2d 183, 187-188, 189, n. 6 (1973); Prosser, The Borderland of Tort and Contract, in Selected Topics on the Law of Torts 380, 424-427 (Thomas M. Cooley Lectures, Fourth Series 1953). Tort damages are analogous to reliance damages, which are awarded in contract when there is particular difficulty in measuring the expectation interest. See, e.g., Security Store & Mfg. Co. v. American Railways Express Co., 227 Mo.App. 175, 51 S.W.2d 572 (1932).

they do so by relying on a far murkier line, one that negates the charterers' contention that permitting such recovery under a products-liability theory enables admiralty courts to avoid difficult line drawing. Cf. Ultramares Corp. v. Touche, 255 N.Y. 170, 174 N.E. 441 (1931); Louisiana ex rel. Guste v. M/V Testbank, 752 F.2d 1019, 1046-1052 (CA5 1985) (en banc) (dissenting opinion), cert. pending sub nom. White v. Testbank, No. 84-1808.

D

For the first three counts, the defective turbine components allegedly injured only the turbines themselves. Therefore, a strict products-liability theory of recovery is unavailable to the charterers. Any warranty claims would be subject to Delaval's limitation, both in time and scope, of its warranty liability. App. 78-79. The record indicates that Seatrain and Delaval reached a settlement agreement. Deposition of Stephen Russell, p. 32. We were informed that these charterers could not have asserted the warranty claims. See Tr. of Oral Arg. 36. Even so, the charterers should be left to the terms of their bargains, which explicitly allocated the cost of repairs.

In the charterers' agreements with the owners, the charterers took the ships in "as is" condition, after inspection, and assumed full responsibility for them, including responsibility for maintenance and repairs and for obtaining certain forms of insurance. Id., at 11, 16-17, 35; App. 86, 88, 99, 101, 112, 114, 125-126, 127. In a separate agreement between each charterer and Seatrain, Seatrain agreed to guarantee certain payments and covenants by each charterer to the owner. Id., at 142-156. The contractual responsibilities thus were clearly laid out. There is no reason to extricate the parties from their bargain.

Similarly, in the fifth count, alleging the reverse installation of the astern guardian valve, the only harm was to the propulsion system itself rather than to persons or other property. Even assuming that Delaval's supervision was negligent, as we must on this summary judgment motion, Delaval owed no duty under a products-liability theory based on negligence to avoid causing purely economic loss. Cf. Flintkote Co. v. Dravo Corp., 678 F.2d 942 (CA11 1982); S.M. Wilson & Co. v. Smith International, Inc., 587 F.2d 1363 (CA9 1978). Thus, whether stated in negligence or strict liability, no products-liability claim lies in admiralty when the only injury claimed is economic loss.

While we hold that the fourth count should have been dismissed, we affirm the entry of judgment for Delaval.

It is so ordered.

Index

(References are to page numbers)

Note on Use of the Index

This index contains references to pages on which the indicated term is explicitly mentioned. Because many concepts appear only or first in the answers to the questions posed, not in the questions themselves, the index cannot be used to find every page in the book on which a concept is raised. To identify all the pages on which any given issue appears, the reader of this book should use a combination of the index, the table of contents, and the table of statutory authorities.

"FAIR QUANTUM" TEST (See LIMITATION OF REMEDIES)

FAULT (See EXCUSE)

FINAL EXPRESSION (See PAROL EVIDENCE RULE)

FIRM OFFER (See also OFFER)
Comparing availability in goods and services contracts, 28
Defined, 50

FITNESS, IMPLIED WARRANTY OF (See IMPLIED WARRANTY OF FITNESS)

FLOWCHART
Example, 8, 13

F.O.B. (See CARRIER CONTRACTS, CARRIERS)

FOOD AND BEVERAGE SALES (See IMPLIED WARRANTY OF
MERCHANTABILITY)

FORCE MAJEURE CLAUSES
Excuse doctrine, relationship with, 241-242

FORMATION OF CONTRACT (See CONTRACT FORMATION)

FREEDOM OF CONTRACT
UCC encouragement of, 42

FUTURE PERFORMANCE, WARRANTY AS TO (See STATUTE OF LIMITATIONS)

GAP-FILLERS (See DEFAULT PROVISIONS)

GOOD FAITH
Merchants, 106, 109

GOOD FAITH PURCHASER FOR VALUE (See also TITLE)
    Generally, 231-233
Buyer in ordinary course, compared with, 235-236

GOODS
Amended definition, 26
Applying definition, 23-24
Defined, 21-23
Future goods, 26
Identification of, 191

ISBN 0–314–14975–9